The Whole and Divided Self

The Whole
and
Divided Self

Edited by
David E. Aune and John McCarthy

A Crossroad Herder Book
The Crossroad Publishing Company
New York

1997
The Crossroad Publishing Company
370 Lexington Avenue, New York, NY 10017

Printed in the United States of America

Library of Congress Cataloging-in-Publication Data

The whole and divided self / edited by John McCarthy.
    p.   cm.
  Includes bibliographical references.
  ISBN 0-8245-1668-0
  1. Self–Biblical teaching.   2. Man (Theology)–Biblical teaching.
3. Man (Christian theology).   I. McCarthy, John.
BS661.W52   1997
233'.5–dc21   97-6807
                                                                CIP

Contents

Part 3: Paul Ricoeur on Self and Bible

Preface

*I*n November 1990, the executive committee of the Lilly Endowment made a generous grant for the "Project of Bible and Theology." The present volume collects the final product of one of the working groups of this project.

The Project of Bible and Theology was dedicated to the goal of providing a forum that could help to overcome the fragmentation of theological studies by bringing into conversation areas of specialization that too frequently have no vital contacts with each other. During its four-year duration, the project developed two primary centers of activity.

1. The project assisted in the formation of three working groups whose members agreed to pursue a topic of significant importance in joint work which extended over several years. Members of each working group represented most areas of theological studies, but there was in all groups a preponderance of specialists in contemporary theology and in biblical studies. Each working group consisted of ten to twelve active participants, who met together, submitting to each other their proposals about the selected topic, engaging in extensive dialogue about their several positions, and finalizing their own views of the subject as it emerged after long and repeated dialogue. The idea behind this aspect of the project was to provide the opportunity for a representative group of scholars in different areas of theological work to engage in substantive, collaborative work on a single theme in order to find new avenues through which the fragmentation of theological education might be addressed by examples of joint theological efforts.

2. The project provided the means for an annual Plenary Meeting, to which approximately 120 scholars of all theological disciplines were invited. Between fifty-five and sixty-five persons participated in three annual Plenary Meetings. The agenda for each of these plenaries was set by one of the three working groups who presented for discussion their papers along with reports about the methods employed in their common research. In this way, reactions by a larger group of colleagues to the proposals of one working group could be subsequently considered and incorporated into improvements of individual contributions.

The Project of Bible and Theology was, from its inception, guided by a steering committee that initiated the planning, supervised the implementation, and contributed constant adjustments in the course of the project's four-year history. The membership of the steering committee evolved over a period of time, and some of its members served only for a limited time. But thanks are due to all of them for the vital assistance they gave to the project. They are Lisa S. Cahill, Ronald H. Cram, John R. Donahue, Paul D. Hanson, Patrick D. Miller, Andrew Purves, Sharon H. Ringe, Katharine Doob Sakenfeld, and Michael Welker. The undersigned, who served as director of the project, owes special thanks to two other persons who accompanied the project from its inception and who gave a great deal of time and care to its work: Charles M. Wood was appointed evaluator of the project on behalf of the Lilly Endowment, and Cynthia L. Rigby served as assistant to the project and organizer of the annual Plenary.

Without the constantly encouraging support of Craig R. Dykstra, Vice President for Religion of the Lilly Endowment, no part of the Project of Bible and Theology could have been accomplished. All of us involved in the project thank him and the executive committee of the Lilly Endowment for their help.

Ulrich W. Mauser

Introduction

John McCarthy
Loyola University Chicago

There has never been a golden age when scripture has functioned in an unproblematic manner in the life of the church. There have always been attendant difficulties. So if we find the issue beset with difficulty, we are not in that respect in a totally different position from our forebears in the faith. On the other hand, critical study of the Bible has enabled us to see things about the nature of the scriptural texts that were not so evident before and whose general truth cannot seriously be questioned. . . . We may not be in a totally different position from our forebears in the faith, but we are in a significantly different position. Neither theology nor the church more generally has yet taken full measure of that significant difference.[1]

*M*aurice Wiles draws attention to an undeniable fact regarding the relationship among the Bible, theology, and the church over the last few centuries: things have changed significantly. But what has changed and how can we take some measure of that change? This introduction serves to respond to this question in two ways: first, by reflecting in a more theoretical way on "our significantly different position," and, second, by introducing the work of a group of scholars who chose to engage the issues of "our significantly different position" through a focus on the contributions that biblical and theological thought might make to a better understanding of the complex issues of "the self." There is no pretense here to the solution of the complex problems that beset the discussion of the relation of Bible and Theology today, or the understanding of the "contemporary self"; rather, what follows in this book is an attempt to do what Wiles calls for—to take some measure of how contemporary

1

biblical and theological reflection can contribute to better understanding significant matters of faith.

History As It Bears on the Relation of Biblical and Theological Studies

"Bible" and "theology" are themselves topics with a long history. Several variables regularly condition any specific relationship between Bible and theology. Among these variables are the relation of theology to reigning forms of knowledge and wisdom; the explicit and implicit roles of philosophy; the understanding of faith and reason; the role of authority in religious positions; the relation of canonical scripture to various rules of faith, liturgical expressions, and dogma; canonical questions; concerns with "heresy"; denominational conflicts; the relationship of the written scriptures to "the Word of God"; and more.

For a figure such as Augustine the relation of Bible to theological reflection allowed for a relatively clear exposition. The distinction between wisdom and knowledge was significant. The object of wisdom was eternal and unchangeable reality; the object of knowledge was changeable and temporal. The words of scripture were understood as signs of the transcendent, and their correct understanding was achieved in relation to the eternal. Thus, the understanding of the biblical material was essentially theological insofar as the Bible is properly understood as a sign of eternal reality. The achievement of this understanding was not the end product of an academic method, although clearly the understanding of language, rhetoric, and literature was important. A moral and spiritual purification was essential, however; for the relationship between the Bible and theology was rooted in the eternal plan of God and not essentially in the historical and literary events.

For someone like Thomas Aquinas the scene was changing. Theology was understood more as a "science" in the Aristotelian sense, as a study of first principles. Moving away from *lectio* (reading) to *disputatio* (disputation), theology began to develop its own questions and ordering schemes separate from canonical and liturgical order. Clearly *sacra doctrina* and *sacra pagina* relied on scripture, but increasingly did so as the primary authority in understanding a faith resting on revelation to the apostles and prophets. Reflecting an early and high medieval world in which positions authorized by revelation were assumed to be compatible with those authorized by reason and experience, theology for someone like Thomas was a critical part of the university, and the Bible was its primary book. Both dealt with the first principles of a faith that sought understanding and whose understanding was communicable through reflection, disputation, argument, and philosophy.

The unifying convictions of a medieval university and its summa, however, did not hold. Increasingly philosophy began to be understood as a science in its own right whose authority was human experience and reason unaided. With the Renaissance and the rise of empirical science in the West, the very meaning of human experience became increasingly more positivistic. The divisions between faith and reason as sources of knowledge were accented. The Bible became a book of faith, and theology an articulation of the faith positions of various sects, communities and denominations. The Bible could surely be studied with methods that would divulge its historical and literary importance, but as a source of authoritative knowledge it had largely been replaced. No longer wisdom or science, theology became a reflective confessional articulation, and the Bible a variously interpreted source for the confession.

The history of theology and the relationship between Bible and theology is of course immensely more complex than this sketch conveys. But even this short history suggests at least two conclusions: (1) the relation of Bible to theology in the Christian tradition has not been the same in all periods; (2) the current context of academic biblical and theological scholarship itself has a specific history which influences any contemporary discussion of the relation between Bible and theology, particularly in the context of the complex institution called "the modern Western university." Scholars in this institution frequently confront issues, the resolution of which is not easily attained: What is the relation of contemporary, academic biblical study, with its emphasis on historical, literary, and linguistic questions, to study within a department of theology? What, if any, distinctive elements do denominational affiliations contribute to the university enterprise? What authorizes the positions and conclusions advanced in contemporary biblical and theological studies? How, given the plurality of methods and questions characterizing biblical and theological studies, could the unity for a common discipline be found? Does theological reflection contribute to knowledge in any way that the modern university might understand? All of these questions have deep roots in the issues, advances, and controversies of our past. Thus, while our "distinctly different position" seems to bring certain

issues and questions to the forefront, these are not without their histories, contexts, and forebears.

The Loyola Group

The university as a place of scholarly study is the major unifying context
for all of the contributors to this volume. It is in fact the shared university locale that brought all of these scholars together in the first place.
At the earliest stages of the project all the members of this group were
affiliated with Loyola University Chicago. No university is without its
background, and Roman Catholicism is the explicit background of this
originating university context. Being in a modern Roman Catholic university has had two major effects on this group of scholars: first, it provided a source of encouragement to pursue each of the individual studies
with a sense of academic freedom; second, it has kept the issues of biblical and theological studies together, sometimes more with the hope of
compatibility than its execution, but nevertheless with the consistent
underlying conviction that each enriches the other.

The contributing scholars are by no means all Roman Catholic in
explicit church membership; even those who identify themselves as
Roman Catholic do so with various understandings. The context of the
contemporary Roman Catholic university, however, allows for the free
interchange of scholarship among all individuals who bring competency,
concern with the issues, and an openness to listen to a plurality of viewpoints. While the Roman Catholic tradition was quite slow to adopt officially the approaches and methods of modern biblical scholarship, it has,
since the middle of this century encouraged a real breadth of scholarly
investigation in all fields associated with biblical studies. The recent
statement titled "The Interpretation of the Bible in the Church," issued
by the Pontifical Biblical Commission in 1993, is a clear example of the
Roman Catholic advocacy of plurality and freedom in the academic
study of the Bible. Likewise the contemporary Roman Catholic study of
theology displays an equally wide variety of approaches and methods to
its study, taking full advantage of the social sciences, critical theories, literary studies, and—what it has always felt a special affinity for—philosophical investigations. For the scholarship of this group, then, the
Roman Catholic tradition of the university has meant the freedom to
investigate responsibly, and in close dialogue with others, the areas that

each contributor's study has indicated as important, utilizing the criteria and standards of scholarship shared by all scholars in the field.

The Roman Catholic tradition has always held that there is a close link between theological investigation and the Bible. This same tradition displays a wide variety of interactions between the Bible and theology, at some points almost eclipsing the Bible with dogmatic and philosophical understandings, at others almost eclipsing any interpretive sophistication with a reliance on biblical passages. The contemporary Roman Catholic context is quite aware of the potential for extremes in the relation of Bible and theology. The following passage from the statement of the Pontifical Biblical Commission referred to above is characteristic of the variable mixture of breadth, hope, conviction, history, and caution that characterizes the contemporary Roman Catholic scene:

> The points of view of both disciplines [exegesis and theology] are in fact different and rightly so. The primary task of the exegete is to determine as accurately as possible the meaning of the biblical texts in their own proper context, that is, first of all, in their particular literary and historical context and then in the context of the wider canon of Scripture. In the course of carrying out this task, the exegete expounds the theological meaning of texts when such a meaning is present. This paves the way for a relationship of continuity between exegesis and further theological reflection. But the point of view is not the same, for the work of the exegete is fundamentally historical and descriptive and restricts itself to the interpretation of the Bible.
>
> Theologians as such have a role that is more speculative and more systematic in nature. For this reason they are really interested only in certain texts and aspects of the Bible and deal, besides, with much other data which is not biblical—patristic writings, councilor definitions, other documents of the magisterium, the liturgy—as well as systems of philosophy and the cultural, social and political situation of the contemporary world. Their task is not simply to interpret the Bible; their aim is to present an understanding of the Christian faith that bears the mark of a full reflection upon all its aspects and especially that of its crucial relationship to human existence.[2]

A second unifying context for the "Loyola Group" was the Lilly Foundation Bible and Theology Project, which provided the financial support for the "Loyola Group." The Bible and Theology Project chose as a whole not to devote the energies of its participants to theoretical discussions of the factors that condition the difference of today's questions from those of our forebears: critical theories, post-structuralism, deconstruction, gender studies, political theory, ecological issues, liberation movements, and so on. Such a choice capitalized on the current strength, training, and long years of scholarly productivity of the assembled participants. But it may at the same time have confirmed by repetition habits of scholarship that tend to be systematically immune to the questions disclosed through other forms of analysis, and by a sharper awareness of the results and limitations of current methods. While metacritical investigations often seem prone to airy speculations, righteous high grounds or gnostic codes, "local studies," including specific textual studies, often seem prone to doing "more of the same," further sharpening the knife of valid method without engaging wider questions of the presuppositions of the method itself. Recognizing this general dialectic of the precision of local studies and the reflective clarification of contemporary contextual issues, the "Loyola Group" chose to do each of its projects within this dialectic and to indicate specifically how such study might or might not contribute to a better understanding of the relation of Bible and theology. Thus each of our projects is a specific one, local in its textual choice or topic. At the same time, each author self-consciously remarks on the relation of this local topic to larger contextual issues. The balance varies in each of the contributions, but none loses sight of the dialectic.

Further Specifying the Significantly Different Position

No matter what predispositions individual members brought to the investigation of the relation of Bible and theology, the participants found themselves confronted with at least four issues that further specified what was understood to be part of today's "significantly different position": (1) the distinction between analysis and interpretation; (2) the university context of study; (3) the self-understanding of theology; and (4) the possible nonrelation of Bible and theology.

The Distinction between Analysis and Interpretation

What fuels historical, social, and literary-critical analyses of scripture is, among other factors, the conviction that the distances—cultural, temporal, linguistic—between biblical writings understood today and their more original contexts is significant and, to varying extents, identifiable. With the use of methods that allow scholars to analyze and clarify these distances we are able to have more informed and thus "better" interpretations of biblical materials. This conviction acts as a preface to what we might understand as the "critically informed" reception of the biblical text.

While realizing the undeniable success of this methodologically controlled and careful analysis, there has been increasing attention to what might be termed in the language of Wittgenstein, a category mistake. More information, as reliable as it might be, in one area does not necessarily lay issues to rest in another. For some it is not evident that the literary, historical, and social analyses that make up much of contemporary biblical scholarship has contributed, or even should, in its present form, to the more adequate investigation of contemporary religious and theological issues. There is a sense that the text of modern biblical scholarship has become almost entirely its preface so that the well-trained contemporary biblical scholar knows the languages, histories, and literary forms of ancient Near Eastern and Mediterranean cultures but finds herself less at ease dealing with what falls under the rubric of an interpretive understanding of the religious and theological contributions of biblical study. In a recent article Francis Fiorenza, drawing on Jürgen Habermas's critique of expert cultures, states this side of the issue with some precision:

> This specialized focus of the historical method as technical method results in a reading of the Scriptures that is not directly translatable into concrete life and everyday practice. The specific application of the historical-critical method to the texts has fostered a type of exegetical knowledge that leads to an increased distance between the expert cultures and the broader public. The split is not simply the result of increased specialization and professionalization by which even other experts within theology, for example, historical, pastoral theologians, often are not able to keep abreast. It is the reduction of the study of scripture to a particular rationality that cuts it off from everyday life.[3]

But while for some the preface of contemporary biblical analysis eclipses biblical interpretation, for others the situation is the reverse. Unless we are willing to do the hard, often tedious work of historical, social, and literary analysis precisely in the contexts of the original texts, we are bound to superimpose our own hardly formulated, even hardly self-aware, issues on the written residue of humanity whose problems were neither modern nor postmodern. The argument is yet another reiteration of the charge of a category mistake: even when we are able to clearly focus our concerns with religion in a contemporary culture with a well-formed theological question, we should not assume that our religious concerns will find a soothing echo in seventh century B.C.E. Jerusalem or first century C.E. Galilee.

Surely no modern scholar of religion would argue with a demand for competency, and most would consider it an honor to be called "one of the most competent in her field." In the context of analysis and interpretation, however, the locations of competency are becoming less easy to identify. It is not self-evident that biblical scholars do competent "analysis" while theological scholars do competent "interpretation," or that the often lazy distinction between science and art finds a natural analogue in the relation between rigorous scriptural study and theological scholarship. Nor is it self-evident that analysis must be somehow in the singular tension of corrective to interpretation, or interpretation in the singular tension of prophetic relevance to analysis. Other schemata do exist, and yet they do not seem to characterize the interactions at large between biblical and theological scholars.

The contributors to this volume have each struggled in various ways with the issues, the limits, and the demands of analysis and interpretation. For some, text and history become the most significant criteria by which to mediate the biblical and theological issues. For others these more conventional categories of professional biblical scholarship are much less an issue. However the individual scholars have chosen to exercise their task, each has in some way been consciously aware of this distinction between analysis and interpretation as part of our "significantly different position."

The University Context of Study

One significant and unifying context for raising the question of the relation of Bible and theology shared by all the volume contributors is the university. Clearly there are other contexts for investigating the relationship: church, seminary, social action, the courts, legislation, and so on. And clearly even the studied relationship between Bible and theology need not occur exclusively in the university. Yet to be a scholar in the field of Bible or theology today generally means to share the accepted training, practices, publications, and responsibilities of other university scholars, but with a specific focus on the selected subject matters of biblical studies or theology. Because of this at least two sets of issues arise in the contemporary university context.

The first is the easiest to state, namely, that the "problem of the relation of Bible and theology" is best understood as a problem of method. Current biblical scholarship has consistently proved the worth of historical studies both to contextualize the canonical texts and to dispel the sense that these same canonical texts should be able to answer any number of peculiarly modern questions, or support any number of peculiarly modern dogmatic positions. Likewise, current theological scholarship has become acutely aware of the possible methods by which it may advance its studies, most of which are as highly suspicious of dogmatic control as were methods of the nineteenth and twentieth centuries. Even though both biblical studies and theology share an increasing concern with methodological sophistication as one means to support scholarship, the methods, questions, and expected results are often dissimilar. The analogue in the university for biblical studies more often than not is classics or history; for theology, it ranges from philosophy to social sciences. Not unlike disciplines within the university as a whole, theologians and biblical scholars carry out their work in largely parallel ways, sometimes with polite appreciation, sometimes with aggressive, not to say informed, suspicions. If it happens to be the case that something "interesting" comes up in classical studies, it will more likely attract the attention of the New Testament scholar than of the theologian. This is because the New Testament scholar shares with the classicist the methodological training and appreciation of texts and histories of a similar period. If the ecologist, or philosopher, or literary theorist on the other hand, were to advance a significantly enlightening clarification of the relation between the individual and nature or gender, the theologian might be more than willing to engage in disciplined co-reflection, the scripture scholar probably less so. Again the point of contact is the shared methodological training and appreciations.

A second university issue bearing on the relation of Bible and theology is the way in which human meaning is clarified by scholarly reflection. Meaning seems to suggest a shared or communal context which may be, and at times ought to be, clarified by the available scholarly tools. Thus, for instance, the involvement of self-worth patterns with patterns of exchange might be clarified by the analyses of economics, communication, or political science. In various ways the scholarly disciplines involved in biblical studies and theology deal with facets of the question of meaning, be they textual clarification or ultimate concerns and limit situations. But it is not always clear how the disciplines exercised in contemporary biblical studies and theology clarify human meaning, and to what extent they limit its possibilities. Again Francis Fiorenza helps shed light on some issues at hand.

> This development of a historical approach to the past does not simply mean that now the historical sciences present their results to theology and that theology must then integrate them. The effect of the historical sciences upon theology is much greater. The dominance of the historical approach has splintered the unity of the theological enterprise as theology has itself become historical. In addition meaning itself has become historical, and the question of the authority of the past has become related to the question of the meaning of the past in its relation to the meaning of the present. The issue of authority becomes integrated with the issue of meaning. It is no longer simply a question of whether the scriptural text has authority or not. Instead, the question of the meaning of the text takes priority and only in the context of the resolution of the issue of meaning can the issue of authority be resolved. Differences in meaning entail differences in authority. Moreover, just as expert as well as popular interpretations of a text differ, so too are there correspondingly different conceptions of authority.[4]

If the relationship to the past is a historical one, if the biblical writings are historical, if the reigning methods of historical scholarship are those that best illumine the relationship to biblical texts, if the meaning of these texts is historically mediated, if any claim for an authoritative hearing or authoritative meaning must pass through the fiery brook of historical method, then biblical scholarship, precisely as scholarship, in the university should be largely carried out by historical methods. But so many "ifs." And so many counterquestions. Has our profound awareness of the relation of history and meaning eclipsed other equally important relational patterns: nature, gender, language, ethnicity, mysticism, to name but a few? Is the only adequate approach to the "past" the historical approach? Are other methodological patterns specifiable for alternative approaches? Are such approaches candidates for "authoritative" hearing and meaning? Is it possible to retrieve a nondogmatic understanding of revelation, inspiration, or scripture, or a poetics of theological interpretation that can make claims for authoritative understanding in a scholarly context on warrants other than those characteristic of historical methods? Major institutional programs are behind the historical approach, as likewise are major theoretical agenda behind the counterquestions. And clearly there are scholars who neither dismiss the tensions nor revel in polemic opposition but seriously engage the issues: James Barr, Hans Frei, Charles

Woods, Sandra Schneiders, Elisabeth Schüssler Fiorenza, J. Severino Croatto, to name only a few. Likewise, each of the contributors to this volume consciously engaged in the tensions of the methodologically historical mediation of meaning, a part of our "significantly different position."

The Self-Understanding of Theology

The recent work of Edward Farley, Randy Maddox, Joseph Hough, Stephen Toulmin, Frank Whaling, Max Seckler, and others on the specific historical development of theology as a discipline and its place in the field of academic scholarship, as well as the work of David Tracy, Schubert Ogden, Sallie McFague, Peter Hodgson, and others on the divisions of labor within the theological field, mark another set of issues characteristic of our "significant difference." The issues here tend to respond to two interrelated questions: What is theology in a university supposed to accomplish? And how does the field of theology divide the kinds of questions it most often poses? Both questions have a direct bearing on how the scholar of religion views the discussion of the relation of Bible and theology, and thus both questions deserve some comment.

These questions are particularly complex today. Historically the goal of theology has not always been clarification or understanding of first-order "religious" belief or activity, but has often been "wisdom" or "salvation." While the contemporary modes of reasoning in the university are surely not monolithic, still "wisdom" and "salvation" seem to slide so easily into the realms of privacy, opinion, and the nonfalsifiable as to be first-line candidates for suspicion. For some the slide is inevitable and constitutes sufficient warrant for dismissal, marginalization, or simple, polite neglect of theological questions. For others, strategies of explanation, often academic apologetics, are advanced to ensure the voice of theological reflection as an important one in the academy. Such strategies seem to take three avenues at present. The first is to limit theological questions to the history of information regarding the shapes and results of previous theological questions. Thus, theology in the university is best accomplished as the history of theological texts, questions, trends, dead ends, and persons. While recognizing that these texts, trends, and persons most often placed whatever specific conceptions, if any, in much larger and, to them, more important contexts, the engagement of these contexts is best noted but not co-engaged. To do so would exceed the bounds of the methods geared to inform, not convert. A second strategy recognizes the essential role of information but at the same time ventures arguments about the inevitability, even truth, of theological positions. With varying degrees of acceptance of transcendental positions, these strategies suggest that it is inevitable for humans to be ultimately concerned, to make fundamental options, to be influenced by a history of religious classics, to be part of a community that consciously or not uses a syntax and grammar of hierarchy or perfection, to be forced to make value-laden decisions. As such, the very makeup of human being, history, and culture is religious. The choice for academic scholarship is either to recognize this or to turn away from its investigation, but this must not be confused with the very different suggestions that religion is essentially nonpublic. A third strategy suggests that theology take up its past history of wisdom in the context of knowledge as praxis. Here the critique is from the side of theology on the modes of knowing and reasoning dominant in the contemporary university. Typically "cool" university knowing, it is argued, is self-satisfied with an abundance of information, the balance of theoretical display, or the objectivity of its methodological results. At the same time this tends to displace the possibility that knowledge is transformation, that such knowing takes place of necessity in more local and active contexts and communities, that its goal, while clearly not excluding information, concept, and theory, is change, understood and argued as betterment, liberation, authenticity, and so on. The distinction between fact and value, information and point of view, which often authorizes "cooler" models of knowledge and reason is itself rejected as a naïve, even oppressive.

When the question of the relation of Bible and theology is raised within the context of these strategies and their variations, not only do methods vary, but so also does almost everything else from relevant information, to questions, to the conditions that would put the questions to rest. Often it seems that this conflict of strategies is ordered by the suggestion that the theological enterprise includes it all, and that what seems apparent conflict does have an order (e.g., Tracy's distinctions between fundamental, systematic, and practical theologies; or McFague's between heuristic and hermeneutical theology) or even a sequence of distinct but interrelated procedures (Bernard Lonergan's method). Others— particularly those unenamored by further theoretical clarifications or impressed by the urgency of ecological, social, or political issues, or attuned to those whose voices are systematically excluded from the academic roundtable, or unimpressed with the current goals or standards of success of institutionalized education—suggest that theology's self-definition must be more in accord with various transformative patterns: social prophecy, exodus, apocalyptic.

The various strategies for incorporating theology within the university—strategies of information, philosophical/transcendental clarification and transformation—are not new in the history of theology, but they are, it seems, the significant alternatives, and at points the means by which one clear formulation of what ought to be expected of an investigation of the relation of Bible and theology can be formulated. If the goal is information, then one set of methods may take priority; if transformation, then another; and the problems that attend each concerning the relation of Bible and theology may be quite different. Again, each of the contributing scholars faced this issue as part of our "significantly different position."

The Non-Relation of Bible and Theology

One feature that characterizes the above three facets of our "significant difference" is the shared sense that there should be some specifiable relation. But even this should not be taken for granted, either for theology or for biblical studies. To return to F. Fiorenza:

> An adequate description of the present situation of Christianity should acknowledge that the scriptures have value for many Christians and Christian communities but not for others. This split raises the dilemma: What is it about modernity and modern Christianity that leads to this dual relation to the Scriptures? The question of the nature of Scriptural authority, therefore, should be related to the larger issue of the transformation of Christianity within modernity.[5]

In a period of so many "posts"—postmodern, postliberal, post-Christian —it is not surprising to find pleas for a postscriptural Christianity, or variations that chasten the role of scripture precisely within theological reflection. While some of these forms of theological reflection may take the characteristically deistic and/or post-Kantian form of blurring any boundaries between religion and human reason "correctly understood," or religion and ethics, others would call into question the canonical limits of the received text, or the authority of Semitic and Hellenistic sets of worldviews for today's global society, or the sense that Christianity is basically textual, or the sense that the figure of Jesus as the Christ known through the apostolic witness is normative for Christianity. These

approaches tend to marginalize the Bible and biblical study, either theoretically or functionally, which precludes the need to discuss in any sustained way the relation of Bible and theology.

From another perspective, John Collins writes the following in a discussion of the possibility of "critical biblical theology":

> Rather the decline [of biblical theology] is evident in the fact that an
> increasing number of scholars no longer regard theology as the ultimate
> focus of biblical studies, or even as a necessary dimension of those stud-
> ies at all. The cutting edges of contemporary biblical scholarship are in lit-
> erary criticism on the one hand and sociological criticism on the other.
> Not only is theology no longer queen of the sciences in general, its place
> even among the biblical sciences is in doubt.[6]

This time not from the side of theology and its relation to modernity,
but from the side of scripture scholarship, the need to conceive a relationship between theology and scripture is muted, in practice if not also
in theory. Collins himself goes on to present a survey of the history of
"biblical theology" and ends with a cautious view of the possibility of a
"critical biblical theology" that emphasizes the rightful role of historical
and literary studies to clarify the genre of biblical material:

> . . . in the broad sense of the way in which it should be read and the expec-
> tations that are appropriate to it. . . . Theological language is an integral
> part of the biblical material, and should not be simply by passed in the
> interests of secular interpretation. We can only ask that the methods we
> endorse in historical and literary research be applied consistently also to
> the theological problem.[7]

Collins's strategy is a conditional one: *if* theological questions are to
be raised, and these are not, to be sure, out of place, *then* the prior work
of historical and literary scholarship must set the appropriate expectations. But theological questions are not, it seems, the necessary or sufficient questions to be raised in the practice of biblical sciences. The
relation of Bible and theology is simply not, and need not be, a focus for
biblical studies.

None of these four facets of the "significantly different position"
admits of simple solutions, nor easy escape. The relation of analytic
methods to interpretive results, of the university to the methods of
reflective human investigation, of academic perceptions to theological
self-definition, of the conventions that relate Bible and theology to the
questions of social context and practice—these conditions among others
shape the questions, the methods, the suspicions, the criticisms, the

results, and the frustrations that the contributing scholars dealt with. Clearly the attempt to characterize the complex context of our own scholarship in the "significantly different position" of theology in a Roman Catholic university at the end of the twentieth century is inevitably reductionistic and incomplete, but even so it serves to draw attention to elements that, although not always articulated, are at work within each of the local studies.

The Whole and Divided Self

The collection of texts that makes up this book is the fruit of a four-year-long collaborative process financed by the Lilly Foundation's Project on Bible and Theology. The scholars involved in this process took seriously what Maurice Wiles had written, that we are in a significantly different position than many before us in our understanding of scripture, and that we have not taken full measure of this difference. In accord with the Lilly Foundation's instruction to focus on specific topics, the "Loyola Group" directed its attention to the question of biblical and theological anthropology. Discussion over the last two decades has brought to the surface several shifts in the modern understanding of the "self," a notion difficult to define but seemingly indispensable for human understanding. Regarding biblical/theological study and the "self," the Loyola Group came to two conclusions early on: (1) the contemporary understanding of the relations between biblical study and theological reflection is pluriform, even to the point where those engaged in contemporary biblical studies have little in common with those engaged in theological reflection and vice versa; (2) the contemporary understanding of "self" seemed to be polarized between those who envisioned "self" to name an ideal point of wholeness and those who interpreted "self" as an intentional position inescapably, and not unfortunately, divided. These two conclusions created the genuine set of conundrums which the working group chose to engage. The topic of "The Whole and Divided Self" was thus the focal point for a series of conversations, colloquia, and research projects which took seriously the various ways that the investigation of the Bible might inform and be informed by theological reflection on the "self." There was no single method, no single theological perspective, no single denominational affiliation, nor any single result that the group utilized or sought. Plurality in all these areas was recognized as one of the marks of our "significantly different position." Yet this plurality seldom impeded true conversation. The result of this conversation and research is thus a collection that reflects the ways in which this group of scholars engaged the scriptural material with a host of questions generated by the contemporary concern with the "self."

The result of the group's scholarship is divided into three major sections beginning with a contemporary "map" of the discussion of the "self" and its importance, followed by six individual studies displaying ways in which biblical and theological reflection contribute to understandings of the "self," followed finally by a text and an interview with Paul Ricoeur on aspects of the relation of Bible and "self."

The contemporary "map," titled "The Self in Context: The Issues," is co-authored by Robert Di Vito and William French. It concentrates on two dimensions of the phenomenon named "self": *depth*, which includes interiority, self-consciousness, the unconscious, and subjectivity; and *breadth*, which includes social, communal, historical, political, and ecological relations. The dimension of depth is discussed through a critical summary of Charles Taylor's *Sources of the Self*. The Loyola Group had the unique opportunity of discussing our project at length with Professor Taylor in Montreal in September 1994. Augmenting this discussion is a summary analysis of four major contemporary locations for the discussion of the "self": the liberal-progressive, the communitarian, the postmodern, and the ecological. These contexts both confirm and expand the analysis of Taylor by providing a statement of the ways in which the contemporary discussion of the "self" is carried on and the problems, especially theological and ethical, that these discussions raise.

The first study of the second part of the collection provides a thorough presentation of the issues surrounding the discussion of the "self" in canonical Hebrew scriptures. Robert Di Vito argues that, while there may be an absence of explicit language that deals with the "self," especially language of interiority and self-consciousness, this does not entail an absence of the understanding of "self." The "self" of the Old Testament, however, is substantially different from the modern "self" described, say, by Taylor. Di Vito carries his analysis forward by constant engagement with Taylor's positions and through four discussions: the embedding of the individual in society, personal unity, human interiority, and heteronomy. The result of this discussion is a clear set of alternatives to the discussion of the modern "self" which warrants the position of an understanding of the "self" in contrast to the modern problematics rather than an absence of "self" *in toto.*

In the second article of this section, "Two Pauline Models of the Person," David Aune offers explicitly theological conclusions regarding the plural, even contesting, senses of "self" in the biblical writings. Beginning with an analysis of the eclectic character of Paul's statements on human nature, Aune develops two basic models by which he locates Paul's thought on the "self": (a) the irrational behavior model, and (b) the apocalyptic macrocosm-microcosm model. On the other side of a thorough analysis of these models, Aune raises the specific question of whether Paul's views of human nature, clarified by historical-critical method, have anything to contribute to a modern understanding of the "self."

The third article, "Singing the Psalms: Augustine and Athanasius on the Integration of the Self," by Pamela Bright, moves the study of the "self" away from canonical scripture to instances of its reception. Bright focuses first on book 10 of Augustine's *Confessions* and the role of memory in the creation of an interior. But this interior "self" is not the only "self" that Augustine offers for reflection. Bright provides an analysis of how the reading and singing of the Psalms play a role in creating the integrated "self" that Augustine displays. Along with Augustine, Bright offers a distinctive analysis of singing the Psalms in the work of Athanasius, focusing on the need for an embodied "self" in harmony with other singers and with divine order itself.

Willemein Otten continues this focus on the reception of scripture in her investigation of two autobiographies from the Middle Ages, those of Otloh of St. Emmeran and Peter Abelard. Beginning with an analysis of autobiography in the Middle Ages and the role of reading the Bible in the monastery, Otten moves on to study precisely how the reading of scripture acted differently for these two monks in the creation of a literary "self" embedded in autobiography. Neither whole nor divided, these two autobiographies display a "self" that is at the boundary of communal definition and aesthetic creation.

William French's work, "Soil and Salvation: Theological Anthropology Ecologically Informed," mounts a strong argument for a fundamental reorientation of modern theological scholarship away from an anthropological focus. By using his own narrative of a farming home transformed into a nuclear reactor, French highlights the effects of placing the "self" outside, and in control, of nature. Using both scripture and theology, he argues that the modern, individual, introspective "self" has established its own conditions for self-destruction. As an alternative, he presents the vision of an ecologically informed "self."

The sixth and final work in this second section, entitled "Narrative Selfhood," is offered by John Haughey, S.J. Haughey investigates the multiple layers of narrative that create self-identity. He notes that "identity" is not all that the "self" bears; it likewise may be described as "character," and with the topic of character Haughey enters into the ethical and theological interpretation of the metanarratives which structure self-identity. Turning to specific passages, Haughey reflects on the appropriation of scriptural narratives mediated specifically by religious traditions.

The final part of the book is composed of two works from Paul Ricoeur. The first is the unpublished eleventh Gifford Lecture, "The Self in the Mirror of the Scriptures." In this lecture Ricoeur displays the pluriform unity of the biblical canon, focusing first on the linguistic mediation of faith in scripture, second on the unity of the biblical material created by various forms of literary imagination, and third on the simultaneous pluriformity of this unity observed through the various genres that constitute these writings. This lecture concludes by correlating the reference of biblical genres, the effort to name God, with the "self," understood as the simultaneous pulsation between the quest for a center and the disappearance of the ego.

The final piece is a wide-ranging conversation with Paul Ricoeur conducted in December 1994. The discussion touches on several issues including the role and importance of canon, the place of liturgical reading, the understanding of testimony and attestation, approbation as a final moment of textual appropriation, and the issues of misreading.

Final Observations

David Tracy, in his 1987 work *Plurality and Ambiguity*, wrote the following:

> At times interpretations matter. On the whole such times are times of cultural crisis. The older ways of understanding and practice, even experience itself, no longer seem to work. . . . Then we need to reflect on what it means to interpret.[8]

It may be that the "significant difference" of our own situation constitutes one of these times of cultural crisis, or at least a crisis with the configuration of the religious scholar. If so, then maybe dialogical collections of papers and positions such as this volume are not a luxury but a necessity for critical, even self-critical, biblical and theological study. It is one way to respect the unities and divisions of both the Bible and the "self."

Notes

1. Maurice Wiles, "Scriptural Authority and Theological Construction: The Limitations of Narrative Interpretation," in *Scriptural Authority and Narrative Interpretation*, ed. Garrett Green (Philadelphia: Fortress Press, 1987), 43–44.

2. Pontifical Biblical Commission, "The Interpretation of the Bible in the Church," *Origins* 23:29 (January 6, 1994): 519–20.

3. Francis Fiorenza, "The Crisis of Scriptural Authority: Interpretation and Reception," *Interpretation* 44:4 (1990): 356–57.

4. Ibid., 358.

5. Ibid., 355.

6. John J. Collins, "Is Critical Biblical Theology Possible?" in *The Hebrew Bible and Its Interpreters*, ed. William H. Propp, Baruch Halpern, and David Noel Freedman (Winona Lake, Ind. Eisenbrauns, 1990), 1.

7. Ibid., 14–15.

8. David Tracy, *Plurality and Ambiguity* (San Francisco: Harper and Row, 1987), 7.

Part One

The Self in Context: The Issues

The Self in Context: The Issues

*William C. French
and Robert A. Di Vito
Loyola University Chicago*

[T]he field of my labours is my own self. I have become a problem to myself, like land which a farmer works. . . .

(Augustine, *Confessions* 10.16)

Whether he [Mr. Kurtz] knew of this deficiency himself I can't say. . . . But the wilderness had found him out early. . . . I think it had whispered to him things about himself which he did not know, things of which he had no conception till he took counsel with this great solitude—and the whisper had proved irresistibly fascinating. It echoed loudly within him because he was hollow at the core. . . .

(Joseph Conrad, *Heart of Darkness*)

The Depth and Breadth of the Self

*F*or us in the late twentieth century, in ways foreign to Augustine, the "self" has become a problem. Accordingly works on the self proliferate. Basic social confidence rooted in stable institutions, entrenched social practices, and shared religious and cultural beliefs has weakened. The familiar has been rendered strange, the simple now appears complex, the normal as one option among many.[1] Modern transportation technologies have escalated the flow of world trade and travel, and these, coupled with revolutions in communications and media, heighten almost everyone's consciousness of cultural and religious pluralism. This throws individuals and communities into a pattern of questioning as a result of the awareness of other life options and modes of being human. Additionally, in Michel Foucault's terms, we have distinctly modern "technologies of the self" displayed by different streams of psychological therapy that have profoundly shaped our cultural assumptions about personal identity and a well-lived life.[2] Similarly, new social movements challenge entrenched disciplinary canons and working assumptions, raising new possibilities of interpretation and analysis. The stable, individualist views of traditional liberalism are being probed and rejected in distinctive ways by feminists, communitarians, and postmodern thinkers.[3] Further destabilization is caused by attention paid to the juggernaut of human power and numbers that has surged across the planet in this century. The unprecedented tripling of human population (now about 5.8 billion) and the fiftyfold expansion of the gross world product since the turn of the century have had a massive impact on human communities and planetary ecosystems. Expanding industrialized agriculture, urbanization, and fuel and resource consumption heighten levels of species loss, soil erosion, greenhouse gas emission, global warming, and ozone depletion. Where Augustine and earlier generations could marvel at the majesty and vast scope of God's creation and take solace in its massive stability, this generation marvels at the scale of our newfound human powers and worries about what these bode for the community of life on this planet in the next century. Like communitarians and feminists stressing a "relational self," those attending to humanity's emerging environmental fears understand the self as deeply relational, but relational both socially and ecologically.[4]

Recently in philosophical, theological, and culture-theory circles discussions of the "modern or postmodern self" have generated a rich array of analyses and perspectives on the distinctive ways contemporary society and culture allow individuals to think of themselves. For most, talk of the "self" seems obviously at home in modern psychology and continental philosophy, and yet talk of "the self" inevitably engages notions of community and morality. To be a "self" is to recognize one's social relations and loyalties and participation within one or multiple communities (family, neighborhood, tribe, nation); likewise it requires the recognition of the borders of these social groupings and the class of "outsiders," lumped collectively as "the other."

Abstract discussions of the self are not generally useful, for one cannot isolate some core "self" from the various narratives and categories that each person inhabits. Psychotherapy, for example, is thought of not as a project of recovery of the self's core but rather a process by which the therapist's questioning, coupled with a nonjudgmental context, elicits from the patient the recovery of repressed experience, which, in turn, makes possible a new constructive reappropriation, understanding, and self-acceptance. Healing occurs via the patient's speaking about hurt and anxiety and reincorporating these experiences into a reformulated personal narrative. While therapy is a private matter, the healing occurs by means of a verbal formulation which thus makes personal experience both public and personally accessible.

If the notion of a "core self" seems foreign to current discussion, other dimensions do not. Humans have both *depth* (interior subjectivity, self-consciousness, complex emotions, layers of anxiety and hurt, drives, deep memory, anticipations about the future) and *breadth*, both in social relations—that is, in connections to other individuals, human communities, and institutions—and in natural relations—that is, in participation within the ecosystem of a local "land community" and, more broadly, within the planetary biosphere.

These two dimensions of persons—depth and breadth—offer the two dominant historical trajectories for thematizing the self in Western culture, the first, the path of introspection, and the second, the path of the expansive attention to horizons of relationality. The introspective path, the progressive probing of the "inner depths" of the self, has enjoyed dominance in classical, intellectual, and religious circles. As Charles Taylor, Karl Weintraub, and others so well describe, this dominant account is explored by Plato, St. Paul, Augustine, Luther, Descartes, Pascal, Kant, and other giants. The association of the self with the "inner depths" of interiority, not in social role or public relations, enjoys a classical philosophical and theological pedigree as well as widespread philosophical influence through the impact of modern existentialism and phenomenology. Likewise the rise of modern psychology has given this introspective location of the self a powerful modern idiom and broad cultural appeal. Accordingly, the dominant theoretical discussions of "the self" tend to refer back to the history of the rise of this "introspective self" in Western culture and to the classics of Western intellectual history where watershed understandings of the self's depths were promulgated. Below we will consider in some detail Charles Taylor's important recent contribution to the history of the rise of the Western self.

The second trajectory for thematizing the self—while not as prominent in the philosophical, psychological, or literary-critical literatures—finds its development primarily in modern sociology, social theory, and moral philosophy. For these disciplines the self is social, front and center. This trajectory too enjoys classic expression in Aristotle's politics, in the Thomistic stress on the common good, in modern sociology and ecology, and in both ancient and contemporary streams of ethics. This trajectory holds that the self must be understood explicitly in light of its multiple social and natural relations. Psychological formulations or philosophical and theological anthropologies that fail to frame understandings of the "contemporary self" in its concrete and multiple social and natural communities will necessarily distort our understanding of the contemporary human condition and its distinct moral responsibilities and resources. This trajectory too provides a critical reminder that we are not really dealing with "the self" but with quite diverse selves, with distinct histories in diverse societies, cultures, classes, and social groupings. Some live in cosmopolitan centers, some in towns and villages, and others in rural regions. To hold that the self is social is to take seriously the social location of discourse about "the self" and any understanding of it. This is an important check against discourse of the self slipping wildly into broad and untestable generalizations.

Depth and the Path of the Introspective Self: Charles Taylor

Charles Taylor in his *Sources of the Self: The Making of the Modern Identity* has given great energy to the discussion about the formation of the modern sense of self.[5] According to Taylor, the contemporary understanding of the self has been constituted above all by what can only be called a certain sense of inwardness, a sense of there being an "inside" as opposed to an "outside," a world "within" and a world "without."[6] Developing especially under the impact of the Enlightenment and romanticism, the various forms taken by this sense of inwardness have grounded in turn salient features of modern identity and the marked individualism that is so prominent in it. Two of these features of the modern identity may be highlighted as representative of a whole cluster of broader associations: (1) a self-responsible independence achieved through powers of disengagement and self-objectification, and (2) a conviction of individual uniqueness founded upon moral and religious self-exploration and self-expression.

The first of these features owes its origin to Plato's insistence on self-mastery through the use of reason, or more precisely, on the reign of order within the soul as a result of the submission of human desire to reason and its vision of the Good. As the single locus of human thought and feeling in all its variety and complexity, the soul thereby achieves within itself a kind of unity or harmony, indeed a "calm" and a self-possession. The person who is genuinely ruled by reason is both at one with himself or herself and centered within oneself, rather than driven this way and that by conflicting desires. In fact, this centering and unity with oneself become so important in Plato's thinking that success in the world is no longer decisive, as he sees it, for personal happiness: the just life is the most advantageous life even if one should have to suffer for his/her acts of virtue.[7]

But, as Taylor sees it, Plato's theory is only the precondition for the rise of a sense of inwardness. Its real emergence must await Augustine's transformation of Platonic epistemology and ethics, because only with Augustine is a distinction between "within" and "without" consistently introduced into the discussion of these topics. In ethics it is seen, for example, in the typical Augustinian emphasis on the goods of the soul "within" the person over the goods of the body "without"; in other words, in the insistence on those goods that are spiritual and immaterial over those that are merely corporeal and fleeting. And in Augustine's epistemology it is clear in his transformation of the vision of the Good, once a transcendent principle of cosmic order, into an interior "light," a light shining within the person, which makes thinking possible, and is, in fact, an invariable standard grounding the very activity of human reason itself. In other words, with Augustine one can observe a shift toward a "radical reflexivity" grounding a sense of interiority, insofar as what becomes decisive epistemologically is not the direction of one's attention to the world but rather attention to one's activity as a thinking person, the act of knowing itself. For Augustine, that is where God above all is to be found—within one's very self. And this shift of attention makes the language of interiority "irresistible."[8]

While with Augustine the distinction between "within" and "without" for the first time becomes significant, it is Descartes who transforms this notion of interiority into the peculiarly modern sense of self-sufficiency and self-containment. This happens as a purely mechanistic conception of the universe gradually replaces the classical notion of a cosmic order which is good; once the embodiment of eternal Ideas, the universe is reduced instead to a realm of unthinking mechanical law. As such, the order of reason ceases to be something to be *discovered* by the knower and becomes rather something requiring his or her construction. In fact, to know reality for Descartes can only be to form a correct representation of it, a correct picture *within* oneself of the reality outside *oneself*.

Of course, the consequence of these cosmological and epistemological shifts is a far-reaching transformation in the definition of the ideal knower. Where formerly the ideal lay in a certain attunement of the knower to the Good embodied in the world, now the ideal, attainment of a genuine certainty about what one knows, can be defined only by reference to a soul disengaged from the world and thus even from its own body. Since Descartes's mechanistic cosmology precludes the soul from sharing any essential properties with the world, only the soul's capacity, precisely as disengaged, to *construct* order according to criteria proper to itself as reason establishes its rationality. In other words, rationality has become for Descartes purely procedural, and the certainty that reason achieves has become itself a self-achievement. This is most certainly not Augustine's "self." It is the characteristically modern self, self-sufficient and self-reliant, radically disengaged both from the world and the body, both of which are now conceived merely instrumentally.[9]

The Cartesian notion of disengagement provides, then, the foundation for the modern ideal of rational self-control as well as for the modern self's instrumental stance toward the world. Both are only possible insofar as the subject has disengaged itself from the world by "objectifying" its own experience, that is, by adopting a purely neutral and impersonal stance toward it. For Descartes, of course, that meant recognizing that our ordinary perceptions—sight, color, smell, taste, pain, etc.—are all merely "in the mind," "secondary qualities" of the objects we experience rather than real properties of the objects themselves (viz., figure, number, and size).[10] Only by stepping back from those perceptions, and by implication from *our* own experience of the objects we wish to know, can one know those objects, including our own self, as they really are and not simply as they appear to us.

Of course, this also deprives the subject's normal experience of whatever normative force it might have had in the past for knowing and puts the disengaged knower into a position of control, or mastery, over the objects of its experience in the world. Thus, disengagement becomes the very condition of rationality, which for Descartes is nothing if not the capacity of the subject to construct a representation of reality based on its own internal criteria. And for the sake of that power the knowing subject cannot in the end identify itself by its association with any concrete and particular order or domain of being, even if the latter should be identified as the "right" one.[11] Thus, for Taylor the modern self is already foreshadowed. It is a "punctual self," "extensionless" and found only in its "power to fix things as objects."[12]

No wonder, then, that for Locke the very dignity of a rational being lies in this power of the disengaged subject. Not only does he argue passionately for an ideal of independence and self-responsibility; he argues for nothing less than a complete liberation of reason from the shackles of established custom and traditional authority. Thus, the only real knowledge is that which one develops for oneself.[13] This involves the subject in such a radical stance of disengagement from its own spontaneous mental activity (viewed as the quasi-mechanical assemblage of ideas imposed by tradition and external authority) that it must engage in an unprecedented labor of deconstruction as a precondition to a no less radical remaking of oneself. Is it any wonder that under the impact of this program language turns increasingly to purely "reflexive expressions," such as the "self," the "I," the "ego"?[14]

Of course, the development sketched here with Descartes and Locke undergoes further elaboration in the course of Taylor's exposition of the contemporary sense of self. New emphases inevitably emerge, such as Kant's insistence on a morality that is grounded on nothing but the human rational will and his rejection of any and every form of heteronomy.[15] But even so one can see that with Descartes and with Locke the major elements of modern identity are already in place: a free, autonomous, disengaged, self-sufficient, and self-responsible unity.

Only one additional element needs to be identified for this picture of modern identity to be complete, namely, that form of inwardness which depends on "self-exploration." Here is a form of inwardness that works not through disengagement from oneself, but rather through a more radical attention to individual particularity and unrepeatable difference.[16] The result is the quite modern sense of the individual as one who has profound "inner depths,"[17] the peculiarly modern conviction that there are whole "worlds" to explore within oneself. As Taylor traces its development, it originates with Montaigne, who initiated the movement toward self-exploration by recognizing that the search for a universal human nature can never resolve the issue of who we as individuals are; and the movement gained further momentum in the eighteenth-century theory of natural moral sentiments.[18] The rise of the modern novel also furthered it, with its detailed portrayal of the lives of particular people. Instead of the archetypes of mythology, the modern novel taught the lesson that it is in the particular stories of their individualized characters that the real truth is to be found. The true nature of a thing now lies precisely "within."[19] Ultimately we are who we are because of the purposes and capacities that are there to be discovered within us.

It is this strain of inwardness which romantic expressivism deepened and developed, especially in its insistence that each individual is unique and original. But what is really significant here in the insistence on human uniqueness and originality is romanticism's rejection of the classical and medieval notion of individual difference as merely "accidental," or inessential, to human identity. Indeed, for the romantics, it is the very difference or originality that marks individuals that ought to determine how each of us lives our lives. It–and not any kind of rule imposed from "without"–ought to set the measure, for ourselves as well as others, according to which we ultimately will be judged.[20]

It is out of the necessity, then, of articulating one's inner nature that the modern notion of inner depth finally comes. Although Augustine's concept of *memoria* might suggest a similar sensibility, one cannot forget that, for Augustine, to plunge the "depths" of memory would inevitably take the subject outside of itself to God. In romantic expressivism, however, the vast domain we are talking about lies simply "within," a deep reservoir upon which one can always draw and to which one can always return.[21] "Self-expression," "self-realization," "self-fulfillment"–all find in this notion of inner depth their ground and justification. Inner "depth," as the story of the self unfolds in *Sources of the Self*, has come to be one of the essential elements of the modern identity.

While Taylor's is one of the most comprehensive and influential of recent analyses of the self, it is, of course, neither the first nor the last attempt to chart this terrain. Karl Weintraub in *The Value of the Individual*, like Taylor, assesses Augustine as achieving a breakthrough in the emergence of the Western self. In Augustine's *Confessions* Weintraub believes we see the first true emergence of "the self" in Western culture and the first genuine autobiography.[22] Like Taylor, too, Alasdair MacIntyre in his influential *After Virtue: A Study in Moral Theory* believes that the "peculiarly modern self" in the West is "the emotivist self," which has purchased its moral agency and sense of freedom through cutting bonds with social identity and classical views of "human life as ordered to a given end."[23] This contemporary self freed from substantial relations and a rooted history guides its action via personal preference and decision. It is for MacIntyre a "democratised self" for, on his reading, the Enlightenment attempted to prescind from any substantial accounts of the self to allow liberty where the agent can step back from social roles or particular commitments in substantial histories of relationship and loyalty.[24]

Breadth and Four Frames for Thinking Through the Self

But the self as internal, introspective depth is not the only voice of the self today nor the only path that self-reflection has taken. Any fuller mapping of the contemporary self will need to draw on the resources which underscore the expansive breadth of self.

While there are multiple currents in contemporary discussions of the self we will distinguish among them four prominent streams of analysis: (1) the liberal progressivist, (2) the communitarian, (3) the postmodern, and (4) the ecological. The story of the contemporary self in the West has tended to be told in variations of the first two dominant social and political traditions. In recent years these ways of framing the self have been joined by varieties of the second two critical approaches—the postmodern and the ecological. Of course, these four models of analysis often intertwine in complex ways, and thinkers frequently mix varieties of these models in their work.

The Liberal Progressive Frame

The progressivist view affirms the Enlightenment emphasis on personal freedom and subjectivity. Peter Berger argues that modernization undercuts the identification of the self with communal and institutional roles and thus weakens the conditions that energize the concerns for honor and shame that are so prominent in tribal and heroic societies. By contrast, the "solitary self of the modern consciousness" gives rise to concerns for personal "dignity" and rights inhering in each person regardless of social status or occupation. Concerns of honor arise in communities that have "relatively intact, stable institutions" allowing the individual to find identity in social roles. Modernization pushes individuals to "discover" their "true identity" by emancipation from "socially imposed roles." In honor/shame societies authentic existence is a matter of communal role. In modern culture, "authenticity" is thought to be achieved via liberation from public role.[25] Often this history of the self is narrated as a dramatic epic where individual wholeness is understood as a personal achievement of self-creation.

Emile Durkheim has provided a more optimistic assessment of the possibilities of the public sphere in modern society. Against the notion that modern selves are isolated and separate, he believes that the division of labor in fact gives rise to a new type of "social solidarity." In traditional communities prior to the rise of complex economies there is "a more or less closely organised totality of beliefs and sentiments common to all the members of the group." This "collective type" enjoys "mechanical solidarity," high cohesion because the "individual consciousness" is a "simple appendage of the collective." "Solidarity which comes from resemblance is at its *maximum* when the *conscience collective* completely envelops our whole consciousness and coincides in all points with it. But, at that moment, our individuality is nil."[26]

By contrast "organic solidarity" arises with the division of labor and social and institutional differentiation. Where mechanical solidarity arises to the extent "that individuals resemble each other," organic solidarity arises in proportion to the way individuals differ. Organic solidarity is "possible only if each one has a sphere of action which is peculiar to him—that is, if he possesses a personality." Where mechanical solidarity is threatened by emerging individuality, the organic solidarity is stabilized by increasing individuality. "[E]very individual depends more directly on society as labour becomes more divided; and . . . the activity of every individual becomes more personalised to the degree that it is more specialised."[27]

The Communitarian Frame

Where Durkheim views organic solidarity as the norm, and anomie as disordering pathology, communitarians tend to see privatization and alienation as the norm in modern individualism.

Ferdinand Toennies's account in his 1887 book, *Gemeinschaft und Gesellschaft*, has proved broadly influential, and it well illustrates the rhetorical power of imagery of decline. Powerful metaphors are invoked to praise community as "real and organic," and condemn society as "a mechanical aggregate and artifact." Community is an "intimate . . . living together." Society is moving "into a strange country," the spheres of "business, travel, or sciences," the "public life." While in community humans are "essentially united," in society they are "essentially separated." A "fundamental characteristic" of society is "negation."[28]

Where progressivist theories present an epic of the ascendancy of self-reflective consciousness, freedom, and authenticity, communitarian theories tend to tell a tale of sad decline, an unraveling of genuine community into distorted individualism and inauthenticity. The rise of the self then is a narrative of a painful loss of "wholeness" through a journey into personal dividedness and social separation.

In Berger's view the modern self feels "homeless" because of the "pluralistic structures of modern society" which make the "life of more and more individuals migratory, ever-changing, mobile." Society's "solution" to the "discontents" of modernity, according to Berger, is the "creation of the private sphere" as a "segregated sector of social life." Personal identity located amidst the private relations of the self offers "shelter" against the "threats of anonymity" raised by the impersonality of large-scale corporate institutions. The private realm—family life, voluntary associations, religious community—arises in the "interstitial area left over by the large institutions of modern society" and is accordingly "under-institutionalized" and experienced as unstable and fragile.[29]

In a major study, Habits of the Heart, Robert Bellah and colleagues chart the emergence in, and corrosive impact on, American culture of what they dub "ontological individualism," the "idea that the individual is the only firm reality."[30] Like Berger, Taylor, and MacIntyre, they fear that the rise of a "therapeutic culture" prizes community as long as it is personal and private and freely contracted. However, the vocabulary of "therapy" tends to disparage politics as alienating and moral claims of "oughts" or "duties" as an "intrusion" of "authoritarianism."[31]

Bellah argues that the private-versus-public split must be healed through a reconnection to the languages of community and substantive morality kept still vital in "communities of memory," particularly our religious communities and our republican civic traditions. Where the "me generation" feels free from any history, "communities of memory" maintain richer understandings of how selves are participants in traditions that stabilize communal life. These communities are shaped by vocabularies and loyalties that connect them substantively to the civic world even as they provide narratives that link them in memory to previous generations and in anticipation of future ones.[32]

The Postmodern Frame

In this section we rely primarily on David Tracy's analysis of this important movement in contemporary thought. In contrast to both the progressivist account of the modern self in liberal theory and the regressivist account of the communitarians, postmodern thinkers offer a transgressivist understanding of the self as "decentered." Saturated in the realization that all thinking occurs in a particular culture and history and through language which itself is historically informed, limited, and diffuse, postmodern analyses undermine old certitudes about objective reason, autonomous individuals, stable canons and interpretations, and historical progress. Against modern pretensions that science discerns pure data and facts about the world, postmodern science is self-aware that its history is one of constructive interpretations of the world. Against romantic understandings of language expressing some primal, "nonlinguistic truth inside the self," postmodern accounts hold that there is no prelinguistic voice at the core of the self. As Tracy puts it: "I think my best and worst thoughts, I understand my most intense pleasures and pains, I make my most considered and my most rash judgments . . . in and through the languages available to me."[33]

Postmodern thought understands that interpretation of texts, history, society, and oneself must go on within the context of vastly plural interpretive and disciplinary schemas, cultural perspectives, and historical narratives. Postmodern analysts speak of the self as "decentered," no longer the confident, autonomous self employing language as an instrument to express one's depths and to name and thus control reality. The self can no longer claim "full self-presence" because it is inextricably shaped by multiple narratives, histories, and languages which each limit and distort even as they disclose.[34]

The postmodern picture is transgressive in that it breaks the confidence of the self as proud subject and agent by showing how the self is so powerfully acted on by language and culture. Also it is transgressive in that it attends to the underside of modern history, the interruptive breaks, the bloody wars, the silenced victims, the *tremendum* of the Holocaust. Its insistence upon these histories is potently disruptive of confidence in Enlightenment reason, technological progress, or the superiority of Western culture.

"Difference" and "otherness" are central terms in postmodern views of the self. As Tracy puts it:

> The split self of postmodernity is caught between conscious activity and a growing realization of the radical otherness not only around but within us. We name that otherness, after all, the unconscious. . . . Ideologies are carried in and by the very language we use to know any reality at all. . . . And with a heightened sense of language, the interruptive realities of history and society have entered consciousness anew. . . . Otherness has entered, and it is no longer outside us among the "others." The most radical otherness is within.[35]

Where some postmoderns speak of the "disappearance of the self," Tracy holds that there remains a subject, a self who loves, thinks, and acts. Only this self is "chastened" for it is "a more fragile self—open to epiphanies." It is decentered, but with "coherence," even if only a "rough coherence," made rough by its very openness to multiple histories, interpretations, and languages.[36] Following the lead of Marx, Freud, and Nietzsche—the great interpreters of suspicion—the postmodern self employs suspicion and retrieval, to interrogate claims and traditions, so as to empower resistance to oppressive powers and ideologies.[37]

The "open self" of postmodernism, then, shifts the central focus from interiority and "self-centeredness" to a "liberating Reality-centeredness." For Tracy, Judaism, Islam, and Christianity, despite their differences, agree on a similar demand of self-transformation in a shift of our "center from the ego, by means of that new relationship with Ultimate Reality." Only in this conversion can "the self cease to be an ego and find some authentic freedom by being related to nature, history, others, and even the now transformed self."[38]

For Tracy, the great religions hold potent resources for generating resistance to ideology and oppression and for sustaining praxis oriented toward justice. Postmodern Christianity must appropriate the insight of liberation theologies that "God's option for the poor is central to the Scriptures."[39]

The Ecological Frame

Emerging after World War II, troubling data regarding humanity's degradation of the planetary biosphere began to appear. Increasing human population growth coupled with new modes of energy production, industry, agriculture, and weapons prompted scrutiny about humanity's interaction with the nonhuman natural world. Anthropocentric traditions in ethics had tended to restrict ethical attention to human–human interactions and to let human actions upon the nonhuman sphere be evaluated as merely technical questions governed solely by concerns of efficiency. Similarly the center of modern theology came to focus on the God–human relationship, grace and sin, and Christology. The doctrine of creation, especially under the impact of existentialist and personalist thought, came to play a decreasing role in the first half of the twentieth century. History came to be understood as the interesting category for theological reflection because history was viewed as the arena of human freedom and subjectivity and the key realm of God's revelation and saving acts. Nature, by contrast, was often depicted as a realm of impersonality, an object realm, a sphere of unfreedom and necessity. Even as "nature" served as a conceptual foil for "history," so too did "animality" serve as a contrast for understanding the "human." When human "animality" was acknowledged, usually this was to make a moral point about the dangers of drunkenness or lust dragging us down into the world of "brute" instincts.

Instead of allowing the "self" and culture to be located simply within history, the ecological turn in contemporary thought calls for an acknowledgment that the self and human history have evolved within the sustaining and limiting structures of the planetary biosphere. Against an "exclusionist" model of nature which sets the human apart and above, the ecological view requires an "inclusionist" understanding which includes the human within the natural world. The human then is in nature thoroughly, and nature is in the human throughout. It is not that our bodies and passions are natural but our minds are excluded. Rather, mental life is fully natural because mental life arose within the context of earth's complex history of biochemical and atmospheric change and emerged remarkably via evolutionary processes from the stuff of matter. Human history is enfolded within natural history.

The ecological self too is decentered in that the human is no longer considered the sole locus of "intrinsic value." In the words of Aldo Leopold, an ecologic ethic "changes the role of Homo sapiens from conqueror of the land-community to plain member and citizen of it. It implies respect for his fellow-members" and also for the entire "biotic community" within which the human participates.[40]

Where many postmodern thinkers suspect the term "nature" because of its associations with the traditional attempt to generate "natural law" foundationalist claims of a universal ethic based on nature and reason, ecological thinkers insist that human cultures emerge through evolutionary natural history and in their flourishing are still constrained by natural, biospheric limits. Where some postmodern analysts suspect those who stress "nature" as failing to take history seriously, ecologists counter that the complex history of humanity's evolution on earth, and the history of humanity's accelerating technological assault on significant parts of the ecosphere are critical histories that we ignore at our peril. These histories, some suggest, are *the* critical histories of our day.

Like postmodern understandings of the self as needing to respond to otherness within and without, ecological thinking believes that the nonhuman sphere has historically served as the epitome of the "radical other." Both human sinfulness and the "id" have been thematized repeatedly by employing metaphors and imagery of the "brutes" and "beasts." To develop a truly "open and responsive" self, ecological thinking suggests that we must be open to the voice of the oppressed even if the oppressed's "voice" is a nonhuman one. Ecological thinking is suspicious of resting lightly with the notion of nature as radical other, for nature is as radically near as our next breath, or meal, or our next set of neurons firing. So too ecological thinking tends to interpret the contemporary self as located in truly a "crisis time" where the gravity of the ecological threats we face pushes the self to recognize in awe its dependence on a long chain of evolutionary processes and previous generations and to recognize its responsibility to future generations. While many dismiss the threat of global warming as "distant," the "ecological self" is opened to feel suffering and damage possibly occurring fifty years hence as terribly near.

Unlike postmodern understandings, which often employ language of reality being culturally and linguistically "constructed," ecological thinkers find this emphasis deeply misleading. Nelson Goodman illustrates in his *Ways of Worldmaking* the dangerous hyperbole at work in this "constructivist" epistemology. He makes the point that language classifies and constructs *our* world of experience and thought. In his view, however, there is no "world"; rather, there are various "world-versions" each built up for different purposes by different disciplines and described in various ways. He stresses human interpretive freedom and holds that there are multiple "contrasting right versions" of the world.[41] But as

Hilary Putnam (who generally agrees with Goodman) notes, people whose version "told them they could fly" and who "act upon it by jumping out of a window" would, if they are "lucky enough to survive, see the weakness" of their version "at once." Where Goodman depicts the self as a mighty constructor, Putnam holds that the self is a more humble interpreter open to "experiential *inputs*."[42] The self construed as interpreter rightly avoids the overblown rhetoric and controlling arrogance of the "constructive self," making and remaking the "world" through its words and versions. For ecologists there are biospheric and ecological "realities" which simply are not humanly constructed. We certainly must interpret them, but we must take them seriously in their own right as "existents" and not merely as part of the "free play" of our interpreting.

Contributions of the Four Frames

While in some academic circles it is fashionable to critique the "Enlightenment Project" of reason grounding a universal theory of rights and individual freedoms, it remains true that rights theory is a vital tradition and is one that many peoples of the globe would be overjoyed to see applied regularly in their nations. As Berger reminds us, if the rise of modern society has increased "privatization" and a sense of "homelessness," so also has modern society provided us with a belief in the equality of human dignity, human rights, a rejection of slavery, a new sensitivity to suffering and an abhorrence of torture.[43] Despite significant problems, the liberal progressivist view deserves careful critique, not broadside dismissal and sweeping indictment.

The communitarian account helpfully provides balance to the liberal view by understanding the self as firmly located—morally, historically, and mentally—within broader communities and society. The postmodern approach by decentering the self seems to fracture the self into a multi-relational "trace." The postmodern view both radicalizes the self's sociality in its multiple languages and cultural shapings and decenters stable understandings of personal autonomy, objective reason, and Western cultural superiority. The ecological view, for its part, seeks to broaden our notion of community further by locating the self, human society, and the widening web of multicultural interpretations, within the biosphere understood ecologically as a "community of life."

None of the four accounts or frames enjoys a monopoly on moral insight, and none is immune from moral callousness. Certain ecological positions fixate on nature but ignore social justice concerns. Some postmodern fascinations so emphasize the "free play" of our interpretations that they substantively support a fashionable nihilism, always deconstructing and never actually generating any serious policy alternatives. An emphasis on community by itself does not ensure better ethics. The Nazis were steeped in a communitarian ethic that celebrated blood, land, and race, yet insisted on demonizing "other" communities. Similarly "individualist" doctrine can easily promote social callousness.

If these narrative types do not in themselves provide a substantive ethic, what moral contributions might they offer? We believe they provide important hermeneutical resources for "suspicion" and "retrieval" which can only deepen our moral reasoning, our historical understanding, our theological reflection, and our biblical interpretation. The liberal view is most sensitive to historic patterns of tyranny, group domination, and slavery which have caused vast human suffering. The communitarian is attentive to how individualism and unfettered capitalism can legitimate social injustice. The postmodern is sensitive to how centered selves and communities claiming privileged objective reason or access to "inner voices of revelation" too often pridefully dismiss the "other" as "inferior" or worse as "demon." The ecological is responsive to how we have shaped nonhuman nature as the "Great Other," a field passively waiting for our "conquest" and "domination."

The moral affirmations of each frame, even if not entailing a full-blown substantive ethic, are important. Taken together they provide reminders about what any ethic must take account of today if it is to be even relatively adequate. Concerns for human rights, the well-being of the "common good," our situatedness in multiple histories, and our embodiment in, and dependency on, nature are all key elements in any relatively adequate ethic and any relatively adequate account of the self.

Whole Selves and Wide Relations

The affirmations of each of the frames provide resources for raising questions about the way the self is depicted as we read the historical texts of Western religion and culture. Do the selves express themselves in rich self-reflexive language the way moderns do? What types of social solidarity dominate, and what key terms and metaphors are used to name this solidarity? How broad does the range of a person's identification extend? To whom or what do they feel loyal, bonded, and responsible?

There are multiple dimensions along which understandings of self-identity vary from culture to culture and over time. For example, different groups might acknowledge the role of the unconscious, but give it different weight in their full description of the self. These multiple dimensions of self-identity vary along ranges of saliency or emphasis, and they locate the self within various relations: (1) to God, (2) to other individual persons, (3) to other internal voices, (4) to primary social groups—family, clan, (5) to voluntary social associations, (6) to varieties of social categories—race, gender, (7) to coherent personal narratives, (8) to the natural cosmos/biosphere, (9) to one's body, and (10) to history. Attention to these dimensions and the different weightings which occur in any text or period can only enhance our understanding of different periods and different cultures.[44]

The four frames, moreover, thematize in different ways "dividedness" and "wholeness" of the self. The liberal tends to appreciate the dividedness of social roles, for, as Durkheim noted, such role specificity promotes individualism and "organic solidarity." Personal "wholeness" is seen as a project of personal development in the private sphere. Integrity is high, but the breadth of this self is "narrow." The communitarian, against the thin liberal self, seeks to broaden the self by overcoming the private/public split that bifurcates the individual into private/public selves. The dominant metaphor of communitarians is greater individual wholeness achieved through a growth of civic wholeness. The postmodern, for its part, decenters the false image of objective "wholeness" with reference to the self as a dangerous, prideful "mask." This false "wholeness" must be fractured by stressing the radical "dividedness" and "otherness" abroad and within. Through this shock therapy a "chastened self" with a more humble view of integrity and wholeness through radical "openness" can emerge. Finally, ecologists discern danger in how the surging global economy energizes individual wants, pushing the "tragedy of the commons." Danger is seen in expanding human powers becoming liberated from communal controls or moral restraints. The dividedness of corporate interest groups and individuals seeking consumerist notions of the good life (surely *the* culturally dominant narrative of the self) pushes ecologists to stress healing of self and society as necessarily tied to healing our relations with the earth. Ecological thought sees "wholeness" as responsible living with and in nature. The narrow self is made "whole" through an expansion of direct identification with the entire community of life.

Personal "wholeness," then, can refer either to the unity and integrity of the self or to being broad and whole in one's openness to relations with others, to God, to animals, and the land. Traditionally "wholeness" has been the affirmed goal, while "dividedness" has been viewed as an obstacle. However, one need not look to postmodern thought to find many traditional religious affirmations of "dividedness" and radical fracturing as vehicles of healing, realignment, and the promotion of more mature authenticity. Notions of conversion have long contained a stress on the decentering which must occur if the self is to attend to God and to reach out to the neighbor. Shattering is required to destabilize the incurving energy of the ego as it seeks to center life in self-love and not in God and worldly service. One of the services performed by postmodernism is the new opportunity offered for retrieving these disruptive traditional religious insights.

These are sharp reminders that "wholeness" is not always what it is "cracked" up to be. Wholeness in the sense of personal unity and integrity may simply be rooted in high coherence achieved through little personal complexity or broad loyalties, concerns, and identifications. Narrow selves rooted in prejudice and affirming limited relations within a tightly circumscribed community may well have high personal unity, but most would not want to call this genuine personal wholeness. It would seem that wholeness is best understood as a goal where personal integration is sought within a wide openness of relations to others, society, nature, and God.

The Self and Theological Reflection

The trajectories of *depth* and *breadth* can be seen playing prominent roles in the history of Christian theological anthropological reflection. The Christian life has often been thematized in terms of a journey in which "dividedness" is healed and parts are made "whole." It is a journey toward our real "home." Theologies stressing the radical transcendence of God have tended to promote understandings of human life as a journey of interior ascendancy to God. The jangling of the outer world falls away in silence to an opening up to an immediacy of the divine presence. Christian mystics and monks throughout the centuries have followed the path of interior contemplation seeking intimate union with Christ. For example St. Bonaventura in *The Mind's Road to God* follows Neoplatonic notions of "ascent" via contemplation of the world, the spirit, and the mind. In this century Karl Rahner has shaped a whole generation of Catholics to understand God as the horizon and ground of the self discernible in "transcendental reflection" on human understanding, freedom, and subjectivity. Although Rahner differs markedly from Bonaventura, both call for a journey into interiority.

The Theologies stressing God's creatorship have tended to see the broad range of the created world as good and worthy of respect and civil society as deserving of tangible support. The Protestant Reformation energized this Christian "affirmation of ordinary life" by breaking with the notion of priestly celibacy as a higher calling than marriage and by stressing one's duty to one's vocation in the world.[45] The Christian journey in this reading is not into interior ascent; rather it is the journey out into God's world to work for God's people. Recent liberation theologies have gone back to the exodus story, the prophets, and the life and death of Jesus, to locate the center of Christian witness in the promotion of justice and peace and the overcoming of oppression. As in the exodus journey from oppression to "freedom," current Christians are called to promote a new historical journey of social transformation. Recently ecologically minded theologians have begun to point out that the exodus destination was not an abstract state of historical freedom but rather a new life in relation to a good land.

Just as theologians down through the centuries of necessity have attempted to put their reflection in close contact with the thought forms shaping the understanding, reflection, and social practices of each generation, so too contemporary theologians, religious ethicists, and indeed pastors must find points of contact between theological expression and current understandings of the self, of history, and of nature. Without these explicit points of contact, theological reflection may continue to be intellectually and systematically refined but will increasingly lose its ability to be experientially compelling to broad ranges of general society. Just as Thomas Aquinas drew on Aristotelian understandings of human life and the cosmos in order to develop a vital theological articulation of classic Christian belief, so too today theologians and ethicists must draw on the best insights of our age about the dynamics of the self and its complex relations. In this way attention to the two trajectories of thematizing the self and the four frames surveyed earlier may contribute to more adequate and responsible theological reflection and religious practice.

Notes

1. Thomas C. Heller, Morton Sosna, and David E. Wellbery, eds., *Reconstructing Individualism: Autonomy, Individuality, and the Self in Western Thought* (Stanford: Stanford University Press, 1986); and Michael Carrithers, Steven Collins, and Steven Lukes, eds., *The Category of the Person: Anthropology, Philosophy, History* (Cambridge: Cambridge University Press, 1985).

2. Luther H. Martin, Huck Gutman, and Patrick H. Hutton, eds., *Technologies of the Self: A Seminar with Michel Foucault* (Amherst: University of Massachusetts Press, 1988), 16-49, 121-44. On the rise of the "therapeutic sensibility," see Christopher Lasch, *The Culture of Narcissism* (New York: Warner Books, 1979); and Robert Bellah et al., *Habits of the Heart: Individualism and Commitment in American Life* (New York: Harper & Row, 1985), 47-51, 121-38.

3. Seyla Benhabib, *Situating the Self: Gender, Community and Postmodernism in Contemporary Ethics* (New York: Routledge, 1992). For the feminist recovery of the relational self, see Carol Gilligan, *In a Different Voice* (Cambridge, Mass.: Harvard University Press, 1982); Paula M. Cooey, Sharon A. Farmer, and Mary Ellen Ross, eds., *Embodied Love: Sensuality and Relationship as Feminist Values* (San Francisco: Harper & Row, 1987); and Jean Crimshaw, *Philosophy and Feminist Thinking* (Minneapolis: University of Minnesota Press, 1986), 162-86.

4. See Freya Mathews, *The Ecological Self* (London: Routledge, 1991); and Wendell Berry, *Home Economics* (New York: North Point Press, 1987).

5. See J. J. Buckley, "A Return to the Subject: The Theological Significance of Charles Taylor's *Sources of the Self*," *Thomist* 55 (1991): 498; and Paul Lauritzen, "The Self and Its Discontents: Recent Work on Morality and the Self," *Journal of Religious Ethics* 22 (Spring 1994): 189-210.

6. Charles Taylor, *Sources of the Self: The Making of the Modern Identity* (Cambridge, Mass.: Harvard University Press, 1989), 111.

7. Ibid., 111-26.

8. Ibid., 128-31.

9. Ibid., 143-58.

10. Ibid., 162.

11. Compare the portrait of the modern self, the so-called "emotivist" self, by Alasdair MacIntyre (*After Virtue: A Study in Moral Theory* [Notre Dame: University of Notre Dame Press, 1981], 30): "It is in this capacity of the self to evade any necessary identification with any particular contingent state of affairs that

44 WILLIAM C. FRENCH AND ROBERT A. DI VITO

some modern philosophers, both analytical and existentialist, have seen the essence of moral agency. To be a moral agent is, on this view, precisely to be able to stand back from any and every situation in which one is involved, from any and every characteristic that one may possess, and to pass judgment on it from a purely universal and abstract point of view that is totally detached from all social particularity."

12. Taylor, *Sources of the Self*, 171-72.

13. Compare MacIntyre, who describes the peculiarly modern concept of authority as one which excludes the notion of reason. This separation is "fashioned in a culture to which the notion of authority is alien and repugnant, so that appeals to authority appear irrational" (*After Virtue*, 41).

14. Taylor, *Sources of the Self*, 165-75.

15. Ibid., 364. Indeed, Charles Davis identifies modernity precisely with "the affirmation of an autonomous, self-legislating, self-related subject and the insistence upon a doctrine of immanence that refuses submission to anything that attempts to impose itself heteronomously from without as knowledge or value" ("Our Modern Identity: The Formation of the Self," *Modern Theology* 6:2 [January 1990]: 159).

16. Taylor, *Sources of the Self*, 178-82.

17. Ibid., 211.

18. Ibid., 283-84.

19. Ibid., 286-87.

20. Ibid., 375-76.

21. Ibid., 389-90.

22. Karl Joachim Weintraub, *The Value of the Individual: Self and Circumstance in Autobiography* (Chicago and London: University of Chicago Press, 1978), 1-48; Taylor, *Sources of the Self*, 127-42.

23. MacIntyre, *After Virtue*, 32.

24. Ibid., 30-31.

25. Peter Berger, Brigitte Berger, and Hansfried Kellner, *The Homeless Mind: Modernization and Consciousness* (New York: Vintage Books, 1973), 88-93.

26. Emile Durkheim, *Selected Writings*, ed. and trans. Anthony Giddens (Cambridge: Cambridge University Press, 1972), 138-39.

27. Ibid., 139-40.

28. Ferdinand Toennies, "*Gemeinschaft* and *Gesellschaft*," in *Theories of Society: Foundations of Modern Sociological Theory*, ed. Talcott Parsons et al. (New York: Free Press; London: Collier Macmillan, 1965), 191-92, 197.

29. Berger, Berger, and Kellner, *Homeless Mind*, 184-87.

30. Robert N. Bellah et al., *Habits of the Heart: Individualism and Commitment in American Life* (New York: Harper & Row, 1985), 276.

31. Ibid., 139.

32. Ibid., 152-55, 282, 286.

33. David Tracy, *Plurality and Ambiguity* (San Francisco: Harper & Row, 1987), 49.

34. Ibid., 51, 59.

35. Ibid., 77-78.

36. Ibid., 82-83. On the "disappearance of the self" imagery, see Mark C. Taylor, *ERRING: A Postmodern A/theology* (Chicago and London: University of Chicago Press, 1984, paperback ed., 1987), 34-51. On the "contingency of self-hood," see Richard Rorty, *Contingency, Irony, and Solidarity* (Cambridge: Cambridge University Press, 1989), 23-43.

37. Ibid., 77.

38. Ibid., 89-90; see also 74-75.

39. Ibid., 103.

40. Aldo Leopold, *A Sand County Almanac* (New York: Sierra Club/Ballantine, 1966), 240.

41. Nelson Goodman, *Ways of Worldmaking* (Indianapolis: Hackett, 1978), 4-5.

42. Hilary Putnam, *Reason, Truth and History* (Cambridge: Cambridge University Press, 1981), 54.

43. Berger, Berger, and Kellner, *Homeless Mind*, 95. For a postmodern analysis of the advance of the rejection of cruelty, see Rorty, *Contingency, Irony, and Solidarity*, 141-98.

44. Our group owes thanks to our sociologist colleague Mark Chaves, of the University of Notre Dame, for this helpful analysis.

45. Taylor, *Sources of the Self*, 211-33.

Part Two

Studies

Here One Need Not Be Oneself:
The Concept of "Self" in the Hebrew Scriptures

Robert A. Di Vito
Loyola University Chicago

The Problem of Definition and Approach

*A*lthough articulating the concept of self in the Old Testament (OT) might seem a relatively straightforward assignment to those in other fields, for biblical scholars the task is somewhat perplexing. Moreover, the reason for the quandary has little to do with the kinds of problems that ordinarily beset OT studies of a comparable scope: the length of the time span covered by the literature of the OT and the many changes in culture and society to which it bears witness; the multiplicity of genres in the OT and the wide variety of ideological and theological viewpoints they represent; and the limited knowledge we have of the social, economic, and political contexts of even those texts to which scholars can assign approximate dates. In none of these would one have touched upon the cause of the biblical scholar's initial confusion: namely, the simple, if not obvious, fact that classical Hebrew does not have a word that even remotely corresponds in its usage to the English word "self." Of course, Hebrew can, even in the absence of true reflexive pronouns express reflexive thought and action by means of suffixed personal pronouns and, without difference in meaning, by *nepeš* ("person") and a personal pronoun:[1] viz., *haʾōtî hēm makʿîsîm nĕʾum* YHWH *hălôʾ ʾōtām* ("Is it me that they provoke?" says the Lord. "Is it not themselves?" [Jer. 7:19]) and *nišbaʿ ʾădōnāy* YHWH *bĕnapšô* ("The Lord God has sworn by Himself. . . ." [Amos 6:8]). But even so there is no talk of a "self" or the "self." So how does one inquire into the notion of "self" in the OT when it lacks the word, if not the concept, as a category of explicit reflection?

Evidently, one will have to proceed by asking what is involved in the contemporary conception of the self and by determining to what extent *that* conception is actually represented in the OT—the assumption being that an absence of explicit talk about the self does not mean the OT's construction of personal identity actually lacks one. In other words, the issue is not, as some older and even some more recent works have suggested,[2] that ancient Israel lacked a concept of individuality or simply failed to prize any form of personal autonomy and initiative. Such a negative assessment seems completely unwarranted, particularly in view of studies, such as those by F. R. Kluckhohn and F. L. Strodtbeck, which have criticized the simple dichotomies on which these kinds of assessments of traditional societies typically depend—dichotomies such as that drawn between a more or less homogeneous, conformist/collectivist folk society and a more complex, nonconformist/individualist urban one. In other words, all societies share the same basic stock of values, insofar as the values in question here really represent "solutions" to common human problems. Where, then, they finally differ from each other, relatively rather than absolutely, is *not* in their values but only in their *ranking* of these values and in the degree of their *explicitness* about them.[3] So what we are going to find in a comparison of ancient Israel and the modern West on the subject of the self is not really an absolute dichotomy but rather something in between, where the absence of explicit language in the OT may merely reflect a different rank-ordering of values it actually shares to some degree with modernity (e.g., a high valuing of self-mastery).[4] To take a simple example from the *Iliad*: Homer may have no word to express an act of choice or decision by his heroes; but it would be a mistake to infer from this that Homeric society had absolutely no consciousness of personal freedom or decision. The issue of concern for Homer, the one that is reflected in language, is the distinction between "normal" actions and those performed in a state of $at\bar{e}$[5]—and not the distinction between those actions which are voluntary and those which are involuntary. Consequently, it should come as no surprise that Homer has not developed a language of choice or a language of "will" to mark more explicitly the modern interest in personal intent. And in a similar way, perhaps we should not be surprised—given the values of the OT—to find there no explicit talk of the self.

This makes, however, another question all the more pressing. What, quite simply, is this "self" *we* speak of? As vexing as it might be to talk about the nature of the "self" in the OT, it seems no less challenging to say what it means today. While discourse about the "self" is so pervasive in contemporary society that educated and uneducated speakers alike have difficulty even imagining that "the self" is not a universal feature of language, the concept itself remains an elusive one. Indeed, part of our difficulty in defining what we mean by it may be its very currency in everyday language. Talk about the self is so widespread, and the word used in such very different ways even by the same speakers, that any single definition is probably too much to ask for. Charles Taylor in his *Sources of the Self: The Making of the Modern Identity* has, in fact, taken notice of the localized quality modern conceptions of the self have and their time-bound character as historically particularized achievements. As a result, his own effort to sketch a picture of modern identity is essentially the story of its chronological development from earlier notions of personal identity.[6] That historical dimension to Taylor's work, as well as the critical acclaim it has received from scholars of quite varying theological and philosophical persuasions,[7] makes his discussion of modern identity and its concept of the self a particularly attractive starting point. The discussion that follows is obviously indebted to Taylor's work, and the reader is advised to see it in conjunction with the treatment of Taylor presented in the preceding essay in this volume, where it is set in the context of a much broader treatment of current discussions of the self.

An exhaustive review of the OT here is, of course, out of the question, since some understanding of the self implicitly informs the whole range of its literature. It would potentially include not only how characters or subjects in various books relate to each other and how they relate to God in the text but even how the authors of these texts tacitly relate to the subjectivity they create. (In fact, an author's relation to his or her own creation can involve several levels of complexity in the "I" that emerges as the speaking subject.[8]) This complexity might suggest that the scope of our study be limited to a specific book or to a particular genre. Yet, despite some rather obvious limitations, a number of reasons make a broad focus on the whole of the OT advisable here. Not only does a wide focus allow one to see patterns across books or genres that would not otherwise come into view; it also makes it possible to develop a framework for localized studies which subsequently can confirm, refute, or modify the overview's broader results.

The Biblical Perspective on the "Self"

If Taylor's study can claim, at least in its overall lines, to be an adequate representation of what is meant by the "self" today (insofar as we are speaking simply of a particular cultural expression of it), it is clear that the OT knows of nothing quite comparable. The comparison of the self that emerges in the OT with the self of modernity highlights in a way not otherwise obvious facets of personal identity in the OT that contrast sharply with significant aspects of modern selfhood. These include modernity's sense that human dignity lies in self-sufficiency and self-containment, based on the self's disengagement from the world constituted by its social location; its feeling of personal unity and of having sharply defined personal boundaries; its awareness of inner depths; and finally its sense of autonomy, based in part on the conviction that our very humanity depends on a capacity for self-legislation. All these contribute to what is, according to Taylor, the modern self's profound sense of "inwardness," a sense of there being a world "within" the self as well as a world "without," a world whose potentialities somehow also hold the key to our "true" selves.[9] And since this is perhaps the most salient feature of modern identity, it is with an eye especially to this interiority and the various forms it takes in the making of modern identity that the issue of personal identity comes into focus in the OT. Four general headings set the lines of the analysis: (1) the embedding of the individual in society; (2) personal unity; (3) human interiority; and (4) heteronomy.

The Embedding of the Individual

In contrast to the relative atomism, self-sufficiency, and disengagement of the modern "self," the picture of man and woman that emerges in the Bible is one of deep engagement in ever-widening circles of social life, beginning with the "family," the basic social unit. Of course, one cannot think of the latter simply along the lines of today's so-called nuclear family; rather, one ought to think along the lines suggested by the idealized schema that Josh. 7:14–18 provides, an account of the "discovery" and subsequent punishment of a violator of the rules for Holy War.[10] As this text has it, an Israelite male identifies himself by naming first of all the *bayit* ("house") or, more specifically, the *bêt ʾāb* ("house of the father") to which he belongs, then the larger *mišpāḥâ* ("family" or "clan") and finally the *šēbeṭ* or *maṭṭeh* ("tribe"). (Beyond these, to be sure, are even more inclusive categories, such as the ʿam ["people"], the šibṭê Yiśrāʾēl ["tribes of Israel"], and the běnê Yiśrāʾēl ["children of Israel"].) Accordingly, Joshua 7 identifies the individual (geber) Achan by his patronymic "son of Carmi," then by the bêt ("house") of Zabdi, of the mišpāḥâ ("clan") of Zerah, of the šēbeṭ ("tribe") of Judah. Achan's "immediate" family—that is, his sons and daughters who suffer along with him for his crime (no mention is made of any wife)—lacks any generic designation as a unit and is treated instead simply as an extension of Achan himself, viz., part of "all that belongs to him." Similarly, there is no designation for the grouping presumably headed by Achan's father Carmi, but only for the bêt ("house[hold]") headed by Achan's grandfather, Zabdi. In other words, the "household" of Zabdi is treated as the smallest unit in the overall social structure of Israel, even while in this case it includes apparently four generations![11] This, the extended "family" making up the bêt ʾāb, is, then, where the individual Israelite found the ground of personal identification and selfhood.

As the term bêt ʾāb suggests, the ancient Israelite "family" is unequivocally patriarchal. Genealogies are reckoned through the father's line (with only a rare mention of the mother), and the nearest collateral relation is the paternal uncle (Lev. 25:49).[12] In fact, since kinship was reckoned through the male, the mother's kin lack specific kinship designations and are not even counted as relatives genealogically.[13] The identification with the father is further reinforced by the bêt ʾāb's patrilocality. The wife, in other words, left the bêt ʾāb of her father upon marriage and went to live within the bêt ʾāb of her husband, who became her baʿal ("master"). But if the latter was not also the oldest living paternal ancestor, his overall authority was in fact a limited one, since authority over the "household," including over the wives and children of resident sons, actually resided with the paterfamilias.[14] He was the head of his "household," and in this capacity he—along with all the other heads of households—comprised that group known in the Bible as the "elders" (zěqēnîm). Taking their seats of honor "in the gate" (Deut. 21:19; 22:15; Ruth 4:1, 11; Isa. 29:21), they wielded authority over all aspects of village or city life. (Job 29 offers a striking picture of the respect accorded these community "leaders" as well as the important role they played in the maintenance of community life.) And to the extent that a village was made up of a single clan (mišpāḥâ) formed by joining together several "households," one could say that family and village were simply coextensive, so that the former provided the dominant form of social organization within which the individual Israelite lived out the entirety of his or her life.

Among other things, this means that the "father's house(hold)"—under the rule of its head (rō'š)—also provided, as Wright has suggested, the basic framework of legal authority for an individual, from childhood to perhaps well into adulthood.[15] Within it the control of the head theoretically went unquestioned, including as it did the right to act independently and without reference to any external authority, in matters ranging, for example, from parental discipline to marriage and divorce. So far, in fact, did this judicial independence of the head go that members of a household even enjoyed some measure of inviolability vis-à-vis the larger community as a result of it, at least when it came to seizure for criminal wrongdoing (Deut. 24:10f.; Judg. 6:30f.; 2 Sam. 14:7). But the upshot, of course, is that sons, daughters, and wives nonetheless had few if any "rights" apart from those granted them by the head of the house.[16] Several laws even imply that children were regarded legally as assets or property with a monetary value (see designation of Achan's immediate family as "all that belongs to him" in Josh. 7:15), so that a man could sell his daughter even for the purpose of concubinage (Exod. 21:7ff.), and in extreme poverty might sell his children into "slavery" as a pledge against a loan (Neh. 5:1-5; 2 Kgs. 4:1-7). In point of fact, of course, children were not simply property; and finally the power of the paterfamilias was not absolute. Deut. 24:16, for example, expressly prohibits vicarious or substitutionary punishment of a son for a father's offense; while the "law of the rebellious son" in Deut. 21:18-21 suggests that with its arrival there was some limitation on the power of the head of the house, insofar as this law reserves a son's execution to a decision by the elders "at the gate."[17] Yet in all periods the very real power of a father over children can hardly be minimized. Indeed, the practice of child sacrifice (Judg. 11:29-40; Gen. 22:1-14; 2 Kgs. 16:3; 17:17; 21:6), while probably not an acceptable feature of a mature Yahwism in the Bible, nonetheless illustrates just what a father's "possession" of children might be taken to mean.

Not even death severed the links that bound the individual Israelite (male) to his "father's house." On the contrary, a decent burial meant that he might at last "be gathered to" or "sleep with his fathers" (Gen. 49:29; 1 Kgs. 2:10; 11:21; passim), presumably in one of those "family" (communal) tombs which were usually located just outside and adjacent to the settlements. These, in turn, stood as a perpetual witness, not simply to the memory of the deceased, but to the family's enduring hold on its land—and, perhaps even more, to the obligation living sons had to preserve it.[18] Each *bêt ʾāb* had its own *naḥălâ* ("patrimony"), which, as the story of Naboth's vineyard illustrates (1 Kings 21), was in principle inalienable, since it was the sole theoretical basis for the economic viability of the *bêt ʾāb* down through the generations. As such, every effort had to be made to keep the patrimony intact and within the "household," in keeping with the terms of the original allotment. As a result, the head of the household (*rōʾš bêt ʾāb*), holding only the right of usufruct, by means of this system of land tenure was obligated "beyond death" to preserve the patrimony he received in a double sense: not only was he bound to preserve it for his deceased forebears but also for his own posterity, regardless of whether or not he might live to see them.

Personally, socially, economically, and religiously—in all these ways, according to the OT, the individual Israelite, male and female, was embedded in the family and kinship obligations that constituted social life. And the picture is one whose overall lines seem to be confirmed by modern ethnoarchaeological studies of the region, such as the study Stager cites by A. I. Tannous of the Arab village of Beitin, the site of ancient Bethel.[19] There a kind of multiple family household known as *zaʿila* ("the joint family") supersedes the nuclear family's household as the most important domestic dwelling unit:

It consists of the father, mother, and unwed children as well as the wedded sons and their wives and children, unwed paternal aunts, and sometimes even unwed paternal uncles. In short this unit is composed of blood relatives plus women who were brought into the kinship through marriage. Large as it may be, this unit tends to occupy one dwelling or a compound of dwellings built close together or often attached to one another. It is an economic as well as a social unit and is governed by the grandfather or the eldest male. The joint family normally dissolves upon the death of the grandfather. The land, which until then had been held by the grandfather, is divided among the heirs, and the male children separately, each to become the nucleus of a new *zaʿila*.

In many parts of the Near East, according to Stager, this is still the typical organization in agricultural villages, the kinship ties linking several "houses" being reflected in their proximity to each other within the village and with sometimes even whole quarters of villages established for those of a common lineage. The family compound is, in other words, the focus of village life and the basic unit of economic activity within the village. The multiple family group inhabiting the compound (*bayit*) not only is responsible as a whole for the acquisition, processing, and preservation of the food it produces; but it is also the beneficiary of its own labor.[20] It is both a social and an economic unit, collectively farming the land and sharing its produce. And although under premodern conditions extended and multiple families may have constituted not more than 50 percent of the village population at any one time, its obvious advantages for small proprietors living off the land made the multiple family household until quite recently a kind of ideal pattern for all household organization.

While we have no interest in making historical claims here about ancient Israel, this account from ethnoarchaeology of the classic "patriarchal family" appears to find a resonance in the archaeological ruins investigated at several Iron Age I-II village sites in Israel, among them Raddana, ʿAi, Meshash, Tell Beit Mirsim, Tell Fârʿah (N), and Tell en-Naṣbeh. At these sites, clusters of dwellings, each composed of two or three individual houses, are typical, each house having a separate entrance opening out onto a shared courtyard. It is quite likely that these "compounds" represent multiple or extended family households, the ancient Israelite bêt ʾāb corresponding to the modern Arab zaʿila. Moreover, the archaeological and literary evidence indicates that this type of compound was not simply restricted to the Iron Age and the period of national "independence" prior to 587 B.C.E., but actually persisted in Palestine well into the Roman period. In fact, a reference to such a compound may plausibly lie behind the promise of Jesus in John 14:2, "in my father's house are many mansions."[21]

To be sure, more could be said about the relations that enmeshed one, according to the OT, in groups and structures of social life which extended well beyond, in fact, the household and the lineage. One has only to think, for example, of the important socioeconomic role played by the mišpāḥâ ("clan"), particularly as expressed in the institution of the gōʾēl ("redeemer"). According to the latter, since all males within the clan were regarded as "brothers" (ʾaḥîm), they could, precisely as "brothers" (at least theoretically), be required to play the part of "redeemer" for another clan member, in an order strictly fixed by genealogical proximity (Lev. 25:49). This might mean avenging the murder of a kinsman (Judg. 8:18-21; 2 Sam. 3:27; 2 Sam. 14:1-11; buying or redeeming the land of a bêt ʾāb if poor kin were forced to sell it (Lev. 25:23-28); redeeming kin sold into debt-slavery (Lev. 25:47-55); or playing the part of a deceased brother in the levirate marriage (Deut. 25:5-10).[22] But while positive examples of the family solidarity the Bible envisions can easily be multiplied—extending even to the nation as a whole (viz., Abraham's obedience in Gen. 26:4–5 means the ultimate fulfillment of the patriarchal promises)—the tight web of enveloping kinship networks could also have its "darker" side. Thus, YHWH visits the iniquities of fathers upon their children to the third and fourth generation (Exod. 20:5; Ezek. 18:1–3); the guilt/punishment for an individual's crime is explicitly laid upon the *bêt ʾāb* as a whole (1 Sam. 22:16ff.; 2 Sam. 3:29; 2 Sam. 21:1ff.; and 2 Sam. 24:17; cf. Joshua 7); and David's decision to take a census results in a pestilence upon the entire people (2 Samuel 24).

Indeed, the extent to which solidarity implicated all family members in the fate of one of its members is well documented in OT scholarship, where its consequences for the psychology of the ancient Israelite have often been the subject of considerable debate. But here we should like to emphasize only that these familiar examples of family solidarity and social embedding should not be exaggerated or taken, as they have been, simply as evidence for the "primitive Hebrew mentality," some psychic incapacity on its part to distinguish between the individual and the group or to recognize the limits of the individual personality.[23] Even if a movement toward individual responsibility in the religious sphere is a relatively late development (Ezekiel 18),[24] one that comes with a change in the criterion for sin (*ḥāṭāʾ*) to YHWH's law and his *miṣwōt* (Lev. 4:2, 13, 22, passim; Jer. 16:10–12),[25] in the realm of everyday "secular" law the focus of responsibility was on the individual from the beginning. (This is true both in Israel's earliest legal collection, the so-called Book of the Covenant in Exod 20:22–23:19, and in the later Deuteronomic legislation against vicarious punishment [Deut. 24:16; 2 Kgs. 14:5].[26]) Thus, it is perfectly clear that the disengagement of an individual wrongdoer from the solidarity of the family was always both a theoretical possibility and an ordinary occurrence. But this also means that some sense of individuality and/or unity of personality was always operative in Hebrew psychology. Ancient Israelites could point to themselves as individual agents of action (viz., "I") as well as any modern, and would know well enough, if not better, to stand out of the path of a charging bull![27]

All the same, this simple recognition of some individuality in no way diminishes the significance of what we have been referring to as "family solidarity" or the "embedding of the individual."[28] The notion of self operative in the OT remains radically different from the "self" we talk about today. In fact, one ought to suggest, in light of the degree of engagement the individual has in enveloping kinship networks, that a great deal of the language of contemporary moral discourse, with its insistence on notions of "self-responsibility," "autonomy," and "personal freedom," runs the risk of being incoherent when applied to the individual described in the pages of the Hebrew Bible. From the point of view of the modern self, the individual Israelite cannot even quite be considered a "moral person."[29] But this is not to deny, in some absolute sense, a degree of moral responsibility to the historical individual; nor is it finally to succumb to the kind of simple dichotomy that pits the "collectivist" personality of primitives against the modern "individualist." The point is simply to ask from a cultural point of view what one is left with after disengaging the embedded Israelite identity from all those relations that are central to his or her personal definition. Can we say that such an individual, disengaged from a social location, really has an identity? While for the modern self, self-contained and self-sufficient in its determinations of value, disengagement from a social location can be the necessary starting point for moral existence, it is hard to imagine the ancient Hebrew in the same position. Just who would he or she, in fact, be?

This is perhaps just another way of suggesting that in the context of the OT the "family" or kinship group must be considered the primary moral unit—indeed a genuine moral community. The individual Israelite, disengaged from membership in such a community, is simply not a "self" about whom one can meaningfully speak or whose actions one could meaningfully evaluate. The only reality is the socially "embedded self," the one who is identified essentially, both for oneself and for others, by membership in a particular father's "house," a particular clan, or a particular village. And it is to the roles and practices that constitute the stuff of these groups' social life that one must look to locate where an individual, according to the OT, finds value and meaning—not to a "self" whose authenticity somehow lies in the disavowal of any and all social roles. For even as these structures of family and kin define who one is, they determine also the totality of one's obligations and duties. Consequently, in the OT, instead of universal "rights" and universal "duties," based on an abstraction from the particularities of a social context, there is only the notion of ṣĕdāqâ ("righteousness"), the fulfillment of all the demands a particular relationship makes at any one moment upon the individual[30] (see 1 Sam. 24:17; Gen. 38:26). Or there is ḥesed ("kindness"), conduct that is in accord with the social norms governing the life of family and the clan.[31] Apart from this, in other words, there is no "personal morality" in the Hebrew Bible. Biblical "morality" will inevitably be context-bound and specific to the social structure of ancient Israel.[32]

Personal Unity

As Taylor has shown, a precondition for the sense of inwardness, autonomy, and self-containment that marks the emergence of the modern identity is the sense of personal unity or identity characteristic of the Platonic localization of thought and feeling in the soul.[33] From what has just been said about the embedding of the individual in family and larger kinship structures, it should come as no surprise that in this respect too the notion of "self" reflected in biblical literature presents a striking contrast to modernity. Yet this is not as apparent as it might be, because of a strong tradition in biblical scholarship which contrasts a Semitic view of the person as a psychosomatic unity to a Greek dualism of body and soul. Under the guise of the kind of provocative contrast Oscar Cullmann drew between the idea of the resurrection of the body and the (Greek) notion of an immortal soul,[34] the distinction between these two modes of thinking has gone on to become today something of a theological commonplace, dominating almost entirely the whole contemporary discussion of Hebrew anthropology. Even as recent a treatment of this question as James Barr's remains largely confined in its analysis to the parameters set by this misleading view.[35]

All the same, Barr's essay is of real interest, because he has—in spite of the just-named tradition—again called into question the concept of the person as a psychosomatic unity in the OT. As we shall see, there is some merit to his skepticism. Unfortunately, Barr's own analysis labors seriously under the unsubstantiated claim that Hebrew nepeš (traditionally, "soul") does on occasion actually mean "soul" in the traditional sense (i.e., something immortal, in opposition to the body, and separable from it).[36] But on this issue H. W. Wolff has already said what ought to be said: namely, nepeš "is never given the meaning of an indestructible core of being, in contradistinction to the physical life, and even capable of living when cut off from that life."[37]

Consequently, our starting point is not this somewhat tired metaphysical analysis of the relationship of "soul" to "body." Instead we begin with the recognition, in itself not entirely new, that in the OT human faculties and bodily organs enjoy a measure of independence that is difficult for us to grasp today, without dismissing it as merely poetic speech or, even worse, as clear evidence for primitive Hebrew thought categories.[38] So, a sated "throat" (nepeš) tramples on honey (Prov. 27:7); the ear of the wise seeks knowledge (Prov. 18:15); Abel's blood cries out to God from the ground (Gen. 4:10); all my inner parts (qěrābay) bless God's holy name (Ps. 103:1); David's heart struck him, because he had cut off the corner of Saul's garment (1 Sam. 24:6 LXX); kidneys (kilyôtāy) chastise the psalmist (Ps. 16:7); one's heart rejoices (Ps. 16:9); bones that were broken rejoice (Ps. 51:10); "wide jaws" (rěḥab nepeš) stir up strife (Prov. 28:25); death and life are in the "hand" of the tongue (lāšôn) (Prov. 18:21); the Lord stirs up the "spirit" (rûaḥ) of the king of the Medes (Jer. 51:11 LXX); and the heart (lēb) dies within Nabal although he himself lives another ten days (1 Sam. 25:37). Here, and in countless other instances, the individual organs or faculties seem to operate as independent centers of activity, taking for their own characteristics or functions we might associate with another organ or with the person as a whole. Yet among them all a true "center" for the person never emerges—some "place" where the various activities and functions of these organs and faculties get localized, as they are wont to be today, in a "soul" perhaps, or a "consciousness," or a self-contained "self."

In fact, one will only look in vain for suggestions of some deeper organic unity from which everything flows, a "self" that might finally assert control. Even a person's face (pānîm), that by which he or she addresses others and in turn is addressed by them, is always precisely pānîm (i.e., plural)—as if to suggest that there is nothing to look for beyond the plurality of ways in which one appears.[39] For its part, the closest nepeš ("soul") comes to the traditional concept of "soul" is in a usage that merely extends its basic meaning "throat" (if not also the neck) and its characteristic activity, namely, need, longing, or desire. In this extended use nepeš then functions as the seat of a wide range of emotions or feelings beyond desire, such as suffering, sympathy, fear, or bitterness (Job 19:2; 30:25; Ps. 6:4; 1 Sam. 1:10).[40] But these emotions are by no means specific to the nepeš alone, and that remains the extent of the localization. Indeed, when the psalmist cries in Ps. 103:1, "Bless the Lord, my 'soul'" (NAB, NRSV; cf. Pss. 42:6, 12; 43:5), nepeš still retains traces of its original connection with the throat (hence, the association "life," "breath," and "desire"), and thus associations of the person as "needy" or "spurred on by vital desire."[41] On no account, however, does nepeš come to mean "soul" in anything like the traditional metaphysical sense, comparable to Plato's localization of desire and emotion in some central "locale," under the hegemony of reason. Even when it is used as a substitute for a reflexive (see above) or as a simple pronoun (Gen. 12:13), in all cases *nepeš* denotes only the individual as a numerical unit.[42] And not surprisingly, in this sense it is applicable both to humans and to animals alike (Gen. 9:10, 12, 15; etc.).

Just as there is no center in which human faculties and emotions are localized, so too are the boundaries that mark personal identity extremely permeable. This becomes especially evident in the use of the term *rûaḥ* ("wind/spirit") to designate the driving force in a person. In addition to the notion that one's breath is given by God (Zech. 12:1; Ezek. 37:6; Qoh. 12:7), we should note that acts in any sense out of normal character are routinely attributed not to the person's *rûaḥ* but to YHWH and his *rûaḥ*. Thus, YHWH's *rûaḥ* empowers Samson to tear a lion to shreds (Judg. 14:6) and turns Saul into "another man" (1 Sam. 10:6). Uncharacteristically negative states, too, are habitually "explained" in the same way, by recourse to an external, supernatural agency. Saul's bouts with melancholia illustrate the point: when the *rûaḥ* of YHWH departs from Saul, in its place YHWH sends an "evil spirit" (1 Sam. 16:14). Henceforth, Saul's behavior, just like his earlier prophesying, is not in some real sense his own. Nor is it—the text seems careful to assert—properly YHWH's own (evil) spirit (compare the "spirit of falsehood" in the mouths of the prophets in 1 Kgs. 22:21-23). So "whose" is it?[43]

Yet for all this apparent lack of a unified and bounded "self," the kind of personal identity that appears in these texts does not yet show the tortured subjectivity or the psychological-ethical dualism of the Qumran sectarians.[44] As Carol Newsom has observed in connection with the canonical Psalter, the "self" one observes in the OT may be suffering and it may be guilty, but its speaking voice is entirely integrated into its experience. Indeed that particular aspect of its voice is generated out of the suffering or the guilt it is experiencing.[45] It is only with the development of a sense of inwardness such as we see emerge later that the potential for inner conflict becomes a reality. Before that one finds, however, no real evidence of self-division, or any indication of a dramatic rupture— for example, between a person's knowing and "willing" of the sort taken (erroneously) as the basis of Rom. 7:15-19.[46] In fact, one finds just the opposite, insofar as in Hebrew the same word is used for both "hearing" or "perceiving" and "obeying"—*šāmaʿ*—or again for "knowing" and "choosing"—*yādaᶜ*; while *lēb* ("heart") is the seat of both understanding and decision.[47] Thus, to know God is to fear him (Prov. 2:5); and not to know him is, quite simply, to sin against him (1 Sam. 2:25).[48]

In short, a prophet such as Jeremiah might complain bitterly about his lot as a prophet, accusing God in 20:7a of "deceiving/seducing" him (*pittîtanî*), indeed of "overpowering" him (*ḥăzaqtanî*); but the complaint—for all its bitterness—never reaches the point where Jeremiah experiences his frustration at the apparent failure of his prophecy as "self-conflict." A closer examination of Jeremiah's complaint is instructive:

> You deceived me, O YHWH, and I was deceived;
> You overpowered me and overcame me. . . .
> For the word of YHWH has meant for me
> reproach and derision all day.
> When I said I will not mention him;
> I will speak in his name no more;
> it becomes in my heart like a burning fire,
> shut up in my bones;
> and I become weary holding it in;
> and I cannot (hold it). (Jer. 20:7a, 8b-9)

To be sure, it is not easy for the modern reader to take Jeremiah's complaint in any sense other than that the prophet is at war with himself, full of "self-doubt" and "self-division." The reader inevitably imagines the conflict to be one taking place precisely "within" the prophet (indeed NAB titles the pericope "Jeremiah's Interior Crisis"), in fact, a "private affair" (see v. 9). But though the modern reader, whose perspective has been shaped by convictions about personal autonomy and individual integrity, may automatically translate Jeremiah's realistic language of compulsion and constraint into merely the prophet's self-doubt, this is manifestly not the worldview of the text. The language of v. 7a makes it clear from the beginning, in fact, that Jeremiah's struggles are not simply with himself but with his God, and that the prophet is the victim of deception and brute strength.[49] What Jeremiah describes, in other words, is the coercion and duress under which he must proclaim his terrible message. It is a message he cannot contain because, properly speaking, it is not *his* message after all but YHWH's (the subject of v. 9a is the "word of YHWH";[50] compare NRSV "there is something like burning fire . . ."). Jeremiah cannot hold this word in anymore than earlier in 6:11 he could contain the very wrath of God.

Consequently, even Jeremiah's impassioned complaints fail to provide a biblical analogy to modernity's tortured self-conflicts. For the author, the essential point is to describe the overwhelming power of the *word* of YHWH as a force upon Jeremiah, a force that acts upon the prophet as powerfully as YHWH's "spirit" (*rûaḥ*) does in other contexts. It is a power that could never have been simply generated out of the prophet's own imagination. The larger context of the pericope, in vv. 14–18, confirms as much, when Jeremiah concludes his complaint by cursing the day of his birth and even the poor messenger who announced it. Yet he will never think, in the manner of a modern, to curse himself! Jeremiah's conflict is not with his "self" but with his God.

This difficulty modern readers have in assimilating Jeremiah's realistic language underscores the need for caution in interpreting any of a number of passages that speak of loving YHWH "with all your heart and all your soul and all your strength" (Deut. 6:4) or which may refer to the heart as "'entirely' (*šālēm*) with (or not with) the Lord . . ." (NAB; 1 Kgs. 8:61; 11:4; 15:3; etc.). Again, to modern ears the implication of possible self-conflict and "internal" division is never far away. Yet the real point, as Jer. 3:10 suggests ("her faithless sister Judah did not return to me with all her heart but rather in falsehood"), is the possibility of deceitfulness and hypocrisy.[51] M. Weinfeld makes the same argument in connection with the expression to be "'perfect' (*tammîm*) with the Lord" (Deut. 18:13; cf. Gen. 6:9, "he was perfect [*tammîm*] in his generation"): integrity (*tammîm*) here refers not to the "wholeness" that comes from the healing of division and conflict but to that perfect and loyal service which excludes any kind of two-faced hypocrisy.[52]

Human Interiority

One of the most striking features of modern identity is the conviction that each individual, specifically as a result of his/her particularity and unrepeatable difference, represents in some way an innovative possibility of the human spirit. What this possibility is, of course, no human being can legitimately say for another, since it is a discovery that ultimately depends on the courage one has to attend to capacities that lie not outside the self but only deep "within." There, deep within, one comes upon a vast reservoir of previously unknown possibilities and untapped energies, which not only justify modernity's habitual language of "self-expression," "self-realization," and "self-fulfillment," but also set the standard by which ultimately they are to be judged.

Such a conviction about the self's "inner depth," of course, is foreign to the thought-world of the OT. It is entirely absent, as we see, even in a comparatively late text such as Isa. 24:1–2 (part of the so-called Apocalypse of Isaiah), with its image of universal judgment and sense of terror at the irrelevance of all social distinction or class discriminations:

> Behold YHWH is emptying the land and laying it waste;
> he distorts its surface and scatters its inhabitants.
> as with the lay person, so with the priest;
> as with the servant, so with his master;
> as with the maid servant, so with her mistress.
> as with the buyer, so with the seller;
> as with the lender, so with the borrower;
> as with the creditor, so with the one against whom credit is taken.

Here the author conveys a sense of the terrible judgment ahead of the earth, not, as one might expect, through a description of the concrete ways in which this judgment will be carried out, but by directing the readers' attention to the fact that all people will be treated *without distinction*. The judgment comes upon all, without regard for their social class, their status or privilege, their wealth or even their poverty.[53] This is what is frightening about the scene: in a world where one's identity is defined by status, when it should count most, it does not matter at all.

Yet what is significant in the context of the present discussion is that this blindness to distinction does not then turn upon those features that would be most relevant in any personal evaluation according to the modern imagination. Obviously, what we have in mind are precisely those "interior" states and dispositions that moderns privilege, especially in the context of any evaluative judgment of persons: intention, motivation, interior freedom, degree of subjective responsibility—a person's spiritual guilt or innocence. What is really terrifying to moderns is a judgment that fails to discriminate between these features, because they are the ones that define authentic selfhood for modernity. When placed beside these concerns, questions of one's social status or social role—whether one is a lay person or a cleric, a master or a slave, rich or poor—hardly seem to carry weight. Indeed they cannot carry the same weight, because social roles, as determinations which are essentially *exterior* to the individual as such—or so the thinking goes—do not and cannot *define* us.

But in the ancient Near East social roles do define the person, and it is precisely the abolition of such distinctions that occasions the kind of anxiety moderns experience as threats to personal identity and selfhood. The horror of the scene in *Gilgamesh* which Enkidu paints of the underworld in his deathbed dream turns, then, as we might expect on death's apparent denial of the significance of social status and thereby echoes the thought of Isa. 24:1-2. Here mighty rulers from the past, the very representatives of the gods Anu and Enlil, now are deprived of their crowns and, instead of being served, are forced themselves to wait table:

> I looked at the house that I had entered,
> and crowns were heaped up.
> I [   ] those with crowns who had
> ruled the land from time immemorial,
> [Priests (?) of] Anu and Enlil regularly set out
> cooked meats,
> Set out baked (bread), set out cold water from
> water skins.[54]

The reversal of social status highlighted here in Enkidu's vision is, in fact, a recurrent motif in texts from the ancient Near East that depict cosmic or regional catastrophes in which the "natural" order of things is somehow upset. In biblical materials a reversal of the natural order characteristically centers on a day of judgment against the wicked, when heavenly bodies will no longer give off their light (Isa. 13:10-11; Ezek. 32:7-8; Joel 2:10; 3:3-4; 4:15) and thus presage the complete turn of Israel's fortunes for the better. But in several Egyptian texts (e.g., "The Admonitions of Ipuwer") and, notably, in the plaster inscription from the Iron II sanctuary at Deir ʿAllā in southern Transjordan recording the sayings of Balaam, son of Beor, a "seer of the gods" (ḥzh ʾlhn) (cf. Numbers 22-24), the societal implications are more explicit. In these, the description of catastrophe highlights, line after line, a reversal of expected social behavior and customary social roles.[55] Thus, in the Deir ʿAllā inscription from approximately 700 B.C.E., Balaam receives a vision of the gods assembled in council in which cosmic disaster is described in terms not only of the unnatural behavior of birds and other animals (cf. Isa. 11:6-9), but also of a poor woman preparing myrrh as if she were rich, of a prince wearing only a loincloth, and of one who was formerly respected now having to respect others. From the point of view of the text these behaviors are as "unnatural" as a "hare eating a wolf." They are unnatural because they undermine the primary basis for individual and personal identity in the ancient Near East, namely, one's social role and social status. Proverbs, for example, can warn:

> Luxury is not comely for a fool;
>> how much less for a slave to rule over princes. (Prov. 19:10)

It is not right for slaves to rule over princes, because one *is* one's social role; one *is* one's status. And this is true even in a text like the "Song of Hannah" (1 Sam. 2:1–10), which celebrates the social upheaval other texts decry. For it is a change in the fate of individuals which the song celebrates (e.g., "the barren wife bears seven sons, while the mother of many languishes," v. 5b)—not a denial of the characteristic markers of social identity or the centrality of status for personal identity.

Accordingly, in the Bible the *real* self is actually the *public* self. One does not look *within* one's self to discover who she or he is but rather only comes to such an awareness through a recognition of the roles one has in society and the status one enjoys. One *learns* who one is through the concrete behavior expected in particular situations, rather than through any kind of introspection:

> Listen to advice and receive instruction (*mûsār*);
>> so that you may be wise in your end. (Prov. 19:20; cf. 8:33)

> The one who loves instruction (*mûsār*) loves knowledge;
>> but the one who hates reproof is a brute. (Prov. 12:1).[56]

> Give (instruction) to a wise person so that he/she may be wiser yet;
>> inform a righteous person that he/she may add to their
>> learning. (Prov. 9:9)

To this extent, "self-knowledge" is relatively unproblematic for biblical characters—at least if one compares their situation to the existential plight of the modern man or woman of "inner depths," whose entire life can be absorbed in a quest for the knowledge of who he or she uniquely is. The biblical character simply has no "hidden depths" (i.e., hidden from one's self) to worry about:

> A lamp from YHWH is a human being's breath,
>> searching out all the chambers of the belly. (Prov. 20:27)

One has a "lamp" from God, given with the breath of life, by which one can confidently examine his or her own thoughts and intentions without fear of self-deception.[57] And, at least for those who are discerning, even access to another's thoughts and deepest intentions is possible:

> A purpose in the heart of a person is deep water;
> yet the person of understanding will draw it up. (Prov. 20:5)

> As in water the face mirrors the face;
> thus the mind (lēb) of a person mirrors the person. (Prov. 27:19)

In the absence of an effort at outright deception (see Prov. 26:23–27), persons simply "reveal" who they are through their behavior. Better yet, one really is one's behavior, in a way that at times can be utterly mystifying to moderns.

> A tale-bearer goes about revealing secrets;
> while the trustworthy keeps a secret. (Prov. 11:13)[58]

> A truthful witness does not lie;
> but a false witness utters lies. (Prov. 14:5)

> The tongue of the wise drips knowledge;
> but the mouth of the fool bubbles with folly. (Prov. 15:2)

> It is in his deeds that a youth reveals himself,
> if his action is pure and just. (Prov. 20:11)

> The fruit of a tree shows the care it has had;
> so too does a man's speech disclose the bent
> of his mind. (Sir. 27:6 NAB; cf. 27:7)

Given what has been described as the subject's relative lack of a unified and bounded "self," the point to be made here is less that one's action manifests a "self" or is an "expression of soul" than that one's activity belongs to personal identity in the same way as "heart" or "spirit" or "soul."

It follows, then, that the body also is not something one merely "possesses," or even, with J. Pedersen, a manifestation of "soul."[59] On the contrary, one is one's body, to the extent that the appearance of a person provides others a firm basis for judging who or what one is. So, Saul was "head and shoulders taller than all the people" (1 Sam. 10:23) when selected as king (cf. Ps. 45:3) and Gideon's brothers all "appeared" to the Midianites to be princes (Judg. 8:18).[60] In the absence of an "interiority" that can serve as the basis for distinguishing a "real" self from an apparent self, there is only the body and its characteristic activities to go by. And that is also why, in a way utterly alien to modernity, in the OT various bodily flows will render their bearers unclean (Lev. 15:1–33). And physical defects are sufficient to disqualify otherwise qualified individuals from actually exercising the priestly office (Lev. 21:16–24). In fact, the blind, the lame, and the crippled are all explicitly prohibited from such service and from offering sacrifice before the altar.[61] But whatever else these harsh attitudes might imply,[62] on no account does their apparent disregard of intentionality or subjective responsibility (see Lev. 15:16; Deut. 23:11)—an "inner life," if you will—indicate an empty formalism or externalism pervading Israel's ritual life. On the contrary, without "inner depths" that can function effectively as the focal point of self-definition and personal identity in the way they do for moderns, the dissociation of who or what one is from one's bodily integrity simply fails to emerge as a basic principle of self-evaluation.

The same thing can be seen in the relative lack of consideration given in the OT to an agent's intention or motivation in the assessment of ethical behavior. For although the Bible has no problem distinguishing between inadvertent sin and willful transgression (Gen. 20:6; Num. 35:16–21, 22–28; Deut. 19:5–6), it nonetheless treats the two categories of sin alike as objects of real concern, and both categories called for satisfaction (1 Sam. 14:24–25, 36–44; Ps. 19:13–14). Unintentional transgressions are even liable to the death penalty (Num. 4:15, 20; Lev. 7:20–21; Num. 6:9–11; 1 Sam. 14:24–25, 36–44). On this point, the contrast with modernity's own privileging of the intentional sphere could not be more evident, and, not surprisingly, it is reflected at the level of the respective terminologies for wrongdoing. While the Bible possesses a relatively rich vocabulary with which to name the act of sin itself (ḥṭʾ, pšʿ, ʿwn, ršʿ, ʿbr, etc.),[63] the same words (ʿawôn, ʾāšām, ḥaṭṭāʾt, etc.) are also used to indicate the condition of the agent that results from the act. In other words, the identical words come to designate both the agent's sin and the agent's guilt—and even the punishment to which the agent is liable.[64] The one inevitably goes with the other, regardless of the disposition or the intent of the agent.

Yet, again, the suggestion that this lack of interiority means that the OT values mere conformism in personal behavior is completely unwarranted. Evident, for example, in Isaiah's condemnation of Israel's worship of YHWH is a concern precisely for such personal "involvement":

> Thus says the Lord:
> Because this people approaches me with its mouth,
> and with its lips honors me,

> while its heart is far from me;
> and their fear of me is a *human commandment learned by rote*
> (NAB: "routine observance of the precepts of men")—
> therefore I will again perform wonders against this people. . . .
> (Isa. 29:13–14a)

The same thought appears in Sirach:

> Like a eunuch lusting for intimacy with a maiden,
> is he who does right under compulsion. (Sir. 20:3; cf. 34:18–20)

What is missing here is simply the modern language of "interiority." The relative "priority" given to a person's conduct over anything like subjective "intent" or "motivation," in other words, is only apparent and reflects instead what we have been arguing for all along, namely, the absence in the Bible of a real analogue to the modern notion of interiority and inwardness. There is no "inner" self in that sense whose claims can be set over against the individual's concrete bodily activity and manifest behavior.

If that is so, for the OT the praise a person receives from his or her fellows can be a good measure of what one really is:

> The crucible is for silver and the furnace for gold;
> a person is judged by the praise he or she receives. (Prov. 27:21)

Honor, that is, the acknowledgment by society (or by a particular group within society) of a person's value and worth,[65] accurately mirrors the truth of the self, inasmuch as the self is summed up in the role one has in society and one's status (rights and obligations) is a function of the group to which one belongs ("like mother, like daughter," Ezek. 16:44; Isa. 57:3; Deut. 23:2–4; Sir. 23:22–26). In this sense honor is never merely an "external" incidental to the truth of who one really is. In the OT the honor that society accords a person (or a group) quite literally gives that person "weight" and "substance," *kābôd*[66]—the same word ordinarily translated "glory" or "honor." The very identity of the derivation underscores that, while honor requires social recognition, in the OT it becomes a real property of the one to whom it is given.[67]

Yet honor is also not exactly an aspect of "interiority." Just consider some of the ways in which honor is typically acquired. Aside from that honor which comes to a person by reason of belonging to a particular family (Prov. 17:6; Judg. 8:2–3; above),[68] it comes with the possession of strength and deeds of valor (1 Sam. 18:10; 2 Sam. 23:8–24; 2 Kgs. 14:10). It also comes with age (Prov. 16:31; 20:29; 23:22–25; cf. Isa. 3:5)

and by the status one enjoys as a parent (Exod. 20:12; Mal. 1:6), particularly if one is blessed with many sons (Hos. 9:11; Ps. 127:5). Wealth
and honor, of course, belong together also, to such an extent, in fact, that
the same word *kābēd* ("heavy") designates both "honor" and "wealth."
So, Abraham became very "heavy" in cattle, silver, and gold (Gen. 13:2;
see also Gen. 31:1; Nah. 2:10; Ps. 49:17; Eccl. 6:2; Esth. 5:9-11);[69]
while, by the same token, poor Job suffers the loss of his honor when he
loses his property and his wealth (Job 29-31). One's wealth, one's age,
the number of one's sons—all these are constituents of honor in the
Bible. And if from the perspective of modernity they appear merely as
"external" accidents to personal identity or as features lacking in
"depth," in the OT they are essential.[70] Again the modern concept of
"inward depths" really finds no ancient analogue.

To be sure, there is talk in the Bible of the "heart" (*lēb*), "inward parts"
(*ṭuḥôt*) (Ps. 51:8; NAB: "inmost being"), "inner chambers" (Prov. 18:8;
ḥadrê beṭen), or one's "interior" (*bĕqereb*); but the intention behind these
expressions falls far short of modernity's language of interiority. This
can be seen by examining the etymology of the words in question or the
literary context in which they are employed. Repeatedly what is at stake
is simply the distinction between what is observable to others and what
remains hidden from their sight. So, for example, *ṭuḥôt* ("inward parts")
is derived from a root meaning "to overspread, to overlay, to coat, or to
besmear," and in Ps. 51:8 parallels the word *sātum*, that in the person
which is literally "closed" or "shut up" (as springs, or wells, of water).[71]
What the psalmist there prays for, in other words, is a fidelity (*ʾĕmet*)
which will put an end to hypocrisy or an attitude that merely feigns loyalty (cf. vv. 6, 18-19)—dispositions that no one but God can observe in
him (Prov. 15:11; Pss. 7:10; 17:3; Jer. 12:3; 20:12).

The distinction between what is observable to others and what is hidden from their sight is particularly striking in the usage of the word
"heart." As the typical seat of reason and decision,[72] the heart represents
that aspect of a person's being which may especially remain hidden and
inaccessible to other human beings, just like the bowels (Ps. 22:15; Jer.
4:19), the "place" where secrets can lodge (Ps. 44:22; cf. Prov. 14:13).
That is why in 1 Sam. 16:7 YHWH must warn the prophet Samuel in connection with Jesse's older son not to judge by his stature and appearance,
for while mortals judge by these things God alone looks at a person's
"heart."[73] Prov. 24:12 makes essentially the same point (cf. Prov. 15:11):

> If you say, "Indeed! I do not know this person,"
> does not the One who tests hearts understand?

As something hidden from sight, "heart" aptly suggests the potential for treachery and deception that is so frequently at the center of the psalmist's complaint about the enemies he faces:

> His speech is smooth as butter,
> while his heart is set on war. (Ps. 55:22; cf. Isa. 29:13)

Of course, in the same context the psalmist might equally have chosen with no apparent alteration in meaning bĕqereb ("within"):

> With their mouths they bless,
> while within them (bĕqirbām) they curse.
> (Ps. 62:5; cf. Prov. 26:24)

Whether it be talk of what is in one's heart or what is in one's soul, the expressions in question simply lack, in other words, the scope of modern languages of interiority. If the latter express the uniqueness and depth of individual being, the particular capacities and talents a life is given to unfold, and the real measure according to which each and every human being is to be judged—for the Bible the intent is far simpler. What is "within" indicates what is out of sight to one's fellow even if not to God.

The "Heteronomous" Self

Of the several aspects of inwardness Taylor delineates as features of modern identity, none stands further removed from the Bible than its demand for autonomy. Here modernity's uncompromising rejection of any and every form of heteronomy[74] comes face to face with the equally insistent demands of a traditional society, where it is finally in something akin to "heteronomy" (from the viewpoint of modernity[75]) that the lineal group—with its emphases on, for example, hereditary patterns, tradition, and primogeniture—assures itself of survival through and over the course of time. This is what a discussion of Israel's "heteronomy" in this context actually means: the many ways in which for the OT, unlike modernity, the goals of the individual characteristically are subordinated to those of the larger cultural community to which he or she belongs.

Yet this juxtaposition of the OT and modernity cannot be regarded as either absolute or simple. The subordination of individuals to the lineal group, even in traditional societies, is never categorical and complete, any more than autonomy is in the most individualistically oriented modern societies, a point F. R. Kluckhohn insists on.[76] Just as the predominance of the individualistic orientation in contemporary society means that individual goals have primacy over the goals of both collateral groups to which one belongs (e.g., the business corporation) and lineal groupings (one's parents and grandparents) without allowing a person to disregard completely the interests of others for one's selfish pursuits, so even in the most traditional societies there is room for the individuality of the individual. Not everyone within a traditional society such as we suppose ancient Israel to be need represent the dominant (lineal) tendency nor even every subgroup. In sum, then, this talk of "heteronomy" has only a relative validity, being legitimate only to the extent that it suggests as typical the recurrent subordination of individual goals to those pursued by the larger group.

The characteristic form for this subordination in ancient Israel, first and foremost within the family as the basic unit of economic and social life, is obedience, the obedience the son owes to his father (as well as his mother; cf. Deut. 21:18-21; Prov. 1:8; 6:20). The father may or may not be also the head of the "father's household." But if he is, he possesses, as we have noted, unquestioned authority, an authority based simply on his position as the oldest living male within the lineage. This natural claim to authority lies, in fact, at the very heart of the entire education to which the son was subject, the essential lines of which appear in Proverbs' repeated command to one called "my son" "to hear" a "father's" instruction. In other words, the pupil–teacher relationship reprises the relationship between father and son, and, as such, "hearing" in this context can only mean "to obey" (on the identity of the terms, see above). How little the entire process has in common with contemporary educational theory is evident even from the following sample, among which Prov. 1:8-9 includes the demand that the son also obey the "teaching" (tôrâ) of his mother:

> Hear, my son, your father's instruction;
>> do not reject your mother's teaching. (Prov. 1:8-9)

> My son, do not forget my teaching (tôrâ);
>> let your heart keep my commandments (miṣwôt).
>> (Prov. 3:1; cf. 7:1)

> The one who spares the rod hates his son;
>> the one who loves him seeks to discipline him
>> from the first. (Prov. 13:24; cf. 22:15; 23:13-14; Sir. 30:7-13)

> The rod and correction give wisdom;
> a youth let loose will bring shame to his mother.
> (Prov 29:15)

Wisdom comes not to those who explore the "worlds" that lie within one's own soul but only to those who are careful to heed the voice of instruction from "without," the authoritative voice of tradition. To be sure, it is a voice of experience, a voice familiar with the ways of its world. But this rationale is not the basis of its appeal (cf. Qoheleth) anymore than self-discovery and individual experimentation are its educational ideals.

The centrality of obedience in the OT is perhaps nowhere more evident than in the sphere of Israel's religion, where, as Deuteronomy puts it, "taking care to do all these commandments just as He commanded us" (6:25) comes to define Israel's "righteousness" (ṣĕdāqâ) before the Lord and the very essence of covenant fidelity (cf. Exod. 19:5). But as this obedience is articulated in regard to the Law and the Covenant, what ought to be emphasized here in the face of modernity's preoccupation with rational foundations is the decidedly "heteronomous" character of the obedience and the way in which it is everywhere prominent. The only real ground of the law, what warrants obedience to its individual stipulations, is not, in fact, its rationality or pragmatic benefits but, as Jon Levenson has reminded us, the authority of YHWH as Israel's only god. "Reason is not the suzerain. . . . It is because the covenant relationship is founded upon personal fidelity that there can be laws whose only 'explanation' is the unfathomable decree of God."[77] And repeatedly this is the only "explanation" or justification of the law one hears, even in a context where a variety of motivations may be supplied for its observance. It is YHWH alone who authorizes the commandments Moses enjoins on the Israelites, commandments which Deuteronomy insists are not to be added to or diminished in any way (4:2, 5), proclaimed as they were in their hearing in YHWH's own voice (4:9-14, 32-36; cf. 5:22-33).

Assuredly, this view of her relationship to God shapes Israel's faith in ways which profoundly separate it from modern liberal creeds, ways perhaps epitomized in the portrayal of Abraham as the paradigm of obedience.[78] Genesis 22, the story of Abraham's testing and near-sacrifice of his son Isaac, shows how far obedience's demands could go and makes of Abraham in this respect a model for all believers (Gen. 18:19), the one on account of whom a blessing will extend unconditionally to all his descendants (Gen. 26:5).[79] Certainly nothing ought to obscure the mon-

strous nature of the sacrifice demanded here of Abraham—as well as the
perfect obedience of this father who rises early the next morning to carry
it out (22:3). But even so, according to Gen. 26:5, this act is construed
merely as an act of obedience,[80] of Abraham simply observing "my
[YHWH's] charge: my commandments, my statutes, and my instructions,"
phraseology reminiscent of Deuteronomy's description of the Law incum-
bent upon all Israel (Deut. 11:1; cf. Josh. 22:3; 1 Kgs. 2:3). If so, this suggests that Abraham in Genesis 22 is doing no more than is expected of
any pious person. For the true Israelite *nothing* matters except that the
Lord has commanded it; and this *alone* justifies any observance.

Ironically perhaps, this view comes to be promoted even in Israel's
developed wisdom tradition, where the latter's traditional prizing of
understanding and its ability to master a situation is bluntly juxtaposed
to trust in YHWH and true religious devotion:

> Trust in the Lord with all your heart,
>   and on your own understanding do not rely. (Prov. 3:5)

> Do not be wise in your own eyes;
>   fear the Lord and turn away from evil. (Prov. 3:7)

One's own understanding can provide no certain measure of good and
evil. In fact, the suggestion here is that the effort at intellectual self-
determination is actually inimical to discriminating between good and
evil and is bound to end in moral failure.[81] This, of course, was precisely
the charge which the prophet Isaiah leveled against the sages of
Jerusalem:

> Alas, those who say evil is good and good evil,
>   turning the darkness into light and light into darkness,
>   and turning the bitter into the sweet and the sweet into the bitter!
> Alas, those who are wise in their own eyes,
>   and discerning in their own estimation. (Isa. 5:20-21)

To interpret the antithesis supposed here between a person's estimation
of their moral conduct and God's own norms as stemming simply from
"ill will," or the absence of sincerity on the part of the moral agent,
misses the point. The possibility envisioned in this pericope is more radical than that, since it is based on the conviction that moral competence
belongs solely to YHWH. YHWH's appraisal alone determines the ethical
significance of an action (see above), while even the best efforts of the
wise to find the "right way" often go awry:

> All the ways of a person are pure in their sight,
> but it is YHWH who appraises initiatives (*rūḥôt*). (Prov. 16:2)
>
> Every way of a person is right in their eyes,
> but it is YHWH who appraises hearts. (Prov. 21:2)
>
> There is a way which to a person is right,
> but at its end lies the ways of death. (Prov. 14:12; cf. 16:25)

If these texts are right in characterizing the human situation as one where we lack the competence not only to legislate for ourselves what is right but even to know that one's efforts to do right *are* right, then the only hope open to humankind is that YHWH will show it the way. For the OT, at least, only some form of heteronomy can be a genuine ground of morality.

Again the ethical problem turns, then, chiefly on the issue of knowledge. People must know the Law to observe it, and so its commands and stipulations must constantly be taught. ("Teach them to your children," says Deuteronomy, "by speaking of them when you sit in your house and when you go on a journey, when you lie down and when you get up" [11:19].) The problem, Jeremiah says, is that people have instead deceived their neighbors and "taught their tongues to speak falsehood . . . they refuse to know me [YHWH]" (Jer. 9:4-5).[82] Similarly, Hosea warns, there is "no knowledge of God in the land" and so "my people perish for want of knowledge" (Hos. 4: 1, 6). To correct this apparent failure of the community's efforts to educate in the law's genuine demands, the only hope is that in some way the need for teaching the law can be eliminated altogether. In fact, this is precisely what Ezekiel and Jeremiah propose in the wake of the temple's destruction and the loss of Jerusalem. They envision a solution for the future that does away with any mediated knowledge of the Lord and thereby assures observance by Israel of the Law's demands:

> "The days are surely coming," says the Lord, "when I will cut a new covenant with the House of Israel and the House of Judah, not like the covenant I made with their ancestors. . . . I will put my teaching (*tôrā*) within them and on their heart I will write it; and I shall be their God and they shall be my people. They shall no longer teach their neighbor or their kin, saying, 'Know the Lord!' but all of them will know me from their least to their greatest." (Jer. 31:31-34)

Under the New Covenant disobedience will truly be a thing of the past, because the law will be inscribed on the very "heart" of the people.

Indeed, Ezekiel says God will actually remove their old heart and give them an entirely new one. He will give them a new spirit, *his* own spirit, and "make you walk in my statutes and take care to observe my judgments" (36:25-27). So, it is actually God's own spirit that finally guarantees the people's obedience, doing *for* them what they could not do when they were left to themselves.

For moderns this prophetic solution will immediately raise questions about how to reconcile the new dispensation with human freedom,[83] especially as the ground for genuine morality; but apparently it did not for Jeremiah and Ezekiel. Instead, for both prophets, the solution to the problem of Israel's lack of compliance with the Law turns on overcoming the autonomy of the moral agent, as both a knower and as a doer. What matters is that the Law be observed. Yet for neither prophet does this in any way mitigate the degree to which humanity will be held accountable for its conduct (viz., Ezekiel 18). In other words, if today the question of responsibility is synonymous with the question of one's capacity for self-determination—where the "self" at issue is a unified and bounded agent, disengaged from the world and free from any and all "outside" influences—for Jeremiah or Ezekiel there was never such a "self" to be determined. For them and the OT generally, human individuality, constituted by its relationships rather than diminished by them, was always compatible with the sovereignty of God.

Insofar as it portrays the human situation of guilt in a paradigmatic fashion, the story of Adam and Eve in Gen. 2:4b-3:24 turns on this issue of autonomy versus dependence. This is above all evident in the choice of Adam and Eve, where the "knowledge of good and evil" (i.e., simply what is helpful or hurtful) refers to an achievement of adult experience and adult responsibility (cf. Deut. 1:39; Isa. 7:15).[84] By means of this knowledge, Adam and Eve leave behind a state of childlike dependence (where nakedness is appropriate) for a measure of adultlike independence (where clothes are mandatory). But this "achievement" on their part also has its price, since it has been won through disobedience and ends in the loss of "life" (3:22-24). Thus, the wisdom they acquire turns out not to be real "knowledge" at all. Real knowledge begins, according to Israel's sages, with the "fear of the Lord" (Prov. 1:7; 9:10; cf. Deut. 4:1-6) and reaches its goal in a "tree of life to all who grasp her" (Prov. 4:10-18; cf. 2:5-22). In rejecting childlike dependence for an adultlike knowledge, Adam and Eve gain, in other words, a modernity-like "freedom" only to lose life itself.

While Augustine's interpretation of Adam and Eve's sin reveals the distance which already separates him from the biblical world in its thoroughgoing interiorization of their action,[85] he was not far off the mark: as an assertion of human autonomy, pride is for the OT the "original sin" at the basis of all sin. For "pride" and its allied vices frequently function as stock characterizations of the wicked, especially in psalms and in wisdom literature (e.g., Pss. 5:6; 10:2; 17:10; 73:6; Prov. 8:13; 21:4); while the myth about Eden apparently alluded to in Ezek. 28: 11–19 features a literal "fall" and expulsion from God's presence because of pride (v. 17). Indeed, more than one OT text simply sums up a list of moral transgressions by alluding to the "pride" of the sinner (e.g., Amos 6:8; Ezek. 16:49; Isa. 2:6–22; Zeph. 3:11–13).[86]

> Pride (gāʾôn) goes before destruction;
> before a fall a haughty spirit (gōbāh rûaḥ). (Prov. 16:18)

The notion of "pride" figures prominently, then, in the Bible's depictions of human guilt. But what needs to be emphasized here is how, especially in relation to God, the OT's rather frequent denunciations of human pride have as their target nothing less than those forms of individual autonomy, self-determination, and self-sufficiency that are so highly prized today by modernity.

Common to most of the Hebrew roots ordinarily used to express the notion of "pride" and the allied ideas of arrogance, presumption, and insolence,[87] is simply the idea of being "high" and/or "lofty" or of "lifting up" the eyes, the heart, or the head, and so on. While these same figures can be used as well in a positive sense to mean "majesty" or "greatness," occasionally with reference even to humans (e.g., Isa. 4:2; Ps. 47:5), overwhelmingly the more frequent use as far as humans are concerned is for action or behavior that is religiously or ethically evil. The coming Day of YHWH articulates well the Isaianic ideal on these matters:

> For YHWH of Hosts has a day,
>   against all that is proud (gēʾeh) and haughty (rām),
> and against all that is lifted up (niśśāʾ). . . .
> The pride (gabhût) of humankind will bow down,
>   its haughtiness (rûm) will be abased;
> and YHWH alone on that day will be elevated. (Isa. 2:12, 17)

The visual aspect of the language here is as striking as it is characteristic, not only of Isaiah but also of Israel's great wisdom tradition, on which he here seems to depend (cf. Prov. 6:16; 16:5). The only properly human stance before God, seated "on a high and lofty throne" (Isa. 6:1), is an obeisance which signals complete submission and one's unwavering obedience.

Consequently, within the context of the OT any sign of human autonomy and independence comes to suggest the presence in a person of a pride that is ultimately hostile to God. Even more, text after text in the OT makes the further point that human autonomy and its allied notions of arrogance and self-sufficiency are, in fact, the very *essence* of pride. The king of Assyria, chosen by God as the "rod of his anger" to punish an impious nation (Isa. 10:5), illustrates the idea well: in the end he will be punished as he must be—not for the suffering and terror he inflicted on countless peoples—but rather for his pride-filled boast:

> I [YHWH] will punish the speech of the proud heart of the
>   king of Assyria:
> "By the power of my hand I have done it,
>   and in my wisdom, for I am intelligent. . . ."
> But will the axe boast against the one who hews with it?
>   Or the saw exalt itself over the one who wields it?
> As if a rod sways the one who lifts it,
>   or a staff raises one who is not wood! (Isa. 10:12b, 13a, 15)

The king's speech, in fact, is the characteristic boast of the proud: "My own power has made me victorious!" (Judg. 7:2). It is the boast of those doomed to judgment in Amos 6:8–14 (with reference to "Jacob's pride") as well the motive behind Gideon's dismissal of soldiers in Judg. 7:2. And as Deuteronomy insists, it is the ever-present danger lurking behind prosperity and self-content:

> Be careful not to forget YHWH, your God. . . . Lest, when you have eaten and are satisfied . . . you become proud of heart and forget YHWH, your God, who brought you out of the land of Egypt. And you say in your heart: "My own power and the strength of my hand has achieved this wealth for me." Remember that YHWH, your God, is the one who gives you the power to achieve wealth. . . ." (Deut. 8:11–18)

As far as the OT is concerned, a denial of God's sovereignty is implicit in every suggestion of self-sufficiency or independence. And why this should be so becomes clear when one reflects that the world of the OT finally is one where the horizon against which human action takes place always turns on the issue of loyalty, that is, on the question not *whether* one will serve but only *whom* one will serve by the deed. Indeed it is this question, implied in everything an individual does, that transforms a simple assertion of self-sufficiency or autonomy into an act that is actually hostile to God. Thus the psalmist prays:

> May YHWH cut off all deceitful lips,
> and the tongue which boasts,
> Those who say, "We will prevail by our tongues;
> our lips are our support. Who is lord over us?" (Ps. 12:4-5).

Obviously it goes beyond the scope of this essay to pursue all of the factors that might be at work in the OT's emphatic dismissal of autonomy and independence; but surely prominent among them would be a strong desire for social solidarity in the Jewish community, particularly in the postexilic period. The OT's repeated warnings against pride and all forms of individual autonomy unabashedly promote the subordination of individual aspirations to the interests of the family and the larger community. From a sociological point of view, perhaps that is what is really at stake here: the solidarity of the community and its survival through the generations. Instructive in this regard is the role that repeated warnings against *hybris* (understood as the deliberate infliction of shame and dishonor on an individual or a group, above all by the wealthy or powerful) played in maintaining social solidarity in ancient Greece.[88] One can only surmise that, despite perhaps very different social milieus, "pride" played a similar role in ancient Israel,[89] as perhaps the habitual designation of the wicked precisely as "proud" in the complaints of the psalmist would seem to suggest. The solidarity of the community and its survival as a community have been values of the highest order to Israel in all periods, undiminished even by the postexilic period's increasing emphasis on personal responsibility and individual commitment (see Ezekiel 18). In fact, the argument could be made that the need to subordinate the individual to the group actually grew stronger. Speaking of the world of later Judaism (second century B.C.E. on), Peter Brown has made the point that with it one enters the world of an "afflicted nation," where the survival of the group as a whole is at the very heart of all the self's moral anxiety:

> The continuance of the traditions of Israel, the continued loyalty of Jews to those traditions and to each other, was the common, central issue for Jewish figures as various as the followers of Jesus of Nazareth, Saint Paul, and the later rabbinic sages—not to mention the communal experiments of the Essenes and the Qumran community. Seldom in the history of the ancient world are we confronted with such an explicit sense of the need

to mobilize the whole of the self in the service of a religious law, and of the concomitant need to mobilize to the full a sense of solidarity between the members of a threatened community.[90]

Conclusion

From the foregoing examination several facets of the personal identity of those whose stories are recounted in the OT have emerged. Together they suggest a picture of the self quite different from that fostered by modernity. Here was a self (1) deeply embedded and engaged in the larger social world constituted by the family and the clan; (2) relatively de-centered and undefined with respect to its borders; (3) transparent, "fully" socialized, and locally embodied; and (4) heteronomous, obedient, and explicitly dependent. As such, it stands over against the relatively isolated, self-contained, bounded, self-legislating, and autonomous self of modernity, whose inner depths are the very warrant of its uniqueness and originality.

It would be unfortunate if one drew from this result the conclusion that the biblical self, after all, simply mirrors the conditions of any premodern society; or that, as such, it represents a kind of "backward" development, where conformism and the group are prized over the unique contributions of an individual creativity. Again, conformity is a requirement of every society and cultural tradition, and it is not in itself inimical to creativity and individuality. Different societies simply instill different kinds of conformism in their members.[91] The conclusion one ought to draw, in other words, is that the "biblical" admonition against any and every kind of idolatry is relevant here, including as it does, Charles Davis suggests, that "idolatry" which accords an eternal significance to what are merely contingent forms of selfhood.[92] If one did take this admonition to heart, then one's relationship to oneself might become a strategy of "renunciation," whereby one renounces any certainty about the self. For there is no truth of the self which can escape conflict with the evil within oneself, in the thought of St. Ignatius's *Spiritual Exercises* "no truth about the self that could not be utilized by the Evil One as a device for ensnaring the soul."[93] The isolation of the autonomous subject "discovered" by modernity may, in fact, be self-imposed; here the OT suggests exploring another possibility, one where identity is founded on a new kind of (postmodern) intersubjectivity.[94]

Notes

1. R. J. Williams, *Hebrew Syntax: An Outline* (2nd ed.; Toronto: University of Toronto Press, 1976), 25.

2. Bruce Malina would go so far, in speaking of first-century people, as to assert that they have no comprehension of the modern notion of an individual—to such a degree that they are even poor judges of individual character and psychology and "did not know each other very well in the way we know people, i.e., psychologically, individually, intimately, and personally" (*The New Testament World: Insights from Cultural Anthropology* [Atlanta: John Knox Press, 1981], 53–58). Reference to the work of Euripides might suggest otherwise.

3. F. R. Kluckhohn and F. L. Strodtbeck, *Variations in Value Orientations* (Evanston, Ill.: Row, Peterson & Co., 1961), 17, 10. For a basic statement of their position, consider the following (p. 10): "That there is an ordered variation in value-orientation systems is the first major assumption of our study. Basic both to the classification of value orientations . . . and to the treatment of types of variations and their effects . . . there are these three more specifically formulated assumptions. *First, it is assumed that there is a limited number of common human problems for which all peoples at all times must find some solution.* This is the universal aspect of value orientations because the common human problems to be treated arise inevitably out of the human situation. The second assumption is that *while there is variability in solutions of all the problems, it is neither limitless nor random but is definitely variable within a range of possible solutions.* The third assumption, the one which provides the main key to the later analysis of variation in value orientations, is that *all alternatives of all solutions are present in all societies at all times but are differentially preferred.* Every society has, in addition to its dominant profile of value orientations, numerous *variant* or *substitute profiles.* Moreover, it is postulated that in both the dominant and the variant profiles there is almost always a *rank ordering* of the preferences of the value-orientation alternatives. In societies which are undergoing change the ordering of preferences will not be clear-cut for some or even all the value orientations."

4. Ibid., 4–5.

5. That is, a temporary insanity produced by external demonic agency. On the issue of freedom in Homer, see E. R. Dodds, *The Greeks and the Irrational* (Berkeley: University of California Press, 1966), 7–8.

6. Charles Taylor, *Sources of the Self: The Making of the Modern Identity* (Cambridge, Mass.: Harvard University Press, 1989), 111–13. Taylor pays special attention to developments in the modern conception of self which are the result of the Enlightenment and its aftermath in romanticism.

7. J. J. Buckley, "A Return to the Subject: The Theological Significance of Charles Taylor's *Sources of the Self,*" *Thomist* 55 (1991): 498.

8. For examples in lament and thanksgiving psalms, see H. Fisch, "Psalm: The Limits of Subjectivity," in *Poetry with a Purpose* (Bloomington: Indiana University Press, 1987), 104–35, esp. 108–13; C. Newsom, "The Case of the Blinking I: Discourse of the Self at Qumran," *Semeia* 57 (1992): 13–23.

9. Taylor, *Sources of the Self*, 111.

10. See also Judg. 6:15; 1 Sam. 10:20f.; 1 Sam. 9:21.

11. There has been considerable discussion in recent years about the composition of the *bêt ʾāb* and its usage in the Bible (nuclear family, lineage, multiple family, or extended family). While the *bêt* here seems to include as many as four generations, this need not be taken as typical (see below). Biblical usage itself seems to be inconsistent, with *bêt ʾāb* being applied to kinship groups of various sizes, ranging from the extended family (even the nuclear family?) up to and including the lineage. See here J. D. Martin, "Israel as a Tribal Society," in *The World of Ancient Israel: Sociological, Anthropological and Political Perspectives*, ed. R. E. Clements (Cambridge: Cambridge University Press, 1989), 104–5. Here I have tried to follow the usage of L. E. Stager ("The Archaeology of the Family in Ancient Israel," *Bulletin of the American Schools of Oriental Research* 260 [1985]: 20–22), who relates the *bêt ʾāb* to the "lineage," understood as all those who claim descent from a common paternal ancestor and for whom the genealogical connections may be demonstrated. Extended and multiple families represent lineage subgroups.

12. R. de Vaux, *Ancient Israel*, 2 vols. (New York: McGraw-Hill, 1961), 1.

13. C. J. H. Wright, "Family," *Anchor Bible Dictionary*, 2:762.

14. A young unmarried male (*naʿar*, "youth") remained a "youth," regardless of his age until he established himself as head of the household through the death of the *paterfamilias*. Consequently, it was not at all impossible for an "elder" (*zāqēn*) to be actually younger than a "youth" if the elder's *paterfamilias* had already died. "Youth" ended for the *naʿar* only with his ascent to the head of the household. On this and the loose relation of the status of *naʿar* to age, see Stager, "Archaeology of the Family," 26, and Judg. 13:5–12; 1 Sam. 1:22; 1 Sam. 16:11; 17:31; 1 Kgs. 3:7; 2 Chr. 34:3; Gen. 41:12, 16.

15. Wright, "Family," 764.

16. E. Bellefontaine, "Customary Law and Chieftainship: Judicial Aspects of 2 Samuel 14.4–21, *Journal for Study of the Old Testament* 38 (1987): 49–50; G. I. Emmerson, "Women in Ancient Israel," in *The World of Ancient Israel: Sociological, Anthropological and Political Perspectives*, ed. R. E. Clements (Cambridge: Cambridge University Press, 1989), 380–81.

17. Wright, "Family," 767.

18. Stager, "Archaeology of the Family," 23.

19. Ibid., 18–22.

20. Indeed, the need for labor is one of the primary reasons (along with land

ownership) for multiple family compounds (Stager, "Archaeology of the Family,"
20).

21. Ibid., 18, 22. Note also (pp. 23-24) that the organization of Iron Age villages along the lines of kinship—extending from the bêt ʾāb type of compound
to larger lineage groupings—is supported by the fact that place-names are frequently identical to personal names or composed with personal names: e.g.,
Ḥāṣar ʾAddār, "the enclosure of the Addar family" (Num. 34:4), or Gat Rim-
môn, "the estate/press of the Rimmon family" (Josh. 19:45).

22. Wright, "Family," 763.

23. Note in particular the anthropological presuppositions of the once popular theory of "corporate personality," particularly as articulated by H. W.
Robinson ("The Hebrew Conception of Corporate Personality," in *Corporate
Personality in Ancient Israel* [Philadelphia: Fortress Press, 1964], 25–44, esp.
27–31) with the trenchant critique by J. W. Rogerson, "The Hebrew Conception of Corporate Personality: A Re-Examination," *Journal of Theological Studies*
21 (1990): 1–16, esp. 3–10; idem, *Anthropology and the Old Testament* (Atlanta:
John Knox Press, 1979), 46–59.

24. But note that in Isa. 14:21 (cf. Jer. 29:32), probably postexilic, the sons
of the king of Babylon are responsible for the guilt of their father. This shows
that the development toward an individuation of guilt and responsibility was
not unilinear and homogeneous.

25. K. Koch, "ḥāṭāʾ," *Theological Dictionary of the Old Testament*, 4:317.

26. J. R. Porter, "The Legal Aspects of the Concept of 'Corporate Personality' in the Old Testament," *Vetus Testamentum* 15 (1965): 364–66.

27. Jan Bremmer (*The Early Greek Concept of the Soul* [Princeton: Princeton
University Press, 1983], 66–67) reports this last point as a standard criticism of
Bruno Snell's thesis that the early Greeks lacked a concept designating the psy-
chic whole.

28. In terms of what has been said about an "individual" focus of everyday
"secular" law, it may be pertinent to note in this regard the domain within
which this law operated. The "everyday" law we are referring to was, at least initially, only for the regulation of life within the social group to which the
offender belonged, the towns and the villages inhabited by the clan and concentrated regionally (like the clan of the Danites at Zorrah and Eshtaol in Judg.
18:11; see de Vaux, *Ancient Israel*, 21). For matters involving those outside the
"clan," other laws applied, such as the law of blood vengeance, based on the
principle of family solidarity (see 2 Sam. 3:29; 21:1ff.; cf. 14:4–11). On no
account do these laws operate within the clan, inasmuch as their internal oper-
ation could only amount to self-destruction (de Vaux, *Ancient Israel*, 11–12).

29. That is, insofar as "person" is a culturally specific category. On this
point, see here the classic and still valuable essay by Marcel Mauss, "A Category

of the Human Mind: The Notion of Person; the Notion of Self," in *The Cate-gory of the Person: Anthropology, Philosophy, History*, ed. Michael Carrithers, Steven Collins, and Steven Lukes; trans. W. D. Halls; Cambridge: Cambridge University Press, 1985), 1–25: "Who knows even whether this 'category', which all of us here believe to be well founded, will always be recognised as such? It is formulated only for us, among us. Even its moral strength—the sacred character of the human—person' . . .—is questioned, not only throughout the Orient, which has not yet attained the level of our sciences, but even in the countries where this principle was discovered" (p. 22).

30. G. A. Buttrick, "Righteousness in the OT," *Interpreter's Dictionary of the Bible*, 4:80–84; idem, "Righteousness," *Encyclopedia Judaica* (Jerusalem: Keter, 1972), 14:179–81.

31. H.-J. Zobel, "ḥesed," *Theological Dictionary of the Old Testament*, 5:44–54.

32. See Alasdair MacIntyre, *After Virtue: A Study in Moral Theory* (Notre Dame: University of Notre Dame Press, 1984), 121–27, on the notion of moral-ity in heroic society.

33. Taylor, *Sources of the Self*, 111–26.

34. O. Cullmann, "The Immortality of the Soul or Resurrection of the Dead," in *Immortality and Resurrection*, ed. K. Stendahl (New York: Macmillan, 1965), 9–53. Cullmann, of course, did not originate the idea. Its roots may be found in the work of scholars such as H. W. Robinson in the early twentieth century who employed various anthropological theories about prelogical modes of experience to argue for the synthetic and relational cast of Hebrew thinking as opposed to the analytic thought of the ancient Greeks. As Robinson saw it, this psychic limitation of the early Hebrews found expression not only in an undifferentiated conception of personal unity but also in a notion of "corporate personality," based on the idea that the ancient Israelite personality, lacking the psychological unity of the modern Westerner, could fuse completely with that of the group to which he or she belonged, or even that of another individual. See, e.g., Robinson, "Corporate Personality," 29–33 and n. 23 above.

35. James Barr, *The Garden of Eden and the Hope of Immortality* (Minneapo-lis: Fortress Press, 1993), 36–37.

36. Ibid., 37–44: "I submit, then, that it seems probable that in certain con-texts the nepeš is *not*, as much present opinion favours, a unity of body and soul, a totality of personality comprising all these elements: it is rather . . . a superior controlling centre which accompanies, expresses and directs the existence of that totality, and one which, especially, provides the life to the whole. Because it is the life-giving element, it is difficult to conceive that it itself will die. . . . With the recognition of this fact the gate to immortality lies open. I do not say that the Hebrews, in early times, 'believed in the immortality of the soul'. But they did have terms, distinctions and beliefs upon which such a position could be built and was in fact eventually built." In addition to Pss. 42:6 and 103:1,

Barr points to passages where *nepeš* and *bāśār* ("flesh") seem to stand in opposition (pp. 38ff.). But in Isa. 10:18 (*minnepeš wĕʿad bāśār*, "from 'soul' to 'body'") the reference is to the destruction of vegetation and not human life (H. W. Wolff, *Anthropology of the Old Testament* [London: SCM Press, 1974], 233 n. 3); and in the other texts (Job 14:22; Pss. 63:2; 84:3 [where *nepeš* parallels *lēb* ("heart") and *bāśār* together]), the fact that in each case the activities of the *nepeš* and the *bāśār* are identical argues against the assumed opposition. In Gen. 35:18 ("When her *nepeš* left her . . .") and 1 Kgs. 17:21 (". . . let the *nepeš* of the child return within him . . ."), cited to illustrate the mobility of the "soul" (pp. 38–39), *nepeš* is, *contra* Barr, quite rightly customarily translated "life-breath." Note that in the second passage, v. 17 had just noted that no *nĕšāmâ* ("breath") was left in him (Wolff, *Anthropology*, 13). Other texts cited by Barr (1 Sam. 18:2; Pss. 30:4; 86:13; etc.) are on his own admission ambiguous, and *nepeš* is again customarily translated by words such as "desire" or "life." Given that Barr must admit that numerous texts also speak of the (imminent) death of the *nepeš* (Ps. 78:50; Num. 23:10; Judg. 16:30; etc.), he has little unambiguous data to support his thesis. And without the traditional notion of "soul," one would never assume its use in the OT.

37. Wolff, *Anthropology*, 20.

38. On the first alternative, see A. R. Johnson (*The Vitality of the Individual in the Thought of Ancient Israel* [Cardiff: University of Wales, 1964]), who accounts for the phenomenon we are describing simply as the use of synecdoche. On the latter, see H. W. Robinson, *The Christian Doctrine of Man* (Edinburgh: T. & T. Clark, 1911), 22ff.

39. Wolff, *Anthropology*, 74.

40. Ibid., 17.

41. Ibid., 25.

42. Ibid., 21–23.

43. Note in this connection how some of Moses' "spirit" can be distributed by YHWH to the seventy elders of Israel (Num. 11:17), while Elisha asks Elijah for a double portion of his "spirit" (2 Kgs. 2:9).

44. See, for example, the self constructed by the speaker in the Qumran *Hodayot* (Newsom, "The Case of the Blinking I," 13–23).

45. Ibid., 16.

46. See here the classic discussion of Krister Stendahl, "The Apostle Paul and the Introspective Conscience of the West," in *Paul Among Jews and Gentiles* (Philadelphia: Fortress Press, 1976), 78–96, esp. 92–94.

47. Wolff, *Anthropology*, 51–53.

48. G. J. Botterweck, "*yādaʿ*," *Theological Dictionary of the Old Testament*, 5:461–70.

49. On the connotation of sexual violence inherent in the verb "to deceive" in v. 7a, see F. Brown, S. R. Driver, and C. A. Briggs, *Hebrew and English Lexi-*

con of the Old Testament (Oxford: Oxford University Press, 1906), *sub pth*, and Exod. 22:16; Hos. 2:16; and Judg. 14:15. On a similar connotation for "to over-power," see also W. Holladay (*Jeremiah 1: A Commentary on the Book of the Prophet Jeremiah, Chapters 1-25* [Hermeneia; Philadelphia: Fortress Press, 1986], 553); and 2 Sam. 13:14 and Deut. 22:25.

50. So John Bright, *Jeremiah* (Anchor Bible; Garden City, N.Y.: Doubleday, 1965), 132; and Holladay, *Jeremiah 1*, 555. Note that Holladay speaks in this context of the "compulsion of the word of Yhwh on Jrm's psyche."

51. A number of texts that might appear superficially to suggest deep-seated division or radical self-conflict are to be read in this light. Jer. 17:9 ("More tor-tuous than all else is the human heart" [NAB]) is a case in point. The issue is not, as Merold Westphal ("Socrates between Jeremiah and Descartes: The Dialectic of Self-Consciousness and Self-Knowledge," *Philosophy and Theology* 2 [1988]: 206) and Holladay (*Jeremiah 1*, 496) claim, a "heart deeply self-deceived" (Westphal) or a reflection of Paul's perceptions in Rom. 7:14-25, namely, that we "both conceal and disguise ourselves from ourselves" (Holladay). Reforma-tion anthropology is foreign to the spirit of the text, which speaks only of the deceitfulness and hypocrisy of humankind. Similarly, in Ps. 86:11, which the NRSV renders "Give me an undivided heart," the expression in question, *yaḥēd lēbābî*, means, not as it might literally suggest, "Make my heart one," but, with H.-J. Kraus (cited in H. J. Fabry, *"yāḥad,"* *Theological Dictionary of the Old Tes-tament*, 6:45), on the basis of the preceding colon in v. 11a, simply, "Direct my concentration (toward a single goal) to fear your Name."

52. M. Weinfeld, *Deuteronomy and the Deuteronomic School* (Winona Lake, Ind.: Eisenbrauns, 1992), 75-77, 268-69. Note the many linguistic parallels he offers to the language of Neo-Assyrian grants.

53. On the universality of judgment in Isa. 24:1-2 and the larger literary context of the pericope, see, e.g., O. Kaiser, *Isaiah 13-39: A Commentary* (Old Testament Library; Philadelphia: Westminster Press, 1974), 181-83.

54. *Gilgamesh* Tablet VII iv 41-44. The translation is that of S. Dalley, *Myths from Mesopotamia: Creation, The Flood, Gilgamesh, and Others* (The World's Clas-sics; Oxford: Oxford University Press, 1989), 89.

55. On the presence of the motif of reversal in Egyptian literature as well as the Deir ʿAllā inscription itself, see J. A. Hackett, *The Balaam Text from Deir ʿAllā* (Harvard Semitic Monographs 31; Chico, Calif.: Scholars Press, 1984), 75-76.

56. W. McKane comments on "instruction" and "reproof" here as integral elements of an education where the emphasis lies on the authority of the teacher and the need for discipline in the student (*Proverbs: A New Interpretation* [Old Testament Library; Philadelphia: Westminster Press, 1970], 441).

57. On this interpretation of Prov. 20:27, see McKane, *Proverbs*, 547.

58. The proverb appears to be simply a tautology, unless it is seen that an

assessment of human behavior as an expression of personal character and identity is involved.

59. J. Pedersen, *Israel: Its Life and Culture* (London: Oxford University Press, 1926), 226.

60. Ibid.

61. They may, however, enter the temple court and partake of sacred food. See J. Milgrom, *Leviticus 1–16* (Anchor Bible 3; New York: Doubleday, 1991), 721. Eunuchs fare worse. According to Deut. 23:2, they cannot even gain admission into the cultic community.

62. See, e.g., Milgrom's discussions on the ethical foundations of the priestly dietary system (*Leviticus 1-16*, 718-36).

63. R. C. Cover, "Sin, Sinners (OT)," *Anchor Bible Dictionary*, 6:31–40, esp. 31-32.

64. Brown, Driver, and Briggs, *Hebrew and English Lexicon*, 79–80, 309, 833.

65. Malina, *New Testament World*, 27–28, 36.

66. See also the allied terms gĕdūlâ ("greatness"); hādār, etc. ("ornament, splendor, honor"); hôd ("splendor, majesty, vigor"); yĕqār ("preciousness, price, honor"), tip'eret ("beauty, glory, honor").

67. Compare Pedersen, *Israel*, 215, 226-28.

68. Malina (*New Testament World*, 29) makes the distinction between "ascribed honor," which comes to persons for being who they are rather than for what they did, and "acquired honor," as the "socially recognized claim to worth that a person acquires by excelling over others. . . ."

69. Pedersen, *Israel*, 228.

70. Ibid., 224.

71. Brown, Driver, and Briggs, *Hebrew and English Lexicon*, 376, 711.

72. Wolff, *Anthropology*, 40-58.

73. Ibid., 43.

74. See C. Davis, "Our Modern Identity: The Formation of the Self," *Modern Theology* 6 (1990); esp. 159.

75. Strictly speaking, to speak of "heteronomy" in the Bible in the absence of a modern self—an isolated, self-sufficient, free, and unified "self," disengaged from everyone and everything—is anachronistic. The "other" on whom the individual man and woman in the OT is in some way dependent could never be the radically differentiated "other" of modernity.

76. Kluckhohn and Strodtbeck, *Variations in Value Orientations*, 17-24.

77. J. D. Levenson, *Sinai and Zion: An Entry into the Jewish Bible* (San Francisco: Harper & Row, 1985), 53.

78. On the significance of the depiction of Abraham in the late exilic period and Genesis 22, in particular, see J. Van Seters, *Abraham in History and Tradition* (New Haven: Yale University Press, 1975), 227-40, 269-78.

79. Weinfeld, *Deuteronomy*, 75.

80. Van Seters, *Abraham in History*, 273.

81. McKane, *Proverbs*, 292-93.

82. On the problem of knowledge here, see Holladay, *Jeremiah*, 198-99.

83. Holladay raises this very point and makes reference to Rom. 7:21-25 for the New Testament's fresh insights on the question (*Jeremiah*, 198).

84. For a further discussion of this point, see my discussion in "The Demarcation of Divine and Human Realms in Genesis 2-11," in *Creation in the Biblical Traditions*, ed. R. J. Clifford and J. J. Collins (Catholic Biblical Quarterly Monograph Series 24; Washington, DC: The Catholic Biblical Association of America, 1992), 44-48.

85. Obviously, Augustine goes far beyond what the biblical account can justify insofar as he argues in his account for a thoroughgoing interiorization of pride, whereby the sin of pride, being a disordered self-love, had already "secretly" preceded within Adam and Eve their "open" act of disobedience. On Augustine's interpretation, see *City of God* 14.13; and E. J. Hundert, "Augustine and the Sources of the Divided Self," *Political Theory* 20 (1992): 91-92.

86. J. A. Wharton, "Pride," *Interpreter's Dictionary of the Bible*, 3:876.

87. Among the roots that are used in various lexical formations are *g'h, gbh, rwm, ns', gdl, zy/wd*.

88. N. R. E. Fisher, *Hybris: A Study in the Values of Honour and Shame in Ancient Greece* (Warminster: Aris & Phillips, 1992), 493. Note, too, that in the sixth century Solon's legislation with regard to acts of *hybris* had the same goal in view, by ensuring a sense of firm boundaries between groups and classes.

89. Note that the biblical concept of "pride" appears to be decidedly different from the Greek notion of *hybris*. See here Fisher (*Hybris*, 2) and his thoroughgoing critique of traditional views of *hybris*, which see it as above all an offense directed against the gods, in thought, word, or deed, whereby a mortal forgets the limitations of mortality, competes with the gods, or boasts overconfidently. This conception actually stands much closer to the biblical concept of "pride." In fact, if Fisher is correct, one suspects that it is actually the biblical notion of "pride" that is behind the traditional interpretation of the Greek material.

90. P. Brown, "Person and Group in Judaism and Early Christianity," in *A History of Private Life: From Pagan Rome to Byzantium*, ed. Paul Veyne (Cambridge, Mass.: The Belknap Press of Harvard University Press, 1987), 1:253.

91. Kluckhohn and Strodtbeck, *Variations in Value Orientations*, 21-24.

92. Davis, "Our Modern Identity," 169.

93. The quotation is taken from James Bernauer, "The Prisons of Man: Foucault's Negative Theology," *International Philosophical Quarterly* 27 (1987): 379, as quoted by Davis, "Our Modern Identity," 169.

94. The suggestion that, in the wake of modernity, intersubjectivity ought to be explored as the basis for a new identity is that of Davis's "Our Modern Identity," 170.

Two Pauline Models of the Person

David E. Aune
Loyola University Chicago

*T*he purpose of this study is to explore certain conceptions of the human person expressed or implied in the letters of Paul and to place those conceptions in dialogue with contemporary ways of understanding the whole and the divided self. Two factors make this task complex. First, for both Paul and us the self has both public and private dimensions, though there is no clear boundary between the two. Second, Paul's conceptions of the human person or the self were inseparably linked to his experience of God and were attempts to understand the basis and implications of that experience. It is therefore legitimate to ask how the modern Christian's experience of the transforming presence of God can be understood in light of modern conceptions of the whole and divided self. The task of this study is therefore essentially theological, since it attempts to describe accurately important aspects of Paul's theological anthropology and then to reflect on the major configurations of a contemporary theological anthropology. The emphasis on "accurate description" means the rigorous application of the historical-critical method, while the attempt to formulate a viable modern theological anthropology is essentially an exercise in constructive theology.

Paul uses at least two different ancient models of human nature to account for the inner tensions and conflicts Christians experience when they attempt to live in accordance with the will of God.[1] The *irrational behavior model* is clearly reflected in Rom. 7:14–25 and Gal. 5:16–17, and is readily comprehensible to Christians living in the modern world who are similarly faced with the conflicts involved in making moral

89

choices. The *apocalyptic macrocosm-microcosm model* is presupposed, though never explicitly articulated in a variety of texts (Rom. 6:6; 2 Cor. 5:17; cf. Eph. 4:22-23; Col. 3:5-11), and presumes a view of reality that some but not all modern Christians are able to understand or share. Before discussing these two models, it is first necessary to deal with some of the major problems involved in synthesizing Paul's views of human nature. We will conclude with some theological reflections on the role of the Bible in contemporary Christianity and the significance of the Pauline views of human nature for modern perspectives of the self.

The Problem of Pauline Anthropology

Paul's views of human nature, like much of his thought, cannot be understood adequately apart from the cultural and religious context in which he lived and wrote. At least that is what I, as a practitioner of the historical-critical method, have been trained to believe. After more than a century of debate, it is evident that there are still wide areas of disagreement on the complex question of whether Paul's views of human nature are explicable on the basis of Jewish tradition alone (in both continuity and discontinuity with traditions in the Hebrew Bible), or whether he was influenced, consciously or unconsciously, by Hellenistic conceptions of human nature, perhaps refracted through Hellenistic Judaism. There seems to be increasing agreement that Paul did not simply adopt anthropological models from "Judaism," "Hellenistic Judaism," or "Hellenism" (clear boundaries between these cultural designations did not, of course, exist), in part because he had no apparent interest in articulating a consistent view of human nature. While he does use many Greek anthropological terms to explain aspects of human behavior in sections of his letters, he appears to do so in an ad hoc manner so that there is little overall consistency evident when these statements are compared. In this area at least, Paul was an eclectic who drew upon a variety of anthropological conceptions in the service of his more central ethical concerns.

Ancient Monistic and Dualistic Views of Human Nature

One widely held assumption is that ancient views of human nature must be either monistic or dualistic, conceptions often linked respectively to

Hebrew and Greek views of the person. However, the two most popular Hellenistic philosophies during the third and second centuries B.C.E. were Stoicism and Epicureanism, both of which espoused a monistic and hence materialistic view of human nature. Different forms of early Judaism embraced a variety of cultural and religious traditions in which there was no consistent view of human nature,[2] and in which Hellenistic conceptions of human nature were assimilated to various degrees.[3] There were, in fact, many variations and permutations of monistic and dualistic conceptions of the universe and human nature (the two are often understood homologously), though when a dualistic model is prevalent, there is without exception an expectation that plurality will be resolved into unity. Some of the later Stoics, for example (including Posidonius and Marcus Aurelius), were monistic materialists in the Stoic tradition, but had a dualistic psychology.

Despite the many differences that can be registered, there were a number of views of the soul and the body shared by the major Hellenistic philosophical traditions (Platonism, Aristotelianism, Epicureanism, and Stoicism): (a) All distinguished the soul from the body. (b) All regarded the soul as the center of intelligence within the human frame. (c) All thought that the soul was localized or at least centered in a particular part of the human body. (d) All attributed mental and moral qualities to the soul, not the body. (e) All but the early Stoics and Epictetus agreed that the soul had both rational and irrational aspects. (f) All (even Epicureans and Stoics) thought that death could be defined as the separation of the soul from the body. (g) All but the Epicureans and the Stoic Panaetius (Cicero *Tusculan Disputations* 1.79) believed that the soul continued to exist for at least a limited period of time after separation from the body at death. This is a significant list of common convictions, many of which coincide with popular views widely subscribed to in the Hellenistic and Roman world.

Pauline Anthropological Dualism

Paul has more to say about human nature than any other early Christian author (with the exception of later Gnostic writers), yet his concern is not primarily theoretical, nor do the fragmentary expressions of his views of human nature exhibit internal consistency. Further, only in Romans 6–8 and Gal. 5:13–6:10 does Paul explicitly link his views of human nature with Christian ethics. Paul did use a number of dichotomous designations for human nature: (1) *sarx/pneuma* (Rom. 1:4; 8:4–6, 27; 1 Cor. 5:5: the destruction of the *sarx* [i.e., death] will ensure the salvation of a person's *pneuma*; 2 Cor. 7:1; Gal. 3:2–3; 4:29; 5:16–18; Col. 2:5); (2) *sōma/pneuma* (Rom. 8:10–11, 13; 1 Cor. 5:3 [cf. Col. 2:5 *sōma* = *sarx*]; 7:34; 12:13; cf. Eph. 4:4); (3) *nous/sarx* (Rom. 7:22–25; cf. Col. 2:18). Only in 1 Thess. 5:23, does Paul use the trichotomous designation *sōma/psychē/pneuma*, which when taken together function to encompass the entire person.[4] The presupposition, however, is that the person is somehow constituted of these elements. Paul distinguishes between the "spirit" (*pneuma*) and the "mind" (*nous*) in 1 Cor. 14:14–19, and advises against allowing the spirit to do what the mind cannot participate in. According to vv. 14–15:

> For if I pray in a tongue, my spirit prays but my mind is unfruitful. What am I to do? I will pray with the spirit and I will pray with the mind also; I will sing with the spirit and I will sing with the mind also.

Both are clearly aspects of the person, the irrational and rational faculties, not the whole person viewed from two different perspectives;[5] both are qualitatively distinguished from each other; and both belong to the "higher" faculties within the human person. Yet using a term like "higher" is inherently problematic, for it carries with it implications. The term *nous* occurs fourteen times in the genuine Pauline letters, though only here and in 1 Cor. 2:16, Rom. 7:23–25 and Rom. 12:2 is its usage particularly important for our discussion. Richard Reitzenstein argued that Paul and his audience could understand *pneuma* and *nous* as equivalents, based on the equivalency of the phrases *to pneuma tou theou* (1 Cor. 2:11, 12, 14), and *nous kyriou* or *nous Christou* (1 Cor. 2:16).[6] In Rom. 7:23–25, Paul distinguishes between his *nous*, which is equated with his *esō anthrōpos*, and his *sarx*, or *melē*, or *to sōma tou thanatou*. Clearly this psychosomatic contrast reflects a split in human nature that cannot be ignored.[7] Yet the *nous* is not divine, as in Hellenistic philosophy and Hermetic thought, for it must be renewed or transformed (Rom. 12:2; cf. Eph. 4:23).

2 Cor. 5:1–10 is an important passage for understanding Paul's view of human nature, but it is also a passage that has been interpreted in an astonishing number of diverse ways.[8] Verses 1–4 are of particular significance:

> For we know that if the earthly tent [*oikia tou skēnous*] we live in is destroyed, we have a building from God, a house not made with hands,

eternal in the heavens. Here indeed we groan, and long to put on our heavenly dwelling [to oikētērion hymōn to ex ouranou], so that by putting it on we may not be found naked.

There are several observations that can be made about this passage.[9] First, the use the image of the house (oikia) or tent (skēnos) as a metaphor for the physical aspect of human existence (i.e., sōma, cf. vv. 6–8) occurs frequently in Hellenistic tradition from Plato on,[10] but rarely in early Judaism (Wis. 9:15; Par. Jer. 6:6f. where skēnōma is parallel to sarkikos oikos). Second, Paul distinguishes the real person from the purely physical dimension of human existence, so that (despite frequent demurrers among those who have commented on this debated passage), this is essentially a dualistic appraisal of human nature, though it reflects neither common Hellenistic nor common early Jewish conceptions, but rather is (apparently) Paul's own theological construct. Third, running throughout this passage is an undeniably negative evaluation of physical existence in comparison to the positive evaluation of the type of existence possible following death (see Rom. 8:23). Fourth, to be "naked" refers to that state of postmortem existence in which the self is separated from the physical body.[11] Fifth, the oikodomē ek theou (v. 1) or the oikētērion ex ouranou, is a way of referring to the glorified body of the Christian, that is, a form of corporeality in which the dualistic conflict between flesh and Spirit is transcended by a monistic form of existence.

In 2 Cor. 5:6–9 Paul continues to use the first-person plural (representing the view of Christians generally) of the desirability of being absent from the body and present with the Lord.[12] Dropping the tent metaphor that he used in vv. 1–4, he says that "while we are at home in the body we are away from the Lord" (v. 6b), and "we would rather be away from the body and at home with the Lord" (v. 8). Here Paul does not identify Christians with their physical frames, but with the separable "we." Paul does not explicitly label that part of human nature which will be separated from the body upon death. If pressed, however, he might well have preferred the term pneuma to psychē, since the former was used as commonly in Hellenistic Judaism as the latter was among pagans. In Phil. 1:21–26, Paul says of the possibility of his own physical death that to apothanein kerdos, "to die is gain" (v. 21), and that to "depart" and be with Christ would be pollōi mallon kreisson, "infinitely better."[13] He refers to to zēn en sarki, "life in the flesh" (v. 22) and to epimenein [en] tēi sarki, "remaining in the flesh" (v. 24), as the less preferable alternative, and in both instances sarx is used as the equivalent of *sōma*. Obviously it must be Paul's true self that will "depart and be with Christ," though again he does not give this separable element a label. In 2 Cor. 12:2-3, where not death but an altered state of consciousness is in view, Paul uses the term *anthrōpos* for the self, the center of consciousness (whether himself or someone else), in the two contrastive states of *en sōmati* and *ektos tou sōmatos* or *chōris tou sōmatos*. This indicates that Paul could contrast the body with the self.

The discussion of these passages suggests that, while Paul did not simply take over (as did Josephus and the author of 4 Maccabees) one particular model of Hellenistic anthropology, and he does speak of various pluralistic features within the human person that cannot simply be explained using Israelite models.

Refutations of proposals that Hellenistic conceptions of human nature influenced Paul's own views have often been based on caricatures of "the Greek view," often based on an oversimplified understanding of classical sources coupled with superficial understanding of Hellenistic paradigms of human nature. Thus, W. D. Davies has argued that according to Hellenistic dualism the flesh was intrinsically evil, and that the term *sarx* had no dualistic associations in the Hellenistic world. He is wrong on both counts. It was only during the second century and later that Platonic dualism was radically interpreted to mean that matter was evil and spirit good, a position that characterized (but was not restricted to) Gnosticism. Further, while Davies is correct that *psychē* and *sarx* are not used antithetically in classical Greek literature, in the trichotomous psychology of Marcus Aurelius, the term *sarx* is used interchangeably with *sōma* (2.2; 3.16; 12.3), and *sarx* is also used as a synonym of *sōma* by Epictetus (2.1.17, 19; 3.7.4, 9), and Philo (*De gig.* 29-31). The notion that the body was intrinsically evil, and a temporary prison for the immortal soul (exaggerated, to be sure), generally considered an Orphic or Pythagorean view adopted by Plato, has particularly come to be associated with the *Phaedo*. Plato's *Timaeus*, however, was even more influential and was probably one of the most important philosophical treatises in the Hellenistic and Roman period, particularly after Platonism began to dominate philosophical discussion beginning with the first century B.C.E. In his lengthy discussion of the fashioning of the soul and body of the human person in *Timaeus* 69a-92c, Plato makes an observation (*Timaeus* 88b; Loeb Classical Library trans.):

> From both these evils [diseases of the body and soul] the one means of salvation is this—neither to exercise the soul without the body nor the

body without the soul, so that they may be evenly matched and sound of health.

Plotinus, who noted that Plato did not say the same thing about the soul everywhere in his writings, alludes to various passages in Plato's *Phaedo*, *Cratylus*, and *Republic*, and then calls attention to the positive assessment of the soul/body dualism in the *Timaeus* (4.8.1; Loeb Classical Library trans.):

> And, though in all these passages he disapproves of the soul's coming to the body, in the Timaeus when speaking about this All he praises the universe and calls it a blessed god, and says that the soul was given by the goodness of the Craftsman, so that this All might be intelligent, because it had to be intelligent, and this could be without the soul.

A similarly positive assessment of the soul/body dualism is found in Aristotle's *Protrepticus* (frag. B60; Düring), an early exoteric work reflecting the "Platonic" phase of his views of human nature:

> In the soul, there is on the one hand reason (which by nature rules and judges in matters concerning ourselves), on the other hand that which follows and whose nature is to be ruled; everything is in perfect order when each part brings its proper excellence to bear; for to attain this excellence is a good.

The materialistic monism of Epicureans and early Stoics meant that they also had an essentially positive attitude toward physical existence in this world. Posidonius, a middle Stoic, expressed a view similar to that reflected in the *Timaeus*, perhaps based on his reading of that dialogue (Clement of Alexandria *Strom.* 2.21; Edelstein-Kidd, frag. 186), when he says that *to telos* is "to live contemplating the truth and order of absolutely everything [*tōn holōn*], and contributing to the establishment of it [*autēn*] as far as possible (in oneself), without being influenced by the irrational part of the soul [*hypo tou alogou merous tēs psychēs*]." A positive assessment of the relationship between soul and body is also reflected in Ps.-Heraclitus *Ep.* 9 (trans. Malherbe), reflecting a more popular view: "The body, while a slave to the soul, is at the same time its fellow citizen, and it does not irritate the intellect [*nous*] to dwell with its servants."

Though particular lexemes (*sōma*, *psychē*, *sarx*, *pneuma*, etc.) may be used as *termini technici* by relatively sophisticated authors (though there is inconsistency in even the greatest thinkers,[14] such as Plato and Aristotle), one must avoid the erroneous notion that particular concepts are wedded to particular lexemes. We must rather think in terms of the general semantic equivalence that exists between lexical items belonging to the same semantic domains or subdomains rather than restrict our investigation to particular lexical items, and also pay attention to the different meanings conveyed by the same word (i.e., a single lexical item can belong to many different semantic domains). When Jas. 2:26 says that *to sōma chōris pneumatos nekros estin*, it is clear that the psychosomatic dualism of Hellenistic Judaism is in view, with *pneuma* used as a substitute for *psychē*. *Nous* and *kardia* often overlap because in Hebrew *lēb* ("heart") was regarded as primarily the seat of intellectual rather than emotional life, and it is this semantic borrowing that results in the common use of *kardia* for "mind" in early Christian authors, while *nous* is the most common lexeme for "mind" among Hellenistic authors.

The distance between Paul's views of human nature and those of popular Hellenistic philosopical thought is not as great as might first appear. Certainly in Roman Hellenism and early Judaism, it is widely assumed that good behavior and bad behavior can be freely chosen by each person, and for that reason lists of virtues and vices are an integral part of moral exhortation. In Pauline thought, on the other hand, a radical distinction is made between *homo ante gratiam* and *homo sub gratia*. For Paul, the disobedience of Adam introduced an era of death (exacerbated by the giving of the Law) which largely determined human behavior (Rom. 5:12-21).

In spite of the theological distance, there is a striking structural and phenomenological similarity between the anthropological dualism of popular Hellenistic tradition and that of Paul. *Mutatis mutandis*, the ethical dualism reflected in Paul's view of the dilemma of the Christian, expressed in Rom. 7:25 (with his *nous* he serves the law of God but with his *sarx* the law of sin) is structurally similar to the situation of Greeks to whom a philosopher would direct his *logos protreptikos*, offering freedom from the material bondage of weath and reputation. For Hellenistic philosophers, human beings possessed the potential to turn from material encumbrances to embrace the philosophic life. For Paul, on the other hand, freedom from sin and death is impossible for *homo ante gratiam* and is only a possibility for those who have been justified by faith (Rom. 8:1-2). For Paul the central anthropological terms are *sarx* and *pneuma*, and Christians can "set their minds" (*phronein, pronēma*) on either with negative or positive consequences (Rom. 8:5-6).

The Irrational Behavior Model
in Hellenistic Psychology

One of the more lasting assumptions of ancient Greek psychology was the view that emotions (the irrational) could be separated from both cognition (reason) and motivation (will, volition),[15] with the correlative view that cognition belonged to the "higher" aspects of the personality, while the emotions belonged to the "lower." While Platonists, Epicureans, and Stoics had vastly different conceptions of reality, they did share one major point of agreement in their ethical theories (the later Aristotle and the Peripatetics are an exception), expressed in the Socratic paradox *oudeis ekon hamartanei*, "no one willingly does wrong," a notion frequently discussed by Plato (see *Prot.* 345d–e; *Tim.* 86d; *Laws* 731c; 860d). These three philosophical traditions linked moral behavior to human knowledge. According to a widespread ancient tradition, then, people do what is wrong even though they know what is right, and that these impulses to action originate either in ignorance (which inhibits rational planning and deliberation), or from irrational emotions such as anger, fear, and hatred.[16] This theory is dramatized in a speech of Medea in Euripides *Medea* 1077–80:

... but I am overcome by evil [*nikomai kakois*]. Now I learn what evil deeds I intended to perform; but passion [*thymos*] overpowered my wishes [*tōn bouleumatōn*], which is the cause of the greatest evil for mortals.

Medea was a favorite character among mythographers as well as dramatists. In Ovid's retelling of the story, Medea finds herself inexplicably attracted to Jason and makes the following statement as part of a longer soliloquy (*Metamorphoses* 7.19-20; Loeb Classical Library trans.):

But some strange power holds me down against my will. Desire persuades me one way, reason another. I see the better and approve it, but I follow the worse.

The same popular psychology is projected onto the Egyptians in Diodorus 1.71.3 (Loeb Classical Library trans.):

They believed that all other men, in thoughtlessly following their natural passions [*physikois pathesi*], commit many acts which bring them injuries and perils, and that oftentimes some who realize that they are about to commit a sin [*hamartanein*] nevertheless do base acts when overpowered by love or hatred or some other passion.

This not only is true in literary conceptions of human behavior but was also taken up for serious discussion in the various Greek philosophical traditions (e.g., Plato *Protagoras* 352d-e). Epictetus, who held an exclusively intellectualist explanation of behavior, comes close to Paul's language in Rom. 7:14-25 and Gal. 5:16-17, which we will consider below (Arrian *Epict. Diss.* 2.27.1; Loeb Classical Library trans.):

> Every error involves a contradiction. For since he who is in error does not wish to err [*ou thelei hamartanein*], but to be right, it is clear that he is not doing what he wishes [*ho thelei ou poiei*].

Epictetus is very probably familiar with the proverbial formulation "no one willingly does wrong," but assumes in good Stoic fashion that a person who does what he does not want to do is ignorant of what he really wants, whereas in Paul the *epithymiai* ("lusts, desires") of the flesh or the body frustrate the wishes of the mind. While Plato originally took only rational factors into account when determining human conduct, he later complemented this intellectualist approach to behavior (inherited from Socrates; cf. Xenophon *Mem.* 3.9.4), with the recognition of the presence of irrational factors which resulted in psychological conflict (*stasis*).[17] For most Stoics, however, who saw no split between reason and emotion, behavior was based exclusively on the rational faculties (Epictetus 1.28.6-8; citing Medea's speech in Euripides *Medea* 1077-80), though Posidonius was an exception. In the general Greek view, therefore, moral progress was based on education. The traditional bipartition of human nature into that of intellect and emotion, the rational and the irrational, remained the basic frame of reference for Greek ethical theory.

The Irrational Behavior Model in Paul

In Rom. 7:14-25 and Gal. 5:16-17, Paul attributes the conflicts and frustrations of human moral experience to the basic antithetical constituents of the human person. The constituents, however, are not the same in both passages. In Rom. 7:14-25, the conflict is first of all between the Law, which is external yet *pneumatikos*, "spiritual," and the human person who is *sarkikos*, "fleshly" (v. 14). This has a microcosmic correspondence within the human person in a conflict between a "higher" element (described as the *esō anthrōpos*, "the inner person," v. 22; or *nous*, "the mind," vv. 23, 25), and a "lower" element (variously described as *sarx*, "the flesh," which is enslaved to sin [v. 18], or "my members" [v. 23], or *to sōma tou thanatou touto*, "this body of death," i.e., "this mortal body" [v. 24], all of which are enslaved to sin). These opposing forces are engaged in battle on a field of combat that consists of Paul's self (Rom. 7:23 NRSV):

> But I see in my members another law at war with the law of my mind, making me captive to the law of sin that dwells in my members. Wretched man that I am! Who will rescue me from this body of death?

This conflict is clearly expressed in Rom. 7:25b (NRSV):

> So then, with my mind I am slave to the law of God, but with my flesh I am a slave to the law of sin.

In Gal. 5:16–17, on the other hand, the opposition is between the flesh and the Spirit.[18] As in Rom. 7:14–25, the self is apparently pulled in opposite directions by these two forces. Further, Rom. 7:14–25 has a more decidedly theoretical character, for it does not contain virtue and vice lists (like Gal. 5:13–6:10), but rather speaks in more generic terms of doing *agathos* or *kalos* and *kakos*, "good and evil."

The argument in Rom. 7:15–21 is based on the acceptance of the widespread proverbial theme (discussed above) that a person's behavior often contradicts his or her desires, which Paul repeats three times (NRSV):

> I do not understand my own actions. For I do not do what I want, but I do the very thing I hate (v. 15).
> I can will what is right, but I cannot do it (v. 18b).
> For I do not do the good I want, but the evil I do not want is what I do (v. 19).

This threefold variation does not advance the argument so much as underline the truth of the formulation through repetition and rhetorical variation. The reason Paul gives for the conflict between willing and doing is simply that sin—that is, "nothing good"—dwells in him (also emphasized three times [vv. 17b, 20, 18a]). It is important to emphasize at this point that in proposing that "sin" is at the basis of the conflict between willing and doing, Paul adds a distinctive Jewish and Christian feature which was foreign to Greek moral theory.

An important parallel to Rom. 7:14–25 is found in Gal. 5:16–17, which is part of a larger parenetic section in Gal. 5:13–6:10, which exhibits internal coherence, though it does not easily fit into the rhetorical analysis of Galatians.[19] Verse 16 specifies the anthropological basis for right conduct based in the priority of the Spirit coupled with the denial of the desires of the flesh, while v. 17 provides an anthropological model explaining the conflict as based on the dualism of *sarx-pneuma*, which he uses to explain v. 16 (v. 17 is introduced with *gar*), but which serves as an explanation for the entire parenetic section in Gal. 5:16–26. Though this model raises more questions for us than it answers, the very fact that Paul felt obliged to provide this pithy explanatory model suggests his awareness of typical Hellenistic questions.[20]

> But I say, walk by the Spirit, and do not gratify the evil desires of the flesh [*epithymian sarkos*]. For the flesh has evil desires [*hē sarx epithumei*] contrary to the Spirit, and the Spirit contrary to the flesh; for these are opposed to each other, to prevent you from doing what you would [*hina mē ha ean thelēte tauta poiēte*].

Here the individual is not identified with the flesh or the Spirit, but is rather subject to a tug of war between them. Though Paul does not explicitly label the self which is subject to this conflict, it appears to be his view that the human *pneuma* has been permeated with the divine *pneuma* (the divine *pneuma* and the human *pneuma* are contrasted in 1 Cor. 2:11, and in 1 Cor. 6:17 Paul claims that the person who has been united with the Lord is *en pneuma* with him).[20] In this passage it is important to notice that the flesh is personified and has desires (in the phrase *epithymia sarkos*, "the desires of the flesh," *sarkos* is a subjective genitive, and in *hē sarx epithymei*, "the flesh desires," *sarx* is the subject of the verb).[21]

Human Nature and the Macrocosm-Microcosm Analogy in Antiquity

Hellenistic Macrocosm-Microcosm Homologies

One of the more pervasive presuppositions of ancient Mediterranean thought was that human nature could neither be understood nor explained without reference to the larger, more encompassing reality of which it was an integral part. According to the prevailing view of the Ionian philosophers after Heraclitus, for example, the human person consists of body and soul; upon death, the body returns to earth and the soul returns to the heavenly aether from whence it came. "Man is made of portions of the cosmos, and in death like returns to like."[22]

The human experience of conflict, whether intra-personal (psychological) or extra-personal (social), could similarly be explained by reference to an encompassing paradigmatic reality. The historians of religion have often recognized the tendency to understand human life as homologous to the life of the cosmos; that is, either the human body was frequently considered a model of the universe, or the universe was considered a paradigm of human existence.[23] In ancient Greek religious and philosophical thought the human person was often understood as a microcosm of the universe.[24] Throughout this discussion I use the term "microcosmos" (Greek: *mikros kosmos*; Latin: *mundus parvus* or *mundus minor*) for conceptions of human nature that are considered homologous to a comprehensive external reality which constitutes the "macrocosmos" (*megas kosmos*).[25] For ancient religion and philosophy, the human dilemma was frequently understood as a macrocosmic encoding in the individual, while the answer to the human dilemma (evident in such experiences as death, disease, suffering, alienation, and frustration) could be achieved through a proper understanding of the macrocosmos, which opened the possibility for the integration of the human microcosmos into some kind of encompassing macrocosm. Whether the ultimate quest was that for "salvation" of religious cults (understood in both intra-mundane and extra-mundane ways),[26] or for the *summum bonum* of the philosophical schools, the answer to the human dilemma could be found in the macrocosmos.

The view that human life is homologous to the life of the cosmos is a supposition generally acceptable to modern science. The operations of nature observable by humans at the microscopic level, for example, are assumed to be valid for regions of the universe otherwise inaccessible to close observation. However, the kinds of homologous relationships between the individual and the cosmos with which we are concerned in this paper are essentially mythological constructs that have no basis in reality and yet are fascinating precisely because of the widespread assumption of the truth of the macrocosm-microcosm analogy.

In order to become aware of some of the basic patterns in this kind of thought, I propose a typology of three basic patterns, though each pattern occurred in many historical variants, and in some instances the patterns are combined in various ways: (1) *Spatial macrocosm*: that is, salvation involves the upward movement toward a more perfect reality. (2) *Temporal macrocosm*: salvation lies in the paradigmatic past or future. (3) *Systemic macrocosm*: salvation involves cognitive and/or behavioral conformity to a more perfect reality (this latter is often part of spatial microcosm).

The Spatial Macrocosm-Microcosm Homology

Two of the more important presuppositions of spatial microcosm are that perfection lies in the highest realms of the cosmos, and that the properties of the higher world are replicated in the lower world. The individual is therefore composed of two or more separable constituents and the process of separation is linked with paideia in this life and ascension to the perfect realm upon death. For Plato the soul can be considered a "prisoner" within the body (*Phaedo* 82e–83a), and the soul wears the body like clothes that will eventually be discarded (*Phaedo* 87b). The imperfections of the cosmos are mirrored in the imperfections of the individual. In Plato's cosmology, that which is higher is better, while that which is lower is coarser and more inferior, while Aristotle distinguished between the sublunary world (defective, perishable) and the superlunary worlds (eternal, imperishable, divine). Plato describes the creation of the cosmos in the form of a living creature (*Timaeus* 30b; Loeb Classical Library trans.):

> He constructed reason within soul and soul within body as He fashioned the All, that so the work He was executing might be of its nature most fair and most good. Thus, then, in accordance with the likely account, we must declare that this Cosmos has verily come into existence as a Living Creature endowed with soul and reason owing to the providence of God.

The cosmology most appropriate for spatial microcosm was the new geocentric cosmology (widely accepted during the Hellenistic period); that is, the earth occupies the lowest place in the cosmos and is surrounded by an enormous cosmos consisting of a least seven planetary spheres, topped by the eighth sphere of the fixed stars.[27] Since the earth itself occupied the lowest place in the cosmos, the traditional location of the underworld was no longer tenable. The atmosphere between the earth and the moon was chosen as the new site for this cosmic urban renewal project, and it was there that the souls of the dead were allowed to loiter until purified to the point where they could rise to the moon. Gnostic anthropology was sometimes bipartite but usually tripartite, consisting of body, soul, and the self.[28] The inner person (for which such terms as *pneuma* and *nous* are used) corresponds on the macrocosmic level to the unknown God; that is, a kinship or affinity exists between the highest God and the inmost core of the person. But this correspondence is known only through revelation.

The Temporal Macrocosm-Microcosm Analogy

Clear examples of temporal macrocosm-microcosm homologies in antiquity occur only in Judaism and early Christianity, in some of the documents from the Qumran community (primarily 1QS and 1QM), and in the letters of Paul and the Pauline circle. According to 1QS 3.13-4.26, God created two Spirits, one good and one evil, called the Prince of Lights and the Angel of Darkness who will exercise power of human beings until the eschatological visitation of God, who will destroy perversity (1QS 4.18-19). Each of these Spirits presides over a human community, the Prince of Lights over the sons of righteousness and the Angel of Darkness over the sons of perversity (1QM 13.9-12). The Spirit of Truth motivates people to live righteously, while the Spirit of Perversity motivates people to do evil (1QS 4.2-11). Yet the Spirits of Truth and Perversity do battle in the heart of each person (1QS 4.23-26). The dualism reflected in these Qumran documents is both intra-personal (psychological); that is, the struggle which goes on in the heart of each individual in varying proportions,[29] and extra-personal (social and cosmic), and will conclude in a final battle between the two antithetical Spirits and their earthly human communities.[30]

Paul's view of reality, like that of Hellenistic Judaism generally, is strikingly different from the prevailing Hellenistic and Roman view. Since the *kosmos* came into existence at a particular point in time and will eventually go out of existence, the *kosmos* itself understood spatially or systemically cannot function as a macrocosmic model for understanding the human person. The *intra-personal* conflict that Paul discusses occasionally in his letters suggests the internalization of *extra-personal* conflict between the supernatural forces of good and evil, which are struggling yet inevitably moving toward an eschatological resolution in favor of the former.

The Systemic Macrocosm-Microcosm Analogy

For Stoics, human beings, like the heavenly bodies, were composed of the four elements (earth, air, fire, water). While this has the superficial appearance of being somewhat scientific, it is actually a mythological construct. Stoics went on to claim that the soul (compounded of fire and air) was the active principle, while the body (compounded of earth and water) was the passive principle, a microcosmic correspondence to the active and passive principles in the macrocosm.[31] Philo reflects Stoic views when he regards the *nous* of the first human as that which was created in the image of the divine *Nous* (*De opif. mundi* 69; Loeb Classical Library trans.):

> It [*nous*] is in a fashion a god to him who carries and enshrines it as an object of reverence; for the human mind evidently occupies a position in men precisely answering to that which the great Ruler occupies in all the world.

The theory of cosmic sympathy, developed as part of a complex philosophical system by the eclectic Stoic philosopher Posidonius, is often considered one of the basic presuppositions of ancient magic and divination in which sympathy (attraction) is understood in the context of the antithetical notion antipathy (rejection). One important aspect of this theory is the widespread acceptance of the analogy between macrocosm and microcosm as the primary mythological framework for ancient magical and divinatory practices as expressed in the ancient aphorism of alchemy: "That which is above is like to that which is below, and that which is below is like to that which is above."[32] The second- or third-century C.E. astrologer Antiochus of Athens saw a bond between the microcosm of the human person (understood trichotomously) and the macrocosm of the planets: Saturn = body; moon = spirit; sun = soul. Yet he did not focus on the human person alone who is linked to the world above, for the elements of the material world (earth, water, and fire) are correlated with certain metals (lead, silver, and gold, all of which are considered living organisms), forming a complex microcosmic structure (see table 1).

Table 1[33]

Color	Element	Metal	Macrocosm	Microcosm
black	earth	lead	Saturn	body
white	water	silver	moon	spirit
yellow	fire	gold	sun	soul

According to the speculations of Zosimos of Panopolis, the body of first man, whether named Thouth (according to the Egyptians) or Adam (according to the Hebrews), was composed of four elements: earth, water, air, and fire.[34] This means that the human person, which Zosimos believes is constituted of soul and body or mind and flesh, is composed of the basic elements of the cosmos.

Paul's Apocalyptic Macrocosm-Microcosm Homology

The structure of Paul's religious thought is largely the product of his adaptation of Jewish apocalypticism as the framework for understanding the significance of the death and resurrection of Jesus. The basic structure of Jewish apocalyptic mythology consisted in a temporal or eschatological dualism in which the present era ('ōlām hazzeh, literally, "this world or age") is regarded as a period of oppression by the wicked, which will be superseded by a blissful future era ('ōlām habbô', literally, "the coming world or age"). The introduction of the future era will be accomplished by the climactic intervention of God (either directly or through a human agent, that is, a messiah), and will be preceded by the destruction of the wicked and the final deliverance of the righteous. The salvation envisaged was both mundane and nationalistic and consisted of such material and temporal "blessings" as health, wealth, length of life, offspring and fertility of both flock and field, and peace, that is, victory over one's enemies. Jewish eschatology exhibits enormous variety since it is, essentially, a folkloristic vehicle for expressing nationalistic nostalgias and fantasies using imagery drawn both from mythical protological conditions and from idealized Israelite kingship traditions.

While it is incorrect to speak of "Jewish eschatology" as if it were a single unified system of thought, it is nevertheless true that the various Jewish eschatologies had a largely futuristic orientation.[35] Paul's recognition that Jesus as messiah was a figure of the past presumably led him to introduce some significant modifications into his eschatological perspectives. The death and resurrection of Christ in the past were regarded by Paul as the eschatological event that separated "this age" (Rom. 12:2; 1 Cor. 2:6), or "this present evil age" (Gal. 1:4) from "the age to come" (Paul uses no consistent term for this future era). Paul does not explicitly use the latter term, but cf. 2 Cor. 5:17; Gal. 6:15, and though the final consummation was still future, for Christians the new age was present. Paul exhibits a tendency to conceptualize human nature and existence as a microcosmic version of a christianized form of apocalyptic eschatology; that is, the apocalyptic structure of history becomes paradigmatic for understanding human nature. Just as Paul's christianized form of apocalyptic thought is characterized by a historical or eschatological dualism consisting of the juxtaposition of the old age and the new age, so his view of human nature can similarly reflect a homologous dualistic structure. This is particularly evident in 2 Cor. 5:17 (NRSV):

So if anyone is in Christ, there is a new creation [kainē ktisis]: everything old [ta archaia] has passed away; see, everything has become new!

Here Paul uses the basic apocalyptic expectation of the renewal of creation (i.e., the inauguration of the age to come) following the destruction of the present evil age as a paradigm for the transformation experienced by the individual Christian who has moved from unbelief to belief. Thus, the apocalyptic expectation of an impending cosmic change from the present evil age to the future age of bliss has become paradigmatic for the transformation of the individual believer. Since this apocalyptic transformation affects only those "in Christ," the external world and its inhabitants remain under the sway of the old age. The phrase "new creation"[36] refers to the renewal or recreation of a new heaven and earth following the destruction of the old cosmos.[37] Is this simply an instance of the metaphorical use of apocalyptic language, or does it reflect the ontological transformation of a Christian? The passage focuses on the effects for the individual believer.

The kata sarka/kata pneuma dichotomy, which occurs with some frequency in Paul, makes more sense if it is regarded as microcosmic homology to the flesh/spirit dichotomy reflected in the two ages. While the antithetical character of the flesh and the spirit is evident (Rom. 8:4). Life "according to the flesh" is a possible way of living which Paul juxtaposes with life "according to the spirit" (Rom. 8:5-6, 12-13); that is, they are contemporaneous possibilities. Yet there is also a temporal relationship between the flesh and the spirit: "you are not in the flesh; you are in the Spirit" (Rom. 8:9).

We also find in Pauline thought the "already"/"not yet" polarity—that is, the juxtaposition of the indicative and the imperative (e.g., Gal. 5:25: "If we live in the Spirit, let us also walk by the Spirit"). It is at this point that one of the central problems of Pauline ethics become evident. If the flesh has been crucified with Christ (Gal. 2:20; 3:24; 6:14; Rom. 6:2, 6-7, 22; 8:13), why are the desires of the flesh still a problem for Christians (Gal. 5:16-18; Rom. 6:12-14; 8:5-8)?[38] The presence of a macrocosmic paradigm does not necessitate a detailed correspondence between microcosmic conception of human nature and Paul's conception of the apocalyptic macrocosm. In short, Rudolf Bultmann's existentialist understanding of Pauline anthropological terms (i.e., the human person as a free agent responsible for his or her own decisions) and Ernst Käsemann's apocalyptic or cosmological understanding (i.e., the human person as a victim of supernatural cosmic forces) are not mutually exclusive categories. In some respects this is a chicken-and-egg problem: that is, did Paul's mythological view of eschatological dualism give rise to a homologous view of human nature in which the old and the new are juxtaposed until the eschatological consummation, or did his mythological view of the structure of human nature provide confirmation for his Christian understanding of Jewish apocalyptic eschatology? Neither of these possibilities is quite satisfactory, for the answer is probably more dialectical. It is more likely that Paul linked his christianized apocalyptic outlook with current conceptions of the human person, since the former was more unified than the latter.

Theological Reflections

In this study I have used the historical-critical method to argue for a number of positions: (1) Ancient views of human nature, were exceedingly complex and exhibited great variety. (2) The statements of Paul that reflect his views of human nature and the self generally exhibit an anthropological dualism with both ontological and psychological dimensions, though he only addresses the subject in the context of ethical issues (i.e., the problem of obeying the will of God); what he does say is not sufficient for reconstructing a consistent and unified Pauline doctrine of the human person. (3) I further argued that Paul used at least two models of human nature, the *irrational behavior model*, drawn from popular Hellenistic thought, and the *apocalyptic macrocosm-microcosm model*, which has analogies in early Judaism. Even if I assume that I have correctly marshaled and interpreted the evidence of ancient texts, and have done so in such a way that the results are argued in a convincing manner, a nagging question remains. What, if anything, do Paul's views of human nature and the self have to do with a contemporary Christian understanding of the human person? It is clear that there is no single biblical view of human nature, for the Hebrew Bible and the Greek New Testament exhibit such a variety of perspectives on this subject that it is not at all obvious what the constituent features of such a view might be. It is extremely doubtful, for example, whether it is even possible to speak of the concept of the self in the Hebrew Bible, certainly not the introspective self found reflected in parts of Paul's letters.[39]

Conceptions of the human person in the Hebrew Bible and the Greek New Testament exhibit great variety because such conceptions, like all modern conceptions of the person are an inextricable part of the social structures of particular societies within which such conceptions are found. Examining particular conceptions of the human person can reveal a great deal about the religious and social assumptions and values of particular societies. Conceptions of the person (or the lack of such conceptions) in various strata of the biblical text cannot be expected to exhibit the kind of unity that one might find in the thought, for example, of a particular philosopher. The variety of biblical conceptions of the person, therefore, is not a fact to be lamented, but rather a rich variety to be celebrated.

Modern conceptions of the self are not "created" but are rather "given" in the sense that they determined by a variety of social, cultural, and religious factors. Since the transforming presence of God was a factor of utmost importance for Paul, the theological problem he faced was that of determing how the experience of the divine presence could be understood and articulated. The very fact that Paul's anthropology exhibits variety and inconsistency suggests that his central concern is that of understanding the presence of God in his life, not that of formulating a consistent view of the human experiencer. Further, since Paul's experience of the divine was expressed in a variety of metaphors, he does not even provide us with a logically consistent account of his experience of God.

The extent to which Paul's tangential and even contradictory views of human nature are useful for constructing, or even contributing to, a modern theological position on human nature or the self, therefore, remains questionable. According to the Pauline appropriation of the irrational behavior model, the human person consists of two aspects or dimensions that are in conflict with each other. In Rom. 7:14-25 he designates the "higher" aspect of the individual using such symbols as the "inner person" and the "mind," and the "lower" aspect as "the flesh," "my members," and "this moral body." Here it is clear that the real self should be identified with the "higher" aspect. In Gal. 5:16-17, on the other hand, the aspects of the person that are in conflict are "the flesh" and "the spirit." The self is identified with neither but is pulled now one way and now another by these aspects. This is in general agreement, as we have seen, with a widespread Hellenistic conception of human nature which conceptualized the human person as a combination of rational and irrational elements, so that proper behavior was the product of knowledge, while improper behavior was the result of incomplete knowledge or ignorance. This conception of the self, however, is comparatively simple or "thin," for the dramatized internal dialogue or tug-of-war that Paul articulates symbolically represents just two conflicting voices representing his conception of good and evil, virtue and vice. In contrast, most modern notions of the self usually involve a more complex or "thick" description. Such description corresponds to the complexity of modern society, which often makes it necessary for each of us to play many, frequently conflicting roles. It is astonishing, is it not, how an apparently normal husband and father can be transformed into a pathological liar once he steps on the lot where he sells used cars? In the end the question still remains regarding how deeply the Pauline perspective on self can inform modern notions. Worlds have changed and homologies are not the same. Dualisms, even richly described ones, may not be the most adequate frameworks with which to engage the complexities of the modern self.

Notes

1. Only the seven indisputably genuine Pauline letters will be considered as sources for Paul's thought: Romans, 1-2 Corinthians, Galatians, Philippians, 1 Thessalonians, Philemon.

2. For a recognition of the anthropological variety in early Judaism, see George W. E. Nickelsburg, Jr., Resurrection, Immortality, and Eternal Life in Intertestamental Judaism (Harvard Theological Studies 26; Cambridge, Mass.: Harvard University Press, 1972), 170-80. The notion of a variety of views in early Judaism is also emphasized by H. C. C. Cavallin, Life After Death: Paul's Argument for the Resurrection of the Dead in 1 Cor 15, Part I, An Enquiry into the Jewish Background (Lund: Gleerup, 1974), 200: "Statements on an immortality of the soul which excludes the resurrection of the body are almost as common as those which explicitly state the resurrection of the body. . . ."

3. For a variety of early Jewish views of death involving the separation of body from spirit, see Wis. 8:19-20; 9:15 (see David Winston, The Wisdom of Solomon [Anchor Bible 43; Garden City, N.Y.: Doubleday, 1979], 25-32); Jub. 23:30-32; 1 Enoch 102:5; 103:2-4; 104:3; T. Asher 6:5-6; 4 Macc. 7:19; 13:17; 16:25; Ps.-Phocylides 105-8). Josephus frequently imported popular Middle Platonic body/soul dualism into his narrative when discussing the beliefs of first-century Palestinian Jews. He attributes psychosomatic dualism to himself in a speech against suicide (War 3.362-88), to the Zealot leader Eleazar at Masada (War 7.344-48), and to the Essenes (War 2.154). This view is clearly expressed

by Josephus in *War* 3.372 (LCL trans.): "All of us, it is true, have mortal bodies, composed of perishable matter, but the soul lives for ever, immortal: it is a
portion of the Deity housed in our bodies." The Pharisees, according to Josephus, believed that the soul is immortal, but only the souls of good people pass
into other bodies, while the souls of the wicked are punished eternally (*War*
2.163). The Sadducees, on the other hand, did not believe that the soul lives on
after death (*War* 2.164). In tannaitic Judaism,the human person was believed to
be composed of various parts (E. E. Urbach, *The Sages: Their Concepts and
Beliefs* [Cambridge, Mass.: Harvard University Press, 1987], 218–22).

4. The trichotomous conception of human nature is common in Gnosticism
and is found also in Origen (e.g., *De principiis* 3.4), though he waffles between
a bipartite and tripartite conception. The trichotomy *sōma*, *pneuma*, and *psychē*
occurs in Inscriptiones Graecae XIV, 1720 (G. R. Horsley, *New Documents Illus-
trating Early Christianity*, vol. 4 [New South Wales, Australia: Macquarie University, 1987], 38–39), an inscription from the imperial period: "To the
underworld gods. The body of [. . .]rios is below; his spirit and soul remain."
Cf. IG XIV, 2068 (Horsley, *New Documents*, 4:32f.). Three Christian papyri
mention "soul and body and spirit" (*P.Coll.Youtie* 91, an amulet [fifth or sixth
cent.]; *P.Harr.* 107 [third cent.], and *P.Oxy.* 8.1161, a letter [fourth cent.]; see
Horsley, *New Documents*, 1:102f.).

5. W. David Stacey tries to force this passage into the Procrustean bed of the
Israelite view of the person: "When dealing with *nous*, it is very easy to forget
that Paul always adopts the synthetic, Hebrew view of man, and not the analytic
Greek view. It is very easy, therefore, to speak of *nous* as a faculty possessed by
man, but this cannot be allowed" (*The Pauline View of Man in Relation to Its
Judaic and Hellenistic Background* [London: Macmillan, 1956], 198). In 1 Cor.
14:14–19, however, such an interpretation cannot be avoided.

6. Richard Reitzenstein, *Die hellenistische Mysterienreligionen* (Darmstadt:
Wissenschaftliche Buchgesellschaft, 1966), 337f. Reitzenstein, however, erred
in describing this *nous* as "göttliches Fluidum" (p. 338). Reitzenstein's view is
rejected (not refuted) by J. Behm, *Theological Dictionary of the New Testament*,
4:959.

7. Samuel Laeuchli, "Monism and Dualism in the Pauline Anthropology,"
Biblical Research 3 (1958): 19.

8. Friedrich G. Lang, *2 Korinther 5, 1–10 in der neueren Forschung* (Tübin-
gen: J. C. B. Mohr [Paul Siebeck], 1973).

9. Egon Brandenburger, *Fleisch und Geist: Paulus und die dualistische Weisheit*
(Neukirchen-Vluyn: Neukirchener Verlag, 1968), 175–77; he discusses the close
parallel between 2 Cor. 5:1–4 and Philo *Heres* 267 (Loeb Classical Library
trans.): "God does not grant as a gift to the lover of virtue that he should dwell
in the body as in a homeland, but only permits him to sojourn there, as in a

foreign country." See also Cicero *Tusculan Disputations* 1.11.24 (Loeb Classical Library trans.): "souls, on their separation from the body, find their way to heaven as to their dwelling-place [*posse animos, cum e corporibus excesserint, in caelum quasi in domicilium suum pervenire*]."

10. Democritus B.37, B.187, B.223 (Hermann Diels and Walther Kranz, *Die Fragmente der Vorsokratiker*, 6. Aufl. [2 vols.; Zurich and Hildesheim: Weidmann, 1951], 2:155, 183, 190); Longinus *On the Sublime* 32.5; Ps.-Hippocrates *Cord.* 7; *Anat.* 1; Ps.-Plato *Axiochus* 366A; Philo *Quaest. in Gen.* 1.28; PGM I.319; IV.448, 1951, 1970, 2141 (here *skēnos* means "corpse"); Timaeus Locrus *On the Nature of the World and the Soul* 45, 60, 62, 86; *Corpus Hermeticum* 13.12, 15; *Sentences of Sextus* 320 (*skēnōma*); PGM 19a.49: "every limb of this corpse and the spirit of this body [*to pneuma toutou tou skēnōmatos*]"; the phrase *thnētōi skēnei* in Achilles Tatius 2.36.3 is an emendation for *kallei* in the manuscripts, and probably incorrect (Ebbe Vilborg, *Achilles Tatius, Leucippe and Clitophon* [Studia Graeca et Latina Gothoburgensia, I and XV; Stockholm: Almqvist & Wiksell, 1955-62], 1:46; 15:62); for this usage in early Christian literature in addition to 2 Pet. 1:13f., *Ep. Diog.* 6:8, and *Apoc. Sedrach* 9:2, s.v. *skēnos* in Lampe, *Patristic Greek Lexicon*, 1237. This metaphor occurs frequently in Neopythagorean literature; see Holger Thesleff, *The Pythagorean Texts of the Hellenistic Period* (Åbo: Åbo Akademi, 1965), 43.21; 49.9; 70.9; 80.2; 124.18; 143.19; 145.2. Philo (*De somn.* 1.122) speaks of *ho oikos tēs psychēs, to sōma*.

11. According to Plato's myth of the Vision of Judgment, told in Plato *Gorgias* 523A-524A (see E. R. Dodds, *Plato, Gorgias* [Oxford: Clarendon Press, 1959], 372-79), and repeated in Plutarch *Consolatio ad Apoll.* 121A-C, people were once judged just before their death, but this resulted in bad decisions, for base souls were sometimes clad with beautiful bodies. Therefore Zeus arranged that people would be judged immediately after death when "naked" (*gymnos*), that is, when their souls had been divested of their bodies. In Plato *Cratylus* 403B, people are said to fear Pluto *hoti hē psychē tou sōmatos par' ekeinon aperchetai* (Hans Dieter Betz, *Lukian von Samosata und das Neue Testament* [Berlin: Akademie-Verlag, 1961], 93). Walter Schmithals's view that "naked" means "dead," that is, the absence of being, is simply impossible (*Gnosticism in Corinth*, trans. J. E. Steely [Nashville: Abingdon, 1971], 264).

12. This is a disputed passage which a few scholars interpret as Paul's use of the language of his (perhaps Gnostic) opponents. Schmithals finds Gnostic conceptuality throughout this passage (*Gnosticism in Corinth*, 259-75). Similarly, Robert Jewett argues that the term *sōma* reflects Paul's use of the anthropological categories of his Gnostic opponents (Robert Jewett, *Paul's Anthropological Terms: A Study of their Use in Conflict Settings* [Leiden: Brill, 1971], 274-77). Similarly, the view that "while we are at home in the body we are away from the Lord" is a slogan of Paul's opponents and therefore does not reflect Paul's own

112 DAVID E. AUNE

views has most recently been argued by Jerome Murphy-O'Connor, "'Being at Home in the Body we are in Exile from the Lord' (2 Cor. 5:6b)," *Revue Biblique* 93 (1986): 214-21.

13. D. W. Palmer argues that death as a gain for those whose life is burdensome is a commonplace in Greek and Latin literature ("'To Die is Gain' [Philippians i 21]," *Novum Testamentum* 17 [1975]: 203-18).

14. The extant dialogues of Plato do not reflect a unified set of philosophical doctrines, nor can Plato's thought be adequately understood without recourse to the *agrapha dogmata* or "oral tradition" of Platonic teaching reflected in the writings of Aristotle and others. Plato's views of human nature changed during his lifetime as reflected in the nearly thirty authentic dialogues that have been preserved. The most obvious change was from his view of the *psychē* as a simple substance in the *Phaedo*, to the tripartite division of the *psychē* in the *Republic*. Plato's views of the relationship between the body and the soul are drawn from both philosophical and popular traditions, but are not forced into a single coherent system. Plato's view of the immortality and imperishability of the *psychē* may not in fact have been widely shared (*Republic* 608d; *Phaedo* 77b; 84b). In the *Phaedo* alone the term *psychē* is used with a relatively extensive variety of connotations: (1) the element within us whose good condition constitutes our true well-being, (2) the "true self" or "real person" (115b-116a), (3) the intellect, reason, or thinking faculty (65b-c; 76c), (4) the "rational self" in contrast to emotions and physical desires (94b-d), (5) the "life principle" or "animating agent" (64c; 72a-d; 105c-d), (6) generic "soul stuff" in contrast to individual souls, just as matter may be contrasted to individual bodies (70c-d; 80c-d). This wide range of meanings of *psychē* is not easily amenable to consistency. How can the soul "bring life" to the body (105c-d), "rule and be master" of the body (80a; 94b-d), and yet be a "prisoner" within the body (82e-83a)? According to Plato, the soul wore bodies like clothes to be discarded (*Phaedo* 87b), the soul is woven through the body (*Timaeus* 36e), or a person is a soul using a body (*Alc.* 129C-E). One of the persistent problems with Plato's conception of the soul-body relationship (and one that was attacked by both Stoics and Epicureans) was the assumption that the incorporeal could somehow associate with the corporeal to form a single substance, a human person.

15. The concept of motivation or will in antiquity has been discussed in detail by Albrecht Dihle, *The Theory of the Will in Classical Antiquity* (Berkeley: University of California Press, 1982). Dihle argues that even an implicit theory of will was absent from Greek philosophical thought (not even in Aristotle), though it was implicit in Hebrew and early Christian thought. Dihle's argument is flawed by a "vague and confused" (Adkins) definition of "will" (see the penetrating review by A. W. H. Adkins, *Classical Philology* 80 [1985]: 364-70; a much shorter but essentially similar critique is that by Christopher Kirwan, *Classical Review* 34 [1984]: 335-36).

16. This widespread view of human behavior, often expressed in aphoristic forms (e.g., *to men pneuma prothumon, hē de sarx asthenēs*, "the spirit is willing, but the flesh is weak," Mark 14:38 par. Matt. 26:41; Polycarp *Phil.* 7:2) is reflected in many passages in Greek and Latin literature, several of which are listed in Johann Jacob Wettstein, *Hē Kainē Diathēkē* (Amsterdam: Ex Officina Domeriana, 1752), 2:57.

17. E. R. Dodds, "Plato and the Irrational," in *The Ancient Concept of Progress and Other Essays on Greek Literature and Belief* (Oxford: Clarendon Press, 1973), 106-25.

18. The term *pneuma* is occasionally ambiguous in Paul, for it is not always clear whether the human spirit or the divine Spirit is in view, or whether the human spirit is thought of as somehow infused with the divine Spirit.

19. The isolated character of this internally coherent textual unit from the rest of the rhetorical structure of Galatians is emphasized by J. Smit, "The Letter of Paul to the Galatians: A Deliberative Speech," *New Testament Studies* 35 (1989): 25, who does not try to fit it into the rhetorical structure of the rest of the letter.

20. The *pneuma tou theou* (1 Cor. 2:11), is equivalent to the *nous kyriou* (LXX quotation from Isa. 40:13 in 1 Cor. 2:16), and the *nous Christou* (1 Cor. 2:16); that is, in conventional philosophic parlance, the *nous* is the divine portion of the *psychē*.

21. According to Gal. 5:24, the *sarx* has *pathēmata* and *epithymiai*, and in Rom. 6:12, *to thnēton*. These passages, together with Gal. 5:16f., clearly indicate the equivalence of *sarx* and *sōma* in these contexts.

22. Walter Burkert, *Lore and Science in Ancient Pythagoreanism* (Cambridge, Mass.: Harvard University Press, 1972), 362.

23. Mircea Eliade, *The Sacred and the Profane*, trans. Willard R. Trask (New York: Harper & Row, 1959), 165.

24. E. Schweizer, *Theological Dictionary of the New Testament*, 7:1029-30 (for primary and secondary literature); cf. Democritus, frag. 34 (Diels-Kranz, *Fragmente der Vorsokratiker*, 2:153): "there is a miniature universe in the individual."

25.The term *mikrokosmos* does not occur in classical or Hellenistic Greek, but is a later formation that first appears (in transliteration in Latin) in Isidore of Seville, *De natura rerum* 3.1; see Walther Kranz, *Kosmos* (Archiv für Begriffsgeschichte 2/1, 2; Bonn: H. Bouvier, 1955, 1957), 130-31.

26. The terms "intra-mundane" and "extra-mundane" have been borrowed from Ugo Bianchi, "Prolegomena: The Religio-Historical Question of the Mysteries of Mithra," in *Mysteria Mithrae*, ed. Ugo Bianchi (Études préliminaires aux religions orientales dans l'empire romain; 24; Leiden: Brill, 1979), 4.

27. Martin P. Nilsson, *Greek Piety* (New York: Norton, 1969), 96-103.

28. Hans Jonas, *Gnosis und spatantiker Geist, 1. Teil, Die mythologische Gnosis* (3. Aufl.; Göttingen: Vandenhoeck & Ruprecht, 1964), "Excurs II: Anthro-

pologische Zwei- und Dreistufigkeit" (pp. 212–14); Kurt Rudolph, Gnosis: The Nature and History of Gnosticism, trans. R. McL. Wilson (San Francisco: Harper & Row, 1983), 88–113.

29. O. J. F. Seitz, "Two Spirits in Man: An Essay in Biblical Exegesis," New Testament Studies 6 (1959–60): 82–95.

30. Helmer Ringgren, The Faith of Qumran: Theology of the Dead Sea Scrolls (Philadelphia: Fortress Press, 1963), 68–76.

31. Johannes von Arnim, Stoicorum Veterum Fragmenta (4 vols.; Stuttgart: Teubner, 1905–1924), 1:85–87.

32. Henry Kahane and Renée Kahane, "Hellenistic and Medieval Alchemy," The Encyclopedia of Religion 1:195.

33. Ibid., 1:193.

34. Howard M. Jackson (ed.), Zosimos of Panopolis on the Letter Omega (Missoula, Mont.: Scholars Press, 1978), 29.

35. The eschatology reflected in the Qumran Hodayot is an apparent exception; see Heinz-Wolfgang Kuhn, Enderwartung und gegenwärtiges Heil: Untersuchungen zu den Gemeindeliedern von Qumran (Studien zur Umwelt des Neuen Testaments 4; Göttingen: Vandenhoeck & Ruprecht, 1966).

36. There is some disagreement whether ktisis should be translated "creature" or "creation." Since Paul seems to be referring to a "new [order of] creation," or a "new acts of creation," the latter translation is preferable.

37. Isa. 65:17; 66:22; 1 Enoch 91:16; 72:1; 2 Apoc. Bar. 32:6; 44:12; 49:3; 57:2; Ps.-Philo Biblical Antiquities 3:10; 2 Pet. 3:11–13; Rev. 21:1.

38. J. P. Sanders interprets these and other passages as instances of "participationist language," which suggests that the significance of the death of Christ for Paul was not only the traditional one of atonement for sin, but more particularly that by sharing Christ's death, one belongs to God (E. P. Sanders, Paul and Palestinian Judaism [Philadelphia: Fortress, 1977], 463–68). However, Sanders does not discuss the problem of the tension between "already" and "not yet" in Pauline ethics.

39. There is obviously disagreement here with Krister Stendahl, "The Apostle Paul and the Introspective Conscience of the West," in Paul Among Jews and Gentiles (Philadelphia: Fortress Press, 1976), 78–96.

Singing the Psalms:
Augustine and Athanasius
on the Integration of the Self

Pamela Bright
Concordia University

*A*t the beginning of the twentieth century, William James delivered the Gifford Lectures in Edinburgh under the title *The Varieties of Religious Experience: A Study in Human Nature*. Wedged between "The Sick Soul" (Lecture 7) and "Conversion" (Lecture 9), James examines the topic "The Divided Self, and the Process of its Unification" (Lecture 8). He illustrates his theme with a selection of material demonstrating certain individuals' acute awareness of a "horrible duality" within the self:

> "*Homo duplex, homo duplex!*" writes Alphonse Daudet. "The first time I perceived that I was two was at the death of my brother Henri, when my father cried out so dramatically, He is dead, he is dead! While my first self wept, my second self thought, How truly given was that cry, how fine it would be in the theater. I was then fourteen years old.
>
> This horrible duality has often given me cause for reflection. Oh, this terrible second me, while the other is on foot, acting, living, suffering, bestirring itself. This second me that I have never been able to intoxicate, to make shed tears, or to put to sleep. And how it sees into things, and how it mocks!"[1]

James goes on to comment that whereas some people have an inner constitution that is harmonious and well balanced from the outset, others experience an inner duality ranging from "whimsical inconsistency" to a severe discordance.[2] He turns to Augustine of Hippo as a classic case of the discordant personality type, tending to melancholia in the form of self-condemnation and sense of sin. "Augustine's psychological genius has given an account of the trouble of having a divided self that has never been surpassed."[3]

The purpose of the present study is not to plumb the depths of melancholy of the divided self but in a somewhat more cheerful vein to focus on the process of the unification of the self that was so acutely observed in Augustine's *Confessions*. Indeed, there are two classic texts in late antiquity that are relevant to the topic. The first is Athanasius of Alexandria's *Letter to Marcellinus*. This extraordinarily perceptive mid-fourth-century study of the "psychological" impact of praying, or rather, *singing* the Psalms was immediately recognized as a spiritual classic.[4] The second text is Augustine's *Confessions*, which not only takes its place in the front ranks of the articulation of the religious self but also shares the Athanasian focus on the central role of the Psalms in the process of the unification of the self. That the actual praying of the psalms is a key element in the logic and the structure of the *Confessions* is a topic of lively debate among Augustinian scholars.[5] It will be the argument of this study that these two texts offer valuable insights more broadly into the development of the understanding of the self in the foundational era of the Christian church and then, more particularly, into the role played by the praying of the psalms in an integration of selfhood that is both personal and communal.

Although Athanasius's *Letter to Marcellinus* was published some thirty years before Augustine wrote the *Confessions*, the present study will reverse the chronological order, devoting the first part of the paper to an analysis of the memory and the self in Augustine's *Confessions*. Rather than focusing on the conversion scene in the garden in book 8 of the *Confessions*, this section will follow Augustine's journey into "fields and palaces" (*Conf.* 10.8) of memory. The second part of the paper will consider the role of the praying and singing of the psalms in the integration of self, in both the Augustinian and Athanasian texts—first in a short study of Augustine's description of the experience of praying Psalm 4 (*Conf.* book 9) set in the period immediately following his conversion in the summer of 395. This study will be linked with a reflection on the theological principles outlined by Athanasius of Alexandria in his *Letter to Marcellinus* on the importance of actually singing the psalms for the unification of the self, bodily, emotionally, and intellectually, as a Christian believer.

Memory and the Self in the *Confessions* of Augustine

The dramatic conclusion of the narration of the passage from anguished duality of will to self-surrender in conversion tempts many readers of

Augustine's *Confessions* to close the book soon after the author himself closes his mother's eyes in death in book 9. The last four books of the *Confessions* seem a strange admixture of speculations on time and eternity, and of obscure and dated scriptural interpretations, forming an intellectual labyrinth to weary and confuse the reader when compared with the riveting narrative of the autobiographical section from book 1 to book 9. (Some editions of the *Confessions* exclude the final four books, either as a concession to the reader or to the constraints of economy![6]) But the soul-searching or, rather, the self-searching is far from over at the end of book 9. Just as Augustine had begun book 9 with the meditation on "Who am I and what manner of man?" (*Quis ego et qualis ego?*), so book 10 begins with a reflection on the things to be lamented and the things to be rejoiced over (*Conf.* 10.1) in the quest to know God and the self.

The quest announced in book 10 is a remarkable journey through the "spacious palaces" of the innermost self. It is a "journal of the soul," which continues and deepens the "external" narrative of the previous nine books. And yet this is not a solitary quest, nor a retreat into the recesses of aloneness; it is entered upon in conversation with the God whom Augustine addresses as "my most private Physician" (*medice meus intime* [*Conf.* 10.8]). It is thus announced as therapeutic in nature, with careful and explicit analysis of the means and the process of healing.

Augustine's awareness of the complexity of self is evident in the care he takes in structuring this self-reflection. The inner journey through memory begins with sensory memories of light and color and form, sounds and smells, "breath of lilies" and of "violets," tastes and sensations of touch—"all these does that great receipt of the memory receive in her many secret and inexpressible windings" (*Conf.* 10.8). He next explores the capacity of the memory for the precepts of the liberal sciences *de doctrinis liberalibus percepta* (10.9)—logic, grammar, mathematics— and then continues through other vast fields of the memories of past emotions, whether sad or joyful (10.14). Finally he recapitulates the stages of the journey by examining the three-fold power of memory:

> Great is this power of memory; a thing, O my God, to be amazed at, a profound and infinite multiplicity; and this thing is the mind, and this thing am I [*et hoc animus est, et hoc ego ipse sum*]. What am I, therefore, O my God? What kind of nature am I? A life various and full of changes, and exceedingly immense. Behold, in those innumerable fields and dens and caves of my memory, innumerably full of innumerable kinds of things brought in first either by the images, as all bodies are: secondly, by the presence of the things themselves, as the arts are: thirdly, by certain

notions and impressions, as the affections of the mind are . . . through all of these do I run and flit about, on this side and on that, mining into them as far as I am able, but can find no bottom. (Conf.10.17)[7]

This recapitulation is but a respite in the course of the inner journey through memory. We are invited not merely to consider the extent and power of memory but to reflect on what is the driving force behind this exploration of the secret recesses of the remembering self. It is the search for happiness, for that highest "rest" that is the integration of the self with itself, and the self with its Source:

> How then Lord, do I seek you? For when I seek you, my God, I seek the happy life. "I will seek you that my soul may live" (Isaiah 4:30). For my body lives by my soul: and my soul by you. (Conf. 10.20)

The following section of book 10 is a richly suggestive complement to the narrative of his journey to God in books 1 to 9. In this section of book 10 (19–27) Augustine focuses on the quest for happiness—the quest for the "blessed life"—a classical topos in antiquity: "See now, how great a space I have coursed over in my memory seeking you, O Lord" (Conf. 10.24). It is a reflection that culminates in the justly famous outburst:

> Late have I loved you, O Beauty so ancient and so new, late have I loved you. And behold you were within me, and I outside and there I sought for you and in my deformity I rushed headlong into the well-formed things you have made. You were with me and I was not with you. . . . You called and cried to me. . . . You broke open my deafness. . . . You scattered my blindness. . . . You breathed fragrance, and I drew in my breath and I now pant for you. . . . I tasted and I hunger and thirst; you touched me, and I burned for your peace. (Conf. 10.27)

The quest did not end at the moment of "hearing" and "seeing" and "breathing" and "tasting." Conversion does not end in the garden (book 8) or at the baptism (book 9); the pilgrim has reached a blessed stage of the journey, but Augustine goes on to examine the three "concupiscences" that remind us that the goal is still far ahead. The true happiness of the self has been recognized, but there is no secure possession yet.

It is at this point that the deftness of the structuring of book 10 becomes clear. The layering of the memory in the three treasured stores of sense perception, of the wealth of human sciences, and finally all the range of human emotions is retraced in the frame of a "self"-reflection on 1 John 2:16: "all that panders to the appetites or entices the eyes, all the arrogance based on wealth, these spring not from the Father but from the world,"[8]—more traditionally, the "concupiscence of the flesh," the "concupiscence of the eyes," and the "pride of life." Here Augustine considers the repercussions of the unruly disorder of sense images ("the concupiscence of the flesh" [*Conf.* 10.30-34]), of the unbridled appetite for "knowing" ("the concupiscence of the eyes" [10.35]), and the wild clangor of emotions under the driving force of pride ("the pride of life" [10.36-40]). "Thus I have considered the infirmities of my sins in that threefold concupiscence: and I have called your right hand to my help" (10.41). "Whom could I find to reconcile me to you?" Christ is placed before us as the true mediator. Many and great are my infirmities, yes many and great; but your medicine is still greater" (10.43). This echoes an earlier section of the *Confessions* (7.18): "And I sought a way of gaining the strength necessary for enjoying you, and I could not find it until I embraced that Mediator between God and Man, the Man Jesus Christ who is over all, blessed forevermore" (1 Tim. 1:15; Rom. 9:5).

The journey into the recesses of memory that recognizes Christ as both goal of the journey and companion on the way as it is recounted in book 10, is not so much an intense exercise in interiority as a complex, shifting gaze in which the interiority of the focus never loses awareness of the outer realities and the many others whose lives have impinged on his:

> The benefit of confessing, not what I have been, but what I am is this: I confess not only before you, in a secret "exaltation with trembling" (Psalm 2:11) and in secret sorrow with hope, but also in the ears of the believing sons of men, companions of my joy and partners in my mortality, my fellow citizens and fellow pilgrims both those who have gone before and those who follow after and my companions on the way. . . . Therefore to such people whom you have commanded me to serve, I shall reveal not what I was, but what I am now and continue to be. (*Conf.* 10.4)

This is far from a simplistic dichotomy of body/soul. In reading the *Confessions*, one becomes aware of both the intimacy and the complexity of the links between this inner and outer self in Augustine's thought. His capacity to keep the ever-shifting levels of awareness in focus is in large part due to his refusal to reduce this complex vision of self to a neat schema. (How many erudite "introductions" to Augustinian thought fall into dreary reductionism!) The "many-mansioned" self is not easily defined or contained. The self that relentlessly turns inward in search of God and self-knowledge (*Soliloquies* 1) is the same self that reaches out to others in word and gesture and song. It is a process of the integration of self that is at once psychologically acute, Christologically centered, and ecclesially directed. Unless these three aspects are kept in mind, there is danger of an anachronistic reading of the *Confessions* as a case study for psychological analysis.[9] It is the integration of the self in the frame of the praying of the psalms that will be studied in the second part of the paper.

The Integration of Self in Praying the Psalms

Augustine Prays Psalm 4

The journey through memory described in book 10 of the *Confessions* is paralleled in book 9, which takes up the narrative in the period following Augustine's conversion, when he, his mother, and his son together with a group of friends left the city of Milan (and their former professions) in late August 396 for the country house of their friend, Verecundus, at Cassiciacum:

> My God, how I poured out my heart to you as I read the Psalms of David, those songs of faith, those songs of piety which admit of no pride of spirit! ... How I cried aloud to you in those Psalms! How they inflamed me toward you! How I burned to utter them aloud, if possible to the whole world against the pride of mankind. ... With what strong and bitter grief I was enraged against the Manichees! Yet I also pitied them for their ignorance of those medicinal Sacraments and for raging insanely against the antidote which might have made them sane. I wished that they might be near me—without their knowing that they were there—and could see my face and hear my words when in that period of leisure I read the Fourth Psalm so they could see how that Psalm affected me! (*Conf.* 9.4)

The importance of Augustine's treatment of Psalm 4 in book 9 of the *Confessions* has been noted by a number of scholars, recently by Paul Burns in his article on the distinctive use of the psalms in the *Confessions*.[10] Burns draws attention to an earlier study by Hermann-Josef Sieben, who examines the role of Psalm 4 in relation to "words" and "feelings" in Augustine's conversion. Augustine "recognizes the intense personalizing of the sacred text, finding there the identification and the clarification of different stages of the personal journey. Augustine in a sense discovers himself in the text of the Psalm."[11] In distinguishing this type of exegesis from more familiar typological or allegorical methods employed elsewhere is his treatment of the Psalms, Sieben calls this exegesis "therapeutic." Augustine's inclusion of the description of his praying Psalm 4 certainly offers an invaluable insight into his method of praying the psalms, but it may well be that what we are offered here is an even more valuable insight into the process of the integration of the self that lies at the center of conversion as an ongoing experience in life. Burns's own study beautifully illustrates the role of the Psalms in Augustine's life: "Augustine's experience of daily recitation and singing of the Psalms with reflection allowing those texts to illumine his own experience gradually over the years had a profound impact on his self-understanding and ultimately on the themes and structure of the *Confessions.*"[12]

The present study focuses on the role of the Psalms as Augustine walks through the "fields and palaces of memory" in the presence of Christ, his Physician. In the alternating shifts between prayers of lamentation and praise that mark the very structure of the Psalms themselves, Augustine is confronted by the memories of those parts of his life that are to be lamented over and to be rejoiced in (*Conf.* 10.1). But it is not just moments of recognition and confrontation. What he learns in the very act of praying the Psalms is what and how and why he is to lament, just as he discovers what and how and why he is to rejoice. This process of the healing and the unification of the "old self" and the "renewed self" (10.17) is well illustrated in his praying of Psalm 4.

Augustine begins with the cry to God in v. 2 of Psalm 4: "When I called, the God of my righteousness heard me; in tribulation you enlarged me. Have mercy upon me Lord and hear my prayer." He sets the scene by announcing, "I was speaking with myself and to myself in front of you out of the intimate feelings of my soul." Then in the mingled emotions of tremulous fear and hope and exaltation, he hears his former Manichean self being addressed by the Holy Spirit, "How long will you be dull of heart? Why do you love vanity so much and seek after lying?" (Ps. 4:3). Augustine listens and trembles, for these words are spoken "to such as I remember myself to have been. For in those phantasms which I had taken for truth there were both vanity and lying. And in my grief at the remembrance I cried aloud many things earnestly and strongly" (*Conf.* 9.4). His former Manichean self had known paroxysms of anger against that "otherness" within himself that had drawn him away from the pursuit of wisdom. Now, as Augustine prays v. 5 of Psalm 4, "Be angry, and sin not," the outburst of anger is directed at himself, "and how I was moved, my God, I who had already learned to be angry with myself; for it was not that some other nature belonging to the race of darkness committed the sin in me, as the Manichees believe" (*Conf.* 9.4).

Verse 6 of the Psalm leads him to consider, "Who will show us good things?" Then, in the frame of praying vv. 6 to 9 of Psalm 4, there is a kind of concentrated preview of the threefold journey of memory that lies at the heart of book 10 of the *Confessions*: first, through the images burned into the mind of the "visible and temporal things," the "concupiscence of the flesh"; in the gyrating search for "enlightenment," "the concupiscence of the eyes"; and in the vaulting ambition "for good things," "the pride of life":

> The good I now sought was not in the things outside me to be seen by the eye of flesh under the sun. For those finding their joys in things outside easily become vain and waste themselves on visible and temporal things, and with their minds starving go licking at images . . . "The light of your countenance is sealed upon us, O Lord" (Psalm 4:6-7). If only they would see the Eternal Light inside themselves. I had seen it and I was frantic that I could not make them see it even were they to ask: "Who will show us good things?" For the heart they would bring me would be in their eyes, eyes that looked everywhere but at you. For there in the place where I had been angry with myself inside, where I had been pricked, where I had made my sacrifice, offering up my old self and beginning my plan for renewal, with my hope set on you—there it was that you began to grow sweet to me and to put "gladness in my heart" (Psalm 4:7). (*Conf.* 9.4)

Through the narration of the praying of Psalm 4, Augustine affords us a privileged insight into the process of transformation of the old self that was his daily practice in praying the psalms:

> With a deep cry from my heart I called out the following verse: "Oh, in peace, Oh, in the Selfsame!" . . . and you supremely are the Selfsame [*tu es id ipsum*] you who do not change, and in you is that rest in which all labor is forgotten, since there is no other beside you, nor are we to seek for those many other things which are not what you are. But you alone O Lord "have made me dwell in hope" (Psalm 4:8). I read and was set on fire (*Conf.* 9.4)

In his book entitled *Resurrection*, Rowan Williams reflects on the relationship between memory and hope, claiming that memory is the authentic ground for acting and hoping:

> This may help us to understand the way in which Augustine in his *Confessions* takes the bold step of identifying memory with "spirit", especially as he embarks in Book 10 upon his great quest for God in the structure of human awareness. Memory is the "self" because it is my presence to myself, the way I constitute myself and understand myself as a subject with a continuous history of experience. I am not trapped and confined in the

present moment: as a conscious subject with a remembered past, I "transcend" these limitations. I can understand them, I can put them in perspective, move on from and through them.[13]

Augustine was engaged in something even more dynamic than "moving on and through" present and past; at the very least it is clear that Augustine was not advocating taking up permanent residence in the "fields and palaces of memory" in an alienated subjectivity. His baptism alone, if not his ordination to the ministry of word and sacrament (11:2) called him to a dynamic interaction between the "inner" world so acutely observed and the "outer" world for which he was constantly learning to love "ordinately" (but not dispassionately!) rather than "disordinately" in these very journeys through memory in the presence of his "intimate Physician." The healing of the old self is at the same time an integration of inner and outer self, the "inner" self focused on his God, who is more present than his awareness of his existence, and the "outer" self (not mere bodily awareness but the self in interaction with other selves).

Athanasius and the Singing of the Psalms

Among the Christian authors of late antiquity, one of the most original contributions to the integrative role of praying the Psalms in the life of the Christian is to be found in the Letter to Marcellinus,[14] a short treatise of Athanasius, bishop of Alexandria, written in the tumultuous years of the so-called peace of the church under Emperor Constantine and his immediate successors. In spite of the distractions of long political exiles, constant in-fighting in the Christian communities on pivotal issues in doctrinal matters, and the frequent threat of personal danger, Athanasius took the time to write a letter to a sick friend to encourage him in his determination to devote the hours of his convalescence to the study of the Psalms.

In a concentrated work, the bishop leads his reader through a remarkable survey of the psalms from many points of view: the relationship of the psalms to the rest of scripture, the specific characteristic of the Psalms as songs, and the different genres within the book of Psalms. Athanasius then goes on to suggest how every Psalm can be "actualized" in the course of everyday life. It is a virtuoso piece, reflecting the bishop's own prayerful assimilation of the Psalms, as well as his pastoral activity over many decades.

In section 27 of this carefully crafted work, Athanasius announces to

his reader that the psalms are not merely to be read or recited but are to
be sung:

> At this point it is very necessary to pass over the reasons why words of this
> kind [the Psalms] are to be intoned with melody and song. For there are
> certain simplistic people among us who, while they believe that the words
> are divinely inspired, yet consider that the psalms have been put to music
> merely for the pleasure of the listener. But this is not the case. For scrip-
> ture does not seek for sweetness or elegance for its own sake, but rather it
> is composed in such a way to be of benefit for the soul.

It is important to note that Athanasius is not advocating a rejection of
human pleasure. He has argued earlier in the text (*Letter*, 9) for the recognition that the Psalms are songs, and that songs in their very nature have
a universal appeal enabling the appropriation of the Psalms by peoples
and cultures far from the milieu in which they were written. The "sweet-
ness" and "elegance" of the psalms are an integral part of their special
"ministry" within the different literary genres of the Old Testament
books. Especially in the last sections of his essay on praying the Psalms,
he insists on the importance of the very "physicality" of singing the
Psalms:

> to recite the psalms melodiously is not to seek the mere pleasure of sound
> but rather it is to give outward expression to the harmony of the reason-
> ing faculties in the soul. And the melodious recitation is a symbol of the
> rhythmical and tranquil restoration of the understanding. For the praises
> to God on well-sounding cymbals, the cithara, and the ten-stringed harp
> again symbolize the natural concord of the members of the body, like harp
> strings. Furthermore by the sound and by the command of the Spirit all
> these move and live. Thus he who sings well puts his soul in order and so
> leads what is of unbalanced rhythm to an equilibrium. Being established
> in its proper nature it may fear nothing, and in freedom from phantoms
> of the future, it may direct itself to longing for the good things to come.
> (*Letter*, 29)

Athanasius offers two reasons for the need for actually singing the
psalms:

> First it is fitting that the divine scripture praises God not only in the single
> tone of prose, but also by the whole range of the voice. While prose tone
> is suited to the recitation of the Law and the Prophets and all the Histo-
> ries, together with the New Testament, on the other hand it is appropri-
> ate to give expression to the Psalms the Odes and the Canticles with the
> whole range of the voice, just as we are to find salvation by loving God
> with the whole of our strength and power. The second reason is this: Just
> as the concord of the sound of flutes plays together in a harmonious unity,

so too when the various motions of the soul are recognized, this is, the reasoning faculties, and the desires and passions of the soul, and the activity of the members of the body originating in these movements, reason does not wish that man be in disharmony with himself, or be alienated from himself. (*Letter*, 27)

In focusing on Athanasius's insistence on singing the psalms, I do not imply that Augustine of Hippo was deaf to the importance of song, even though his early treatise *On Music* may disappoint modern readers hoping for some inspirational text from late antiquity on such a topic. In fact, for the most part, while *On Music* (book 6) is the properly technical and philosophical product of its time,[15] Augustine's sensitivity to the power and inspiration of music is well attested to in the *Confessions*, and especially in relation to the singing of the Psalms. The importance of studying Athanasius's insistence on the *singing* of the Psalms is not the contrast it offers to Augustine's treatment of the Psalms; rather, it is the challenge that it presents to the stereotypes of the dualities of the self in late antiquity.

Conclusion: The Ancient Self and Its Stereotypes

There are profound contrasts between the contribution of these two bishops to the question of the understanding of the self. The serene, pastoral tone of Athanasius's letter of encouragement to Marcellinus seems light-years removed from the intensity and nervous energy of Augustine, his much younger North African contemporary.[16] There is not a comparable awareness of the complexity of the self in Athanasius's writings. He inherited the categories of self from a long and (for him) unquestioned tradition. Athanasius quotes no learned philosophical forebears; he merely assumes them. But in this unassuming(!) assumption of the traditional language of self, there is a sure-footed and clear-eyed awareness of the harmony of the embodied person, renewed in the image of the Eternal Logos who in the divine paradox of the incarnation has shared our griefs and our joys. In joining our many voices with the voice of the Logos who has sung and now sings the Psalms in and with the community of the church, our whole self—body, emotions, will, intellect—is led to a new harmony.[17]

Is this harmony to be equated with the Stoic self-mastery of the reason? Not exactly, (perhaps even far from exactly). Athanasius urges that the Psalms be sung, not just recited, so that the whole range of the vocal chord can be exercised. In the same way he presents the Psalms as a school for the proper exercise of the whole range of human emotions. (The Psalms are often given to inordinate expressions of "unholy glee": the only thing to which they seem immune is political correctness.) It is not self-mastery that he is urging, not even a servile "submission" to the *Logos*/Reason. Rather, the soul "fixes its gaze upon the mind in Christ" (1 Cor. 2:6). What Athanasius reiterates through all his writing is the remaking of our *humanity* "according to the Image," (*kat' eikona*). It is the human being reconstituted, or re-formed, or renewed in the image of God, the incarnate Logos/Reason. This is the central issue in the *Letter to Marcellinus*, as it is throughout all Athanasius's life and teaching.

With Augustine comes the decisive "turn to the subject." It is no longer the nondifferentiated *humanity* of Athanasius, no matter how beautifully the older bishop speaks of our common humanity's renewal through the incarnation of the Son of God. On the other hand, Augustine, in an uncanny, unblinking reflexive gaze, created a new vocabulary and a capacity for experiencing the self. Does the "inner" world eclipse the "outer" world? I would argue that the interior journey through memory does not create a dichotomy between the inner and the outer self in Augustine's thought, as more facile stereotypes of his thinking may suggest. The radical interiority of his "languaging" of the self does not mean that the journey into the depths of self stays "within" and ignores the "without," or rejects the "without." Augustine is neither a man wrapped in silence, nor given to the indulgence of monologues. No one could accuse him of Stoic impassivity in the face of pain or grief, of indifference to slight or to acts of kindness. He is unapologetically driven by the need for conversation, for letters, for the circle of friends. Indeed, he claims that it is a matter of principle that we must seek truth together, with others:

> . . . seeing that your truth is not mine alone, nor his, nor a third's; but belongs to us all, whom you call publicly to partake of it. For whoever challenges that as proper to himself, which you propound for all to enjoy, and would make that his own which belongs to all, that man shall be driven from what is common to all, to what is properly his own, that is, from truth to a lie. (*Conf.* 12.25)

The journey "within" does not create a refuge from the "without." Rather, it is a journey that effects a "reordering" of the attitude toward the "without," not a denial of the "without." For both Athanasius and

Augustine, the "without" is not the world of illusion; it is not the world of dancing shadows. The "without" is just as truly the arena of the Spirit empowering the actualization of the double commandment of love, love of God and love of neighbor, as is the "inner" world where the remembering self addresses God, the very source of selfhood.

In *Sources of the Self* Charles Taylor analyzes the sources of our modern moral identity, beginning with Plato's *Republic*, and then examining the significance of the shifts in the understanding of the self introduced by Augustine at the turn of the fifth century of our era.[18] While Descartes introduced a further shift in self-understanding, this new perspective still lies within the ambient of the "radical reflectivity" of the Augustinian tradition, whereas modernity has disengaged our thinking selves from the material universe.

In studying the Augustinian and Athanasian reflections on prayer, specifically praying the Psalms, the focus has been not so much on the *analysis of the dichotomies* (body/intellect–logos–in Athanasius; old/renewed self and inner/outer awareness in Augustine) as on the *process of reintegration* of the self–the overcoming of the "horrible dualities" within the consciousness of self to which William James referred in the Gifford Lectures at the beginning of the twentieth century. The focus of the present study has been neither the classical duality of body/non-body nor the modern dichotomy of subject/object. The Augustinian and Athanasian texts on the dynamics of prayer are neither classically philosophical nor psychological (which would be anachronistic for these texts). They are pastorally oriented texts.

Writing as a pastor, Augustine insists that the healing of the old self begins when one enters upon an interior journey into the treasure house of memory that leads the whole self (past and present in a continuity of consciousness) to stand in the presence of the Divine Physician (who is always the "self-same" [*Conf.* 9.4]). The old self is not the past self but the unredeemed self, the self in need of healing and renewal. Athanasius's attention is also fixed on pastoral concern, not only for his sick friend Marcellinus but for all those who suffer from a deeper sickness, the fallen condition of humanity–"fallen" into a disintegrative state, as Athanasius explains in the introduction to *On the Incarnation*.[19] In the *Letter to Marcellinus* he speaks to all those who seek to know how to pray the Psalms in order to achieve self-harmony: "Reason (that is, the *Logos*) does not wish the human being to be in disharmony, or to be alienated from oneself" (*Letter*, 27). In praying the Psalms bodily, with full voice and with all the attention of mind and heart, we enter into a process of "renewal" of our humanity in the image of the incarnate Logos. It is a process of integration of the self under the direction of the Logos of God: "He who sings well puts his soul in order and so leads what is of unbalanced rhythm to an equilibrium" (*Letter*, 29).

We stand at least sixteen hundred years from the place of these two author-bishops. In the meantime, our cosmologies and our anthropologies have changed as radically as our sense of self. This reflection on the self in late antiquity was not an exercise in retrieval of a "golden past." Athanasius and Augustine would smile ironically at such a description of their age. Rather it was an exercise in attention to "others" far from us in time, in the hope that the careful attention given to their voices will stimulate a fruitful and continuing conversation among exegetes and theologians today.

Notes

1. William James, *The Gifford Lectures*, Lecture 8 (New York: Longmans, Green, 1902), 141.

2. Ibid.

3. Ibid., 144. An analysis of the "melancholic self" of Augustine to which James refers would need to be set in the context of Augustine's exegesis of Paul's Epistle to the Romans.

4. Charles Kannengiesser, *Early Christian Spirituality*, trans. Pamela Bright (Philadelphia: Fortress, 1986), 10-20.

5. Robert McMahon, *Augustine's Prayerful Ascent: An Essay on the Literary Form of the Confessions* (Athens, Ga: University of Georgia Press, 1989). See also Paul Burns, "Augustine's Distinctive Use of the Psalms in the *Confessions*: The Role of Music and Recitation," *Augustinian Studies* 24 (1994): 133-46.

6. See Mark Vessey, "Saint Augustine: *Confessions*," *Augustinian Studies* 24 (1994): notes 2 and 3, which trace the early history of the omission of the final books of the *Confessions* (11-13) A note on the last page of the 1887 edition of the *Confessions* reads: "The remaining three books in the Latin text consist entirely of a commentary upon the early chapters of Genesis, and are seldom published with the '*Confessions*'" (p. 181).

7. The translations of *Confessions* books 9 and 10 are taken from *Augustine of Hippo: Selected Writings*, translation and introduction by Mary T. Clark (New York: Image Books, 1984).

8. *The Revised English Bible* (Oxford, Cambridge: 1989).

9. A naïve reading of the *Confessions* for childhood maladjustment or the

hundred pathologies to which we are vulnerable may well be valuable, as long as the genre and the literary structure of the *Confessions* are respected. This calls for a conversation between the humanities and the sciences.

10. Burns, "Augustine's Distinctive Use of the Psalms," 133–46.

11. Ibid., 136.

12. Ibid., 143.

13. Rowan Williams, *Resurrection* (London: Darton, Longman & Todd, 1982), 31.

14. Charles Kannengiesser, *Early Christian Spirituality*, 56–77.

15. Burns, "Augustine's Distinctive Use of the Psalms," 138.

16. Athanasius wrote the *Letter to Marcellinus* when Augustine was still a child. Athanasius died in 373, whereas Augustine was not baptized until 387.

17. For a more detailed study of the role of music in the writings of the early church see Everett Ferguson, "Towards a Patristic Theology of Music," *Studia Patristica* 24 (1991): 266–83.

18. Charles Taylor, *The Sources of the Self: The Making of the Modern Identity* (Cambridge, Mass.: Harvard University Press, 1989). For the present study, see chap. 7, "In Interiore Homine": "On the way from Plato to Descartes stands Augustine. Augustine's whole outlook was influenced by Plato's doctrines as they were transmitted by Plotinus. His encounter with these doctrines played a crucial role in his spiritual development. He could liberate himself from the last shackles of the false Manichaean view when he finally came to see God and the soul as immaterial. Henceforth, for Augustine, the Christian opposition between spirit and flesh was to be understood with the aid of the Platonic distinction between the bodily and the non-bodily" (p. 127).

19. Athanasius, *Incarnation of the Word* 3 (Nicene and Post-Nicene Fathers 4, Second Series; Peabody, Mass.: Hendrickson Publishers, 1994), 37.

The Bible and the Self
in Medieval Autobiography:
Otloh of St. Emmeram (1010-1070)
and Peter Abelard (1079-1142)

Willemien Otten
Boston College

*W*hen one thinks about models of Christian autobiographical writing, the example that invariably comes to mind is that of the *Confessions*. This work's fascinating narrative in which the early Christian bishop Augustine describes the chastening struggle to shape his self to God continues to attract attention. It has even transcended the boundaries of the Christian tradition in that it has come to define the archetype of Western autobiography.[1]

In this essay I want to study two Western autobiographies from the medieval period to see how they elaborate on the same Christian theme of a self that understands itself explicitly as restless in its struggle to find the fullness of a life in God. Before examining them, however, I will make a few comments on the self in medieval autobiography and on the role and function of the Bible in the two autobiographical documents under review here.

Autobiography and the Medieval Self

In the *Confessions*, it might be argued, one witnesses how the quest for God leads Augustine to develop a highly introspective and largely individual sense of self.[2] The persistent desire for God, which permeates his entire autobiographical discourse, instigates a turning inward of the soul and thus gradually differentiates the self of the author from its body, from its position in society and from the selves of others.

To preface our study of Otloh and Abelard, two remarks ought to be made to distinguish medieval autobiographies from the Augustinian tradition. First, the structure of medieval society was not conducive to models of self-expression in which the individual self could be highlighted over and against the collective self as defined by order, class, or religious status. Since we are dealing with two monks here, one of our problems will be to draw the boundaries between a so-called individual and a collective or communal sense of self. My second point pertains not to the social but to the religious impact of living in a monastic environment, as Otloh and Abelard did. To the extent that Augustine's overriding concern in describing the self is his persistent search for God, the medieval period, while firmly retaining this religious aspect, simultaneously magnifies and formalizes it, since the monastery has turned contemplation from art into life-style.

This last facet, among others, has led various scholars to consider medieval documents of the self as not belonging in the same tradition of Christian autobiographical writing, so heavily colored by Augustine's novel sense of introspection and interiority. It is easy to disregard medieval autobiographies as vehicles for individual, as opposed to collective, self-expression.[3] Likewise, it is tempting to disqualify them as channels for spiritual reflection, as the use of literary and liturgical conventions makes it hard to press beneath their sometimes stifled and formulaic religiosity. In this essay I will attempt to bring these medieval documents of the self into conversation with the Augustinian model of an individual self struggling to find a balance in a life with God, without losing sight of the more collective medieval setting of the self.

Upon this view, medieval autobiographies such as those of Otloh and Abelard can offer us a remarkable window on the pluriformity of religious beliefs to which Christianity gave rise. As I hope to show, these religious beliefs not only shaped people in serving as their lifelong paradigm, but they seem to have incited them to search beyond this for ways to attach their own individual sense of meaning to it. The fact that Otloh and, to a lesser extent, Abelard tried to embed their individual views in the more collective setting of church and society, characterizes in my view the flexibility and adaptability with which Christianity flourished in early medieval Europe.

The Bible in Otloh's and Abelard's
Monastic Autobiographies

In selecting autobiographical documents for a study of the medieval discourse of the self, I have chosen to dwell on the period of the eleventh and the twelfth centuries since, among medievalists, this period is commonly associated with the "discovery of the individual."[4] Next to the discovery of the individual, a second documented feature of the late eleventh and early twelfth century is the rise of literacy.[5] This aspect of early-medieval literacy, brought into contact with that of individuality, has led me to focus on the Bible as a critical tool that may help us separate out Otloh's and Abelard's individual self from that infused by their corporate, that is, monastic identity. This paper will try to demonstrate that for both authors the reading of the Bible functions as a "textual lens" by which they can zoom in on various incidents of their lives and are stimulated to weave them into a fresh text by composing what amounts in a sense to a new self.[6] Perhaps a few comments can further explain this point.

In line with its strong mark of individuality, it is well known that in the *Confessions* the Bible is at times so intimately appropriated that it appears to be interchangeable with the voice of Augustine's innermost self.[7] However, in a more collectively oriented Christian environment, such as the medieval world, the Bible is likely to take on a much more formal role. This is especially true inside the medieval monastery, which in its Benedictine form is the backdrop of both Otloh's and Abelard's life. With the *opus dei* and *lectio divina* at the heart of the monastic life, the Bible (especially the Psalms) embodies the actual connection between God and the monk. Since the monks see their task as living the angelic life, the Bible is nothing less than the "stuff" of which their angelic discourse is made. This has radical consequences for the way biblical language was appropriated in the monastic environment. As the enclosure of the monastery creates an insulated, spiritual world for the monks, which recalls paradise and foreshadows heaven, it is no wonder that biblical language should predominantly have a strong internal function within the monastic life. For the monks the use of the Bible both depends heavily on and contributes to the collective identity of the self. Instead of exercising personal discretion in quoting the Bible, as Augustine is fond of doing, there seems to be a structural formalization of the

use of the Bible, which alongside the Rule of St. Benedict was the dominant literary influence in the monastic vocabulary. Inside the medieval
monastery, the personal identification of the voice of the interior self
with the voice of the Bible, which so marks Augustine's prose, recedes
behind a more explicit, formal use of biblical turns and phrases.

Yet the remarkable cultural developments of the late eleventh and
twelfth century strangely allow us to construe this monastic use of the
Bible, which it is tempting to dismiss as mere convention, as opening up
an indirect avenue to the medieval self. With the increase in literacy and
the rise of individuality in this period, the reading of the Bible betrays
signs of fermentation, appearing less collective and more individualistic.
For our study of Otloh and Abelard this translates into the following.
Applying what may amount to a roundabout approach, I will try to use
their reading of the Bible as a "seismograph," registering the subtle
tremors with which their individual selves produce slight cracks on their
collective monastic identity. Instead of the equivalent of a full-blown
introspective Augustinian self, we find the early medieval self conditioned by and creatively involved in the attempt to integrate the expanding horizon of individual ambitions with the enclosure of a life devoted
to God. Though we will arrive at portraits of Otloh and Abelard that are
quite different, they can be jointly described as examples of a self in
process, as these monks find themselves both inside and outside the
community, both whole and divided.

The Case of Otloh

In Otloh of St. Emmeram we have an author who, according to his own
statement, at one stage composed a book called De confessione actuum
meorum,[8] its title echoing Augustine's influence while clearly tilting to
the res gestae-motif, which supplied the more common model to early-
medieval autobiography. Though this work has not survived, it was incorporated into Otloh's: Liber de tentationibus suis et scriptis (The Book on
His Temptations and Writings).[9]

The two components mentioned in the title correspond to the book's
division into two parts: an inner and an outer sketch of his life. The first
and longest part deals with Otloh's temptations, his struggle to adapt to
the monastic life-style—in sum, his spiritual quest for a life with God.
The second and shorter part focuses on his career, that is, his professional duties as a monk who was also a writer and a teacher, as he sums
up the works he produced.

Despite its Augustinian ring, Otloh's *Liber* is more accurately characterized as spiritual biography, for in it we find Otloh displaying a remarkable objectivity toward his own life. He heeds a critical distance vis-à-vis
his own self that borders on alienation. The title of the work as well as
its opening segment, which opens in the third person singular, both
reflect this. The impression this creates is that the author is introducing
somebody else, whom only later we realize to be Otloh himself. For a
brief moment there is the suggestion of another presence, an *alter ego* to
the medieval monk. From the fact that this person undergoes severe
temptations, the reader should infer that this monastic *alter ego* is none
other than the medieval saint.[10] Since Otloh's readers were most likely
his fellow monks, who in the *lectio divina* had learned to ruminate on
scenes from the life of St. Anthony and other saints, they would immediately recognize the numerous temptations and conversations with the
devil as familiar characteristics of every saint.[11] The saint is thus the
model Otloh resorts to in organizing and describing the events of his
life. This may also explain why the accounts he gives of his experiences,
before or after his conversion to the monastic life, seem rather stiff and
stylized.

In conformity with these textual indications, it appears that one
should measure Otloh's autobiographical discourse not by the Augustinian standard of interiority or "presentness" of self but as a discourse
about a self that is consciously modeled after that of the medieval saint.
It is not an interiority of self that Otloh wants to express but an overlap
of his own self with its ideal model: that of the saint who instead of per-
forming heroic acts is domesticated into perfectly embodying the virtues
of monastic life.

Be that as it may, the second part does not lend itself so easily to an
interpretation that fits in with the ideal of the monastic saint. What is
rather unusual is how Otloh emphasizes the importance of his writing
activities. Taken in and by itself, this ought not to be seen as too surprising, since from the eleventh century on it seems fairly common for
lives of saints to include some reference to the outstanding performance
of their subjects in the liberal arts.[12] Yet whereas saints would normally
then (i.e., after their conversion) give up their studies to devote themselves to the *lectio divina*, Otloh does not quite do so. Whereas it would
perhaps be acceptable for a monk to be a scribe or a teacher, Otloh makes
clear that he is not merely copying or teaching but is actually composing
original works. Helga Schauwecker, Otloh's lone modern biographer,

detects in Otloh what she calls a *Mitteilungsbedürfnis*, a distinct urge to write professionally.[13] Underneath the model of the monastic saint, then, one can perhaps detect Otloh's true self as the writer, who is a true representative of the *ars dictaminis* that was to become so popular in twelfth-century Europe.

An example of how this underlying self of Otloh the writer impacts the outward life of Otloh the monk can be found at the end of the second part of the dialogue. Being chased away from his old monastery because of a hostile abbot there and unable to return because of warfare in the area, Otloh stays in the monastery of Amerbach and becomes great friends with the abbot there. In fact, the abbot tells him one day around Easter: "If I could order you one thing, it would be that you would give the sermon at the upcoming holiday."[14] Brushing it off at first, Otloh contemplates how pleased the abbot would be if he would actually write this sermon. So, without awaiting a formal request, Otloh construes the Benedictine feature of obedience to the abbot to write the Easter sermon. As it happens, Otloh is called back to his old monastery within a year, so we do not know if the abbot approved of the spontaneous initiative of his monk or if the Easter sermon was ever delivered— but it was written.

If the above account is true, it means that in Otloh we find the resources of the monastic life strained to the utmost so as to be reconciled with the author's true ambitions, that is, those of the writer. This may explain why in the second part Otloh feels an apologetic need to justify his professional ambitions. Though it is abundantly clear that he has put his skills in the service of the monastery and God, he apparently feels the need for an explicit divine sanction. To do this most effectively he resorts to another device of hagiography: that of the miracle story. It is as a way of reconciling his ambitions with the self-styled monastic ideal of the saint that we can understand the remarkable story he recounts of his youth. In it Otloh tells us how he learned to write precociously, a fact he managed to conceal from his parents and would have hidden from his teacher also, had it not been that he drew attention to himself by the unusual way he held his pen. Through this story Otloh seems to communicate to his readers that God has chosen him for his aspirations as a writer and that his unusual way of holding his pen is a sign that he is a true writer-elect.[15]

It thus appears as if only by exploiting the model of the *saint* is Otloh able to reconcile his conflicting tendencies: his profession of being a writer versus his calling as a monk. I want to interpret his ambition as a professional writer as Otloh's understanding of his inner self, while his calling as a monk continues to represent his contact with God. The image of the saint whose life is a continuous struggle for perfection provides Otloh with an overarching framework in which these two forms of self-realization can be integrated within the confines of one personality.

While it marks the success of Augustine's *Confessions* as Christian autobiography that the horizontal axis of interiority or intimacy with self merges with a vertical axis of intimacy with God, in Otloh we never seem to reach such mystical perfection. To find the self in the culture of medieval Christianity, marked as it is by collective models, it may be advisable to look not for possible points of convergence of individual selves with their God but rather for points of divergence. In Otloh, we see that his adoption of the monastic habit comes to clash with his latent ambitions as an individual. Without favoring one model over the other, perhaps Otloh's nascent self may be found in the cracks the image of the monk-saint betrays. I will conclude by giving an example of such a crack, which shows how the Bible comes to function as the seismograph of the self.

The episode I want to draw attention to occurs right at the beginning of Otloh's account but can be fully understood only in light of the whole. Whereas the whole work is naturally interspersed with numerous biblical quotations, these are mostly stock citations which do not reveal anything in particular about Otloh's self. Yet at the beginning of the work we get a remarkable lead which cannot be explained in terms of the standard descriptions of the saint tested by temptations. Otloh, speaking here about the saint whom we do not yet recognize to be him, states that the more this man reads the Bible, the more he starts doubting its truth. Although this is somewhat unusual, it still fits in with monastic culture where the change to the monastic life indicated the beginning of a conversion process (*initium conversionis*) which still lacked perfection.[16] Warned from the beginning, however, the alerted reader will from here on pay more attention to Otloh's allusions to the Bible in search of significant developments. And he/she will not be disappointed.

In *PL* 146, 32C Otloh recounts the most terrible of his temptations. Up to this point the devil has tried to distract him from the monastic life in different ways. He has told Otloh that he violated the sixth commandment ("honor thy parents") by entering the monastery without parental consent, but the temptation subsided and Otloh found contrasting scripture texts that put the devil's voice to rest. The devil also kept him up at night for weeks, so that finally, when he had to get up for his nightly prayers, he was unable to stay awake in church. The last of his temptations, however, is also their culmination point. In it we see the devil usurping the position of the saint—Otloh's self-styled *alter ego*—in an attempt to play out the ambitions of the professional writer against the ideals of monastic life.

This time the devil does not use a particular quotation from scripture, which Otloh could counter with another one, but launches a more fundamental attack. He claims that the biblical authors have indeed written fine and honest things but that there is no reason to view biblical writers differently from other writers by actually abiding by their instructions.[17] Since there is no guarantee that the biblical writers themselves lived by their own words, they can exercise no power or force to make Otloh live by them. Foreshadowing historical-critical biblical scholarship, the devil argues that there is so much diversity in the Bible that the book only provokes doubt and that if God were truly omnipotent,[18] he would not have allowed for so much confusion and diversity in people's minds.

The implications of Otloh's final temptation are enormous. For if the devil is right, the whole concept of monastic life, centered on the *opus dei* and *lectio divina* as the ordered reading of the Bible, would ultimately amount to the living of a lie. As a final mark of irony, the devil even uses a famous quotation from scripture to bolster his position, saying that the Bible appears not even to take itself seriously when in 2 Cor. 3:6 we read: "The letter kills, but the spirit vivifies."[19]

Otloh, who has no scriptural defense against this attack on scripture itself, can do nothing but pray to God. Fortunately, help quickly arrives: God not only dispels Otloh's doubt but brings him the *lux scientiae* so that he will never have to doubt again. Yet the solution of a dramatic prayer to God receiving an immediate answer can only strike the attentive reader as somewhat artificial. Hinging predominantly on the professional creativity of Otloh as writer, it seems to strain the resources of Otloh's chosen model of the saint-monk almost beyond belief.[20] Unlike the devil, who seemed to catch Otloh always by surprise, God's presence appears to be neatly within the author's control, as at the height of despair he arrives on the scene as a true *deus ex machina*. When next Otloh makes the decision to write down his temptations, this marks the triumph of the writer even more, for there is no evidence of an urging on God's part for Otloh to do this, not even a feigned attempt, as with the abbot who seemed to request him to write his sermon. Except for the standard motive of grace, Otloh's decision to write his temptations down is a completely self-motivated one, inspired by the writer as Otloh's underlying self, that is, the identity hidden beneath the self-styled model of the saint-monk.

Yet Otloh will not risk a rupture with the Benedictine ideal by defining a self that transcends the boundaries of his identity as a monk. And for him there is really no need to, as the Benedictine framework proves flexible enough to give him the room he needs. Otloh will thus continue to fulfill his ambitions as a writer, but he professes that his writing from now on will have no purpose apart from serving the goal of edification. Concerned that other monks may have to undergo the same severe temptations, he insists that only by writing them down can he banish the devil forever from the hearts and minds of his fellow monks. Be that as it may, one would seriously underestimate the resilience of Otloh's medieval self in mistaking the topos of edification as the exclusive literary cause of his autobiographical work. In light of the vivid description of his temptations, the motive of edification seems merely adduced to lend divine meaning to what would otherwise be no more than the disclosure of a human struggle. It was this human struggle, however, that first brought triumph for Otloh's true self as a writer. In retrospect, the temptations of the monk can thus be seen as literary expressions of the pangs with which Otloh's hidden *alter ego* came in conflict with his chosen one: the writer haunting the monk as a real devil.

The voice of the devil is forever silenced when Otloh puts his writing skills once more in the service of his chosen identity as a monk. He represses the demonic voice of his *alter ego* definitively by simply replacing it. A new discussion partner, equally invisible but divinely sent, arrives on the scene and takes over as his companion for the rest of the book.[21]

The Case of Peter Abelard

In Abelard we encounter a discourse about the self whose direct example is not that of Augustine's *Confessions*. The most marked difference is that instead of composing a spiritual diary Abelard engages in correspondence. A first hint at how we can still fit him in with the Augustinian autobiographical tradition can be found if we compare Abelard's account not with the sustained intimacy of the *Confessions* but rather with the dialogical form of Augustine's earlier work, the *Soliloquia*, where his soul debates with fictional Reason or, as has been suggested by Peter von Moos, with Boethius's *Consolatio*, in which Boethius has a discussion with Lady Philosophy.[22]

To do so we have to extend Abelard's autobiography beyond that of the *Historia Calamitatum*. As the consolatory letter to his friend, whose troubles he thought minor in comparison to his own, the *Historia* is merely the first in a series of letters and does not contain his whole life story. In the aftermath of the heated discussion about the authenticity of the *Historia* and of Heloise's responses, especially Letter 6, von Moos has suggested considering the whole corpus of the *Historia*, the reciprocal letters between Abelard and Heloise and, finally, his monastic Rule for Heloise's nuns, as a joint literary composition, the deliberate aim of which was to create a semipublic literary evocation of their life and love.[23] In what follows I will thus approach Abelard's life story as a literary narrative that is unfolded throughout his correspondence with Heloise and is completed by the Rule. I will consider Heloise's voice as essentially her own, but analyze it only inasmuch as it influences Abelard's self-portrait, becoming almost an integral part of it.

In Abelard, who like Otloh considers monastic life to be the heart of the Christian experience, we also have a self that is so powerful that it needs some exhortation before it can be molded into a prefabricated framework. When looking at the story of Abelard's life as it is conveyed throughout the entire corpus, one notices how Abelard sees his life as "agonic," that is, rimpled if not fractured by numerous contests and conflicts. Scholars have noted how this feature of division and controversy becomes transposed from the description of his outer life experiences to that of his inner ones as well. Instead of following some scholars in concluding that Abelard is evidently unable to communicate true—that is, introspective—individuality,[24] I want to use this element of division as a starting point in developing a subtler, more indirect approach to the depths of Abelard's self.

In the case of Otloh, we saw how the monk managed to hide the individual ambitions of the writer beneath the self-chosen image of the saint. Otloh's story approximates thus what might be called an *autohagiography*. This essay wants to suggest that Abelard's account is on the whole guided by a movement that is contrary to the development of Otloh's autobiography. Whereas in Otloh the contemplation of the monastic self was interrupted by an interior conflict brought on by the reading of the

140   WILLEMIEN OTTEN

Bible, for Abelard life itself is from the outset defined by conflict. For him, the Benedictine outlook of monastic life as spiritual warfare[25] helps to lend meaning to what otherwise might appear as an array of unrelated conflicts. For him, living the monastic life of continuous penance seems filled with the hope of sublimating random conflict into a pattern of divinely intended, salvific suffering. Abelard thus taps into a model of monastic life that is quite different from Otloh's, as the martyr comes to replace the saint. It is by styling himself as a true monk-martyr and writing what amounts to an *automartyrology* that Abelard attempts to weave the conflicts of his life into a "holistic" autobiographical corpus. In what follows I will analyze how this is played out in his correspondence. In the course of my argument I will again use the reading of the Bible as an indirect avenue to the monastic self struggling to find its balance in a life with God.

When reading Abelard's literary self-portrait, it is important to note that it is the monastic outlook that first awakens in him the realization that the discrepancies in his *outer* life, initially described as jocular incidents, are somehow rooted in an underlying division of the *inner* life: as the human sinner stands before God in need of salvation. Before his entrance in the monastery Abelard sees his life governed by division, but this division seems caused more by unbounded ambition yielding inevitable envy than that it reflects self-doubt or internal conflict. Thus, early on in the *Historia Calamitatum* we read how Abelard simply exchanges the weapons of the knight for the armor of logic.[26] We also see him engaged in a competitive contest with his teachers, William of Champeaux in philosophy and Anselm of Laon in theology, the latter dispute centering on the conflict between *ingenium* (talent) and *longevus usus* (tradition).[27] Even the whole episode with Heloise can be explained in terms of unscrupulous ambition, namely, to measure himself against a talented woman and win her over physically, as he had uniquely triumphed over all his intellectual competitors.

It is no wonder then to hear Abelard say that his entrance in the monastery springs more from shameful confusion over thwarted ambition than from true conversion.[28] In fact, his ambition even lingers, as from a philosopher of the world he changes into a philosopher of God, an illusion rudely to be unmasked when his theological treatise on the Trinity is officially burned. Still, once inside the monastery, it seems the office of the monk gives Abelard's divided self at least a role to play, through which he can curb his ambition and redirect it as *conversio*.[29]

Though his monastic life may not yet be as "coordinated" as it should be, the concept of it at least is, and it becomes Abelard's specific mission to adapt the practice to its original intent.

That his purpose in overcoming division through monastic penance touches on his inner as well as his outer life becomes even more clear when the *Historia* relates how Abelard, unsatisfied with life in the monastery, withdraws further into the wilderness. He there founds a small oratory, named after the Holy Trinity, where he chooses to live in relative isolation. The foundation of this oratory, which marks the intensely personal nature of Abelard's monastic conversion, is accompanied by an individual appropriation of scripture. Enduring unrelenting hostility from his enemies but receiving support from the students who come to live with him,[30] Abelard renames his oratory "the Paraclete" for the comfort God has bestowed on him (2 Cor. 1:3, 4). In a typical misunderstanding of his motives, however, his contemporaries misconstrue the name, as they accuse him of privileging the Holy Spirit over the other persons of the Trinity.[31] The Paraclete will remain at the heart of Abelard's ascetic conversion, as will the theme of finding comfort and consolation in the self-chosen sacrifice of leading a heremitical life. When shortly afterwards in the *Historia* Abelard compares himself to Christ in being constantly persecuted by enemies and hypocrites, this need not be read as a display of excessive personal ambitions,[32] but should be explained in the context of his individual appropriation of monastic life. Since the theme of *imitatio Christi* is deeply embedded in the monastic experience, it rather seems as if Abelard's strong obsession with being a monk-martyr inspires him to read the monastic root metaphor of the martyr back into the life of Christ.

As the first step to wholeness, Abelard thus embarks on a process of exoneration by doing penance as a monk-martyr. Given his need for consolation, Abelard's intention in being the best possible monk is first and foremost to do penance and gain salvation for the world, but most likely for himself also. This may explain why, after his entrance in the monastery and his becoming abbot of St. Gildas de Rhuys, Abelard bypasses any distinction between his inward and his outward life. This can be illustrated by his use of 2 Cor. 7:5, *Foris pugne, intus timores* ("Conflicts without, anxieties within"), where *foris* refers to the despot and his satellites who besiege the monastery, whereas *intus* can refer both to the danger that awaits the abbot from his own rebellious monks and to his own inner unrest.[33] Though the monastery as the embodiment of his stylized monastic self is divided, it seems Abelard can redeem this external division as well as the underlying internal one, through the continued practice of monastic penance. Through his absorption into the monastic life, he does in fact no longer have to distinguish between these two divisions. For the *conversio* of the monk cancels out any discrepancy between them by adopting the circular rhythm of the monastic *opus dei* and *lectio divina*.

Although the *Historia Calamitatum* ends with Abelard's radical submission of his will to the will of God, the correspondence with Heloise makes clear that his monastic "ploy" to find his own salvation by linking it to that of the world backfires, so to speak, or "is shipwrecked" to use the term with which Heloise refers to her husband's plight.[34] Although Abelard will continue to reinterpret his own life as that of a monk, be it a Benedictine one or a pre-Benedictine anchorite modeled after Jerome, it seems that, unlike Otloh, he ultimately deems his own life unfit to acquire monastic penance.

That Abelard sees his own monastic life as a failure can best be illustrated from the mirror image of monastic success he creates for Heloise. As the correspondence progresses, his earlier attempt at exoneration is gradually replaced by the leitmotif of exhortation, as he persuades Heloise to embrace the monastic life she never sought.[35] Whereas Heloise makes clear that she puts Abelard as her true lord over God, according to him this should not deter her from running the course of the martyr and eventually completing it, reaping the reward of the martyr's crown. For her the very custom of monastic life, even though she entered it with fierce opposition, can still be brought in conformity with the divine truth that is meant to be enacted in it. Thus she can successfully harmonize her inner and her outer life. Despite her bitter words, she can become an exemplary abbess, teaching the nuns as her virgins to achieve the crown under her guidance and in her company. It even seems as if she can regain her chastity, for her "clean start" as a nun can even overcome the fact that she gave birth to their son.

From the ensuing dialogue it becomes increasingly clear, however, that Abelard does not regard this crown as within his own reach. Unlike Origen's case, where the self-inflictedness of his castration precluded the entry into the kingdom of God, it is not the physical mutilation that forms the insurmountable obstacle to Abelard's monastic vocation. This is not equivalent to saying that Abelard's dismissal of his castration as only a momentary pain is a sign of aggression against his own body.[36]

Far worse than his injury, in Abelard's own opinion, are the betrayal and the duplicity that have led to all this: his lustful seduction of Heloise and his lies against her uncle.[37] From the earliest indications in the *Historia* it is clear that Abelard's real pain was never the physical mutilation but rather the damaging gossip and the ensuing bad reputation. This emphasis on repercussion as the real harm reveals that what is most troublesome about his castration for Abelard is that one can always construe it as a punishment, not just a legitimate social one but, much worse, one that is rightfully instigated by God as retribution for a guilty conscience.[38]

Whereas Heloise feels justly betrayed in taking the veil before her husband, she can freely decide to reinterpret her entrance as a positive choice, should she succeed in giving up her bitterness. For Abelard, this choice does simply not exist. He is not able, as becomes especially clear from Letter 7,[39] to achieve the constancy that he so admires in the martyr's plight and thereby to arrive at the martyr's crown. For, because of his mutilation, he cannot truly fight the martyr's fight, that is, resist concupiscence. Just as in the famous controversy with St. Bernard Abelard had the opportunity for a real debate taken away from him through a pre-arranged judgment, so in the instance of his monastic life there is always the possibility that it is seen as an imposed or derived one. Castration and conversion thus can never be fully disentangled.[40] This may explain why in Letter 5 Abelard sees himself in opposition to Christ, whose example he so wants to emulate as a true monk-martyr. While Christ is Heloise's *redemptor*, Abelard regards himself as her *corruptor*, and while Christ truly loves her Abelard only loved what was hers.[41]

For Abelard there is no hope of arriving at the martyr's crown by simply becoming a better monk or abbot. In contrast to Otloh, the sheer adoption of the monastic life-style cannot help him to coordinate the divisions in his inner and his outer life as the first step in overcoming them. Thus he is trapped between two radical dilemmas: an earthly and a heavenly one. On the one hand, while he is truly one with Heloise in the flesh through the sacrament of matrimony, in this earthly life he can never reunite with her, as they are forever separated in their vows. On the other hand, while eschatologically he is truly one with her in Christ, she may consider herself fit to be Christ's *sponsa* as a nun and live out the eschatological dimension of monastic life, whereas he will never be able to harmonize monastic and eschatological reality.[42] While Heloise, through her monastic vocation, can turn Eve into Mary[43] and gain absolution for her own bitterness, all that is left for Abelard in his plight as "moine manqué" is pain (*dolor*) and sadness. Seeing the division running through his monastic life as a permanent one, Abelard ends Letter 5 with a prayer to God in whom are his hope, expectation, and consolation.[44]

From Letter 6 on, Heloise remains silent on the issue of their common past and follows Abelard's advice to change from *excusatio* to *exhortatio* and *doctrina*, though not without protest. In conjunction with this change of tone in their correspondence, which is Heloise's initiative, there seems to be a change in Abelard's perception of the self in which his attitude toward scripture plays a definite role. In the face of his ultimate skepticism toward the success of his own monastic life, Abelard displays a double reaction as he continues to strive for "holistic" consolation. In both cases he displays an appropriation of scripture that is equally fresh and creative.

Within the autobiographical corpus, it seems that it is through the transformation from monk/abbot/hermit now to founder and planter of Heloise's community, reflected in the last two letters, that he finds some consolation.[45] By becoming the Rule-giver of Heloise's community, which after having had to flee from their monastery in Argenteuil has now received permission to gather at the Paraclete, Abelard in a sense returns to his original monastic project, when he first cried out to God in the wilderness. It is by founding a new community there, and by reinterpreting monastic life according to *ingenium* rather than reforming its *longevus usus* that he can hope to foreshadow the eschatological unity with Heloise in a monastic setting. While his own monastic life is inadequate, he can find some consolation, if not redemption, in the cooperation with Heloise and her nuns, "for as Christ came to call and redeem both men and women, so he thought fit to unite them (*adunare*) in the monastic profession."[46]

It seems indeed that in the foundation and plantation of Heloise's congregation there are hints that the eschatological unity of monk and nun, of Abelard and Heloise, can to some extent be realized, as is apparent from his reference (following Jerome) to Simon and Anna in the temple.[47] But more importantly, Abelard is able to create a model for Heloise as *diaconissa* and *abbatissa*. In doing so his transformation from monk/abbot to founder and planter opens up a gulf of creativity, so to speak, in his use of scripture, the reading of which he strongly recommends to the nuns at the end of his Rule.[48] In Letter 7 we witness how through a concatenation of biblical figures he weaves a tapestry of remarkable women who serve as examples prefiguring the eschatological triumph of women. It is important that it is through the treatment of a *series* of biblical figures without privileging any particular role model that Abelard unfolds his ideal of female monastic perfection, where unity and constancy prevail. He emphasizes this by using expressions like: *Quod si veteres revolvamus historias,* and *Si totam Veteris Testamenti seriem revolvamus,* and *Si Veteris Testamenti vel evangelicae Scripturae paginas revolvamus,* extending his examples to include pagan women as well.[49]

Outside his autobiographical corpus, though connected in both time and content, we see how Abelard identifies himself with a series of biblical examples: not with heroes or heroines displaying mental constancy but rather with figures experiencing tragic loss. In his famous *Planctus* on various Old Testament figures Abelard reaches remarkable personal depth, as he steps forward to fill in what is left unspoken in the biblical text.[50] In the first lament on Dinah and Sichem (Genesis 34), we do not find the usual condemnation of the rape, but instead the emergence of a fragile love which was needlessly disturbed by the violent intervention of Dinah's brothers. In another example, the Plaint on Jephtha's daughter, the victim, who is lamented by her fellow virgins here, shows more courage than her cruel father. She is even able to give meaning to the arbitrary fate of her nearing sacrificial death. For it may be that God, who rejected the sacrifice of Abraham's son, will accept this one as forgiveness for sins.[51] Thus Abelard's use of a "series" of biblical figures reaches beyond that of an organizing principle for the arrangement of his poems, because he sees the biblical figures themselves as weaving their lives into this plaintive series.

By taking the poetic liberty of rereading the history of the Old and the New Testaments as a revolving series of examples with which to identify one's fate, Abelard appears to recreate himself as a semibiblical figure through a literary process of lamentation. Rather than identifying himself with any particular tragic figure—as it has been said that he equated himself with Christ—it is in the alternation of these tragic roles that Abelard seems to find some consolation.

Through Abelard's series of women figures, Heloise is given the opportunity to recognize herself in the mirror of the eschatological woman bearing the double crown of virginity and martyrdom.[52] Their heavenly crowns within reach, the earthly role of the nuns becomes clear as well: namely, intercession. Through tearful lamentation and compunction they resemble the women at Jesus' tomb who await his resurrection. It is on this point perhaps that Abelard sees himself united with Heloise. Unable to reach the martyr's crown as she can, who is *sponsa Domini*,[53] all he can hope for is that through the prayers of her congregation he is able to receive salvation.

Conclusions

The Whole and Divided Self in Otloh and Abelard

In comparing Otloh and Abelard, I can summarize my findings concerning the medieval view of the whole and divided self by means of the following three brief historical conclusions:

1. In both cases we find a remarkable affirmation of the self, which may be loosely associated with the discovery of the individual in the eleventh and twelfth centuries.[54] In relation to the rise of literacy, however, it is not through the introspective method of Augustine's *Confessions* but rather through the "external" composition of a literary text that the selves of Otloh and Abelard become created and revealed inside a monastic framework that was increasingly seen as restrictive.[55]

2. If we can agree on the Bible as the "textual lens" through which their monastic selves are filtered before being created on the page, it seems in Otloh reading the Bible opens up the abyss of the self, forcing him to close the gap by his literary activity, whereas in Abelard it seems to help him overcome a divided and fractured self. Recourse to the Bible, which functions as a *Fundgrube* of essential human emotions, provides him with the much-needed consolation for his heart that monastic life itself appears unable to yield. Although his eternal salvation cannot be guaranteed, he may hope that his human plight merits his being inserted in the long series of biblical heroes who invoke divine compassion.

3. In addition to what Caroline Walker Bynum has shown, namely, that twelfth-century individuality, far from being an abstract concept, manifested itself for some in personal allegiance to new consciously chosen groups,[56] it is important to note how others seem to have been encouraged instead to test the boundaries of the existing traditional framework, i.e., Benedictine monasticism. Otloh and Abelard were engaged in the specific attempt to reconcile their ambitions with the mission of their community. As a result, they seem to have found themselves

both inside and outside of the community, making it impossible for us to define their identity narrowly as either individual or collective, either whole or divided. Instead we seem to find indications that, while a general fracturing of Benedictine monastic ideals had set in, the reading of the Bible could in individual instances function as a counterpoise to this centrifugal development by allowing the anonymous monastic *persona* to channel his eschatological identity into the literary self of spiritual autobiography.

Bible and Theology from a Medieval Perspective

Just as it appears to be reductionistic to give a simple definition of the medieval theological self as whole or divided, rationalistic or faithful, in the same way it seems impossible to give a uniform interpretation of the medieval relation between the Bible and theology. It would be altogether pushing the merits of this case study too far if one could extract concrete advice from what pertains to be nothing more than a simple experiment. Still, it may be possible to use this case study to correct some simplifications that dominate our modern theological and exegetical conceptions of the Middle Ages as well as find perhaps some analogues with (post)modern culture. In this regard I see my case study as opening up two further areas of theological self-reflection, namely, the role of literacy—perhaps one should add: scholarly literacy—as fracturing traditional, often communal patterns of reading the Bible, and the multiform role of the Bible as spiritual resource when theological self-expression is confronted with restrictive institutional bounds. With this last point I also want to direct attention to the broader issues of anxiety, shame, and tolerance that are involved when the individual undergoing his/her own theological development comes to find him/herself at odds with the religious community—be it a monastic one or the church at large—to which he/she feels loyalty.

One of the general historical themes of my study has been to highlight the link between conversion as an instance of individual religious crisis and the reading of the Bible. The cultural context of this link was the rapidly developing and increasingly literate Christian civilization of the twelfth century, which heightened the collective and anonymous soul-searching of the monks and redirected it among other spiritual alternatives as the creation of a textual self. It has been the specific theological aim of this medieval case study to point out how biblical reading can function as a textual lens, which allowed individuals not just to position themselves on the increasingly rich spectrum of twelfth-century spiritual ideals but in doing so to create their own equilibrium. The broader theological theme of my study, namely, to see the reading of the Bible as a determining factor in the shaping of a Christian (self-)identity, may provide us with a continuum by which we cannot only overcome the artificial compartmentalization of various medieval theological discourses (e.g., scholastic, monastic) but perhaps also remove the unnecessarily rigid historical barriers by which the early church, the Middle Ages, the Reformation and the Enlightenment era seem to be permanently fenced off from the late twentieth century.

Let me end by pointing out just one further analogue. Just as the twelfth century combined a strong commitment to the spiritual reading of the Bible with an emerging interest in the production of academic, biblical commentaries at the dawn of the scholastic era, so our late twentieth century finds academic exegesis confronted conversely by a resurgence of fundamentalist approaches and personalized spirituality. While this reflects on the one hand the basic freedom that Christians have in defining the theological signification of the Bible as their foundational book, it indicates on the other hand that a problem remains. How to connect professional exegesis with the lived experience of various Christian communities is an issue that needs to be brought to the forefront of both theological and exegetical study. Perhaps it is reassuring to know that this problem existed already so long ago—and the twelfth century is by no means its earliest occurrence— yet at the same time it has been the underlying intention of my article to heighten the urgency of our continued need to reflect on it.

Notes

1. An authoritative essay on the autobiographical genre in the West that generally seems to hold this view is K. J. Weintraub, *The Value of the Individual: Self and Circumstance in Autobiography* (Chicago: University of Chicago Press, 1978), esp. p. 1.

2. See, e.g., Weintraub, *Value of the Individual*, chap. 2, "St. Augustine's Confessions: The Search for a Christian Self*" (pp. 18–48). For a postmodern philosophical assessment of Augustine's accomplishment, see Charles Taylor, *Sources of the Self: The Making of the Modern Identity* (Cambridge, Mass.: Harvard Uni-

versity Press, 1989). Augustine finds God by turning inward (see chap. 7, "In interiore homine" [pp. 127–42]).

3. See G. Misch, *Geschichte der Autobiographie*, 3/1 (Frankfurt a.M.: G. Schulte-Bulmke, 1959). Though Misch adopts the view of Martin Grabmann that Augustine was not treated as an explicit example in the Middle Ages (p. 8), he uses him as his main point of reference when dealing with Otloh and Abelard. His overall view is clearly that only at the end of the Middle Ages, in Suso, do we reach the same level of metaphysical-religious unity in an author. Thus, Augustine seems to function as an ideal example that the Middle Ages can never match. Weintraub largely adopts Misch's view on the Middle Ages, altering it somewhat by saying that the cultural models of the medieval period were so strong that "they had no need for complex processes of self-exploration and self-orientation. For them, the notion of individuality might even have been an embarrassment" (p. 71).

4. The standard work on twelfth-century individuality is Colin Morris, *The Discovery of the Individual (1050–1200)* Medieval Academy Reprints for Teaching 19 (Toronto: University of Toronto, 1987). See also nn. 54, 56 below.

5. For an excellent recent study of this theme, see Ivan Illich, *In the Vineyard of the Text: A Commentary to Hugh's Didascalicon* (Chicago and London: University of Chicago Press, 1993).

6. The "autobiographical" authorities Misch and Weintraub are generally skeptical in seeing a direct link between Augustine and the Middle Ages. While to settle the debate on autobiography would altogether transcend the scope of this article, a comparison between Augustine and the more individual twelfth-century texts of Otloh and Abelard may be deemed more feasible. Augustine is indeed somewhat of a model for Otloh, and though not so much for Abelard, he figures prominently as the model for a famous contemporary autobiography, abbot Guibert of Nogent's *De vita sua*.

7. This is especially true for Augustine's use of the Psalms in the *Confessions*. On psalmody as the most prominent so-called kinesthetic principle for Augustine, see Karl F. Morrison, *Conversion and Text: The Cases of Augustine of Hippo, Herman-Judah, and Constantine Tsatsos* (Charlottesville and London: University Press of Virginia, 1992), 32–35.

8. *PL* 146 (see next note), 56B: Scripsi etiam ante plures annos librum *De confessione actuum meorum*, ut si qua infirmitas vel subitanea mors me in extremis impediret a debita confessione, saltem per scripta patefaceret quis ex memetipso, quis ex Dei gratia essem. ("Many years ago I wrote a book called *On the confession of my deeds*, so that in the event that illness or sudden death would at the last moment keep me from the required confession, it might reveal who I was on my own and who due to God's grace.") The English translations of Otloh's text are my own.

9. The text of this work can be found among Otloh's collected works in

J.-P. Migne, ed., *Patrologiae cursus completus. Series latina (PL)* (Paris, 1844–1864), vol. 146, cols. 29A–58C.

10. Helga Schauwecker points to the similarity between Otloh's opening sentence and that of the story of the miraculous cure of the monk Arnold in *De miraculis S. Emmerami (PL* 141, 1064D ff.): Fuit quidam clericus . . . ("There was a certain cleric") (*Otloh von St. Emmeram: Ein Beitrag zur Bildungs- und Frömmigkeitsgeschichte des 11. Jahrhunderts* [Munich: Verlag der Bayer. Benediktiner-Akademie, 1964], 36 n. 113). This story might well have been familiar to Otloh.

11. Cf. Augustine's conversion, which was triggered by his reading of the *Life of Antony.*

12. See Gillian R. Evans, *Alan of Lille: The Frontiers of Theology in the Later Twelfth Century* (Cambridge: Cambridge University Press, 1983), 146.

13. See Schauwecker, *Otloh,* 35–41. Schauwecker concludes: "Unser Ergebnis ist also dies: Ausgang und Ende, erster und letzter Impuls seines schriftstellerischen Schaffens war sein persönlicher Drang nach Mitteilung und Rechtfertigung. Hieraus erwuchs ihm das hohere Ziel der Erbauung und Ermahnung, für das er zugleich andere zu gewinnen trachte" (p. 41).

14. See *PL* 146, 55C. The abbot says: Credite mihi quod si vobis praecipere aliquid possem, absque dubio praeciperem ut in hac solemnitate proxima sermonem faceretis ad populum. ("Believe me, if I could order you to do something, I would doubtless command that on this coming feastday you should give the sermon to the people.") Otloh, of course, is stunned, but then he goes on: Illo vero eadem repetente, coepi mox cogitare intra me dicens: Quid facerem, si aliquis, cujus jussa transgredi non praesumerem, talia mihi praeciperet? Unde hujusmodi opus assumendum est mihi sponte, priusquam ab aliquo compellar potente, ut sic probem quid facturus essem. Continuoque stylo accepto scribere coepi in modum sermonis. . . . ("But when he repeated the same things, I started thinking to myself, saying: 'What should I do, if somebody whose orders I do not dare cross, would order me such things?' I should therefore undertake such a task voluntarily, before I might be ordered by a powerful person, that I may thus try out what I should be making. Having taken up my pen immediately, I started to write in the manner of a sermon. . . .") Note how Otloh cleverly uses obedience to the abbot as his apparent motive for composing the sermon.

15. The incident is told in 56D–57A. Otloh states: Unde adhuc libet enarrare, quanta scientia quantaque facultas scribendi mihi data fuerit a Domino in primaeva aetate. ("And thus it now pleases me to tell how great a knowledge and how great a gift for writing was given to me by the Lord at a very young age.") He uses the term *miraculum* to show the surprise of those who witnessed him.

16. Schauwecker describes how the contemporary usage of the word "conversion" referred simply to entering the monastery (*Otloh,* p. 99). For Otloh, however, his entrance is only the first step or the *initium conversionis.* This is not

unmonastic, as the Rule of St. Benedict distinguished between the *initium* and the *perfectio conversionis* (see ibid., 99 n. 205).

17. Could it be that, at least for a moment, Otloh looks at the Bible as just another book, realizing full well the possibilities writers have to manipulate their readers? Or would this be too modern for a medieval monk?

18. A feature in the center of eleventh-century theological debate between dialecticians and anti-dialecticians (to which camp Otloh seems to have belonged) about the use of dialectical reasoning in theology. For a sample of the anti-dialectical position, see Peter Damian's *De divina omnipotentia*.

19. *PL* 146, 33A–B: Sicut in plurimis maximeque in divinis codicibus facile reperiuntur sententiae, aliam in littera, aliam in intelligentia rationem retinentes. Haec autem omnia ita esse uno Pauli testimonio approbo: Littera enim, inquit, occidit, spiritus autem, id est sensus, vivificat. Nonne satis aperte per haec Apostoli verba doceris quia, si librorum dicta sequeris, maxima pericula patieris? Idem quoque de Dei essentia intelligendum est. Alioquin si aliqua persona aut virtus Dei omnipotentis esset, nequaquam tanta confusio atque diversitas in rebus cunctis appareret. Cf. Peter Damian, *De divina omnipotentia*, chap. 5 (*PL* 145, 604); he quotes the same passage from 2 Corinthians to dismiss the literal arguments of the dialecticians on future contingents.

20. *PL* 146, 33C: Nulla dehinc mora: et ablata est per Dei gratiam non solum omnis illa dubitationis supradictae nebula, sed etiam scientiae lux tanta in corde meo emicuit ut et nunquam postmodum tales dubitationis mortiferae tenebras sustinerem. In 49C, after his temptations are over, Otloh appears to fall back into a more conventional usage of scripture. He says that the necessity to defend himself against numerous temptations has actually opened up areas of scripture to him that were previously unknown.

21. Thus in the second half of the first part, Otloh has a formal discussion partner, an invisible companion whose voice seems to be that of God (34Cff).

22. See Peter von Moos, "*Post festum*—Was kommt nach der Authentizitätsdebatte über die Briefe Abaelards und Heloises?" in *Petrus Abaelardus (1079–1142): Person, Werk und Wirkung*, ed. Rudolf Thomas et al. (Trier: Paulinus-Verlag, 1980), 84. Von Moos states: "Die Rolle des Boethius in der *Consolatio philosophiae* ist eine Fiktion, aber aus ihr und ebenso aus derjenigen der *Philosophia* spricht der reale Boethius über seine wichtigsten Lebensanschauungen. Ist da die männlich-weibliche Doppelfiktion auf Grund einer vorauszusetzenden existentiellen Gesprächssituation nicht noch lebensnaher und autobiographisch relevanter?"

23. Ibid., 84.

24. Various authors make this point in various ways. See, e.g., Weintraub, *Value of the Individual*, 90–91: "When one thus views the form of the autobiography, the prevalence of status features clinging to the knight as well as the monk, and finally the need to lean on models in the critical issue of self-

perception, it is difficult to think of Abelard either as an example of the autonomous, self-defining personality, or as an individuality, or as an earlier version of the 'Renaissance man.'" See also Mary McLaughlin, "Abelard as Autobiographer: The Motives and Meaning of his 'Story of Calamities,'" *Speculum* 42 (1967): 463-88; and Evelyn Birge Vitz, "Type et individu dans l'«autobiographie» médiévale," *Poétique* 24 (1975): 426-45, esp. 443: "Autant que je puisse l'affirmer, donc, la seule manière qu'on avait alors d'envisager, littérairement sinon philosophiquement, «l'individuel», c'était d'y voir le cas particulier d'un principe ou d'une idée universel."

25. See John Van Engen, "The 'Crisis of Cenobitism' Reconsidered: Benedictine Monasticism in the Years 1050-1150," *Speculum* 61 (1986): 269-304. On p. 293 Van Engen comments on the intercessory task of Benedictine monks as related to their self-evaluation as society's spiritual warriors.

26. See J. Monfrin, ed., *Abelard: Historia Calamitatum* (Paris: J. Vrin, 1959), pp. 63, lines 25-28: et quoniam dialecticarum rationum armaturam omnibus philosophiae documentis pretuli, his armis alia commutavi et tropheis bellorum conflictus pretuli disputationum. ("I preferred the weapons of dialectic to all the other teachings of philosophy, and armed with these I chose the conflicts of disputation instead of the trophies of war.") The English text of the correspondence is taken from Betty Radice, *The Letters of Abelard and Heloise* (London: Penguin Books, 1974). The translation of Letter 7 and of the *Planctus* is my own.

27. See *Hist. Cal.*, ed. Monfrin, pp. 68-69, lines 164-221, esp. lines 207-9: Indignatus autem respondi non esse meae consuetudinis per usum proficere sed per ingenium. ("I replied indignantly that it was not my custom to benefit by practice through tradition, but I relied on my own intelligence.")

28. Cf. *Hist. Cal.*, ed. Monfrin, p. 80, lines 623-26: In tam misera me contritione positum, confusio, fateor, pudoris potius quam devotio conversionis ad monastichorum latibula claustrorum compulit. ("I admit that it was shame and confusion in my remorse and misery rather than any devout wish for conversion which brought me to seek shelter in a monastery cloister.")

29. Despite his ongoing arguments, Abelard seems to mitigate his combativeness once he enters the monastery. In the controversy surrounding the identity of Dionysius the Areopagite, for example, he ultimately says that it does not matter who Dionysius really was as long as he had won a bright crown with the Lord. See *Hist. Cal.*, ed. Monfrin, p. 90, lines 967-70: Ego autem respondi nec me hoc denegasse nec multum curandum esse utrum ipse Ariopagita an aliunde fuerit, dummodo tantam apud Deum adeptus sit coronam. ("I said that I had not denied it, nor did it much matter whether he was the Areopagite or came from somewhere else, seeing that he had won so bright a crown in the eyes of God.") One cannot imagine Abelard having settled one of his earlier dialectical debates in this way.

30. Despite the fact that Abelard gets company from his students, he

stresses that they appear to be hermits rather than students. Abelard states that he needs to teach to maintain himself.

31. See *Hist. Cal.*, ed. Monfrin, pp. 96-97, lines 1189-1195: Non tamen hoc ita conicimus, ut cum Paraclitum primo nostrum vocaverimus oratorium uni ipsum persone nos dicasse fateamur, sed propter eam quam supra reddidimus causam, in memoria scilicet nostre consolationis, quamquam si illo quoque, quo creditur, modo id fecissemus, non esset rationi adversum, licet consuetudini incognitum. ("However, in first giving my oratory the name of Paraclete I had no thought of declaring its dedication to a single person; my reason was simply what I said above—it was in memory of the comfort I had found there. But even if I had done so with the intention which was generally believed, it would not have been unreasonable, though unknown to general custom.") At this stage, Abelard has already been condemned for his views on the Trinity. Note, however, how in his typical defiant style he maintains that, even if he had named the oratory after the Holy Spirit, he would have been theologically justified.

32. See Donald Frank, "Abelard as Imitator of Christ," *Viator* 1 (1970): 107-13. On p. 111 Frank overstates Abelard's "proud emulation of the career of the earthly Jesus" as he does the spiritual reluctance of St. Bernard in seeking a loving union of the Bridegroom (Jesus) and the bride (soul).

33. See *Hist. Cal.*, ed. Monfrin, p. 99, lines 1278-82: Foris me tyrannus ille et satellites sui assidue opprimebant; intus mihi fratres incessanter insidiabantur ut illud Apostoli in me specialiter dictum res ipsa indicaret: 'Foris pugne. Intus timores.' ("Outside the monastery wall that tyrant and his minions never ceased to harry me, inside it the monks were always setting traps for me, until it seemed that the words of the Apostle applied especially to my case: 'Quarrels all round us, forebodings in our heart.'")

34. See Letter 2 (Muckle 1 [see next note]) *Mediaeval Studies* 15 (1953): 68: Per ipsum itaque qui te sibi adhuc quoquo modo protegit Christum obsecramus quatinus ancillulas ipsius et tuas crebris litteris de his in quibus adhuc fluctuas *naufragiis* certificare digneris ut nos saltem quae tibi solae remansimus doloris vel gaudii participes habeas. ("And so in the name of Christ, who is still giving you some protection for his service, we beseech you to write as often as you think fit to us who are his handmaids and yours, with news of the perils in which you are still storm-tossed. We are all that are left you, so at least you should let us share your sorrow or your joy.") Abelard cites this passage from Heloise in Letter 5 (Muckle 4) *Mediaeval Studies* 15 (1953): 86. I have numbered the letters consecutively, taking the *Historia* as Letter 1 and adding the other letters as well as the Rule to it. This explains the difference between my numbering and that of Muckle.

35. See J. T. Muckle, C.S.B., "The Personal Letters Between Abelard and Heloise," *Mediaeval Studies* 15 (1953): 83, where in Letter 5 (Muckle 4) Abelard

replies to Heloise that he is not giving her an *excusatio* but rather a *doctrina* or *exhortatio*.

36. In this way we can perhaps draw some legitimate conclusions while avoiding a simple diagnosis of psychological disorder as in Jean Leclercq, "Modern Psychology and the Interpretation of Medieval Texts," *Speculum* 48 (1973): 476–90, esp. 484.

37. See Letter 5 (Muckle 4) *Mediaeval Studies* 15 (1953): 88, where Abelard criticizes their sexual *fornicationes et pollutiones* (before their marriage and after, in the monastery of Argenteuil) as well as his *proditio* of Heloise's uncle. He seems to regard Heloise's uncle's betrayal as a fitting tribute for his own (see pp. 88, 89).

38. Unlike Leclercq, quoting Alan Richardson, I do not think that Abelard's *Ethics* provides what is essentially "a licence for sin" by discriminating between the deed and the conscience of the actor. It seems that Abelard's wrong intentions make him guilty, whereas Heloise is not (see Leclercq, "Modern Psychology," 484 n. 22).

39. In Letter 7 (Muckle 6; *Mediaeval Studies* 17 [1955]: 256–57), Abelard frequently uses the theme of constancy. It seems to refer especially to the perseverance of the martyrs (see p. 269 with reference to the mother of the seven sons in 2 Maccabees 7).

40. See Letter 5 (Muckle 4) *Mediaeval Studies* 15 (1953) p. 93: Refero Domino et in hoc grates, qui te tunc et a poena liberavit et ad coronam reservavit, et, cum me una corporis mei passione semel ab omni aestu huius concupiscentiae, in qua una totus per immoderatam incontinentiam occupatus eram, refrigeravit ne corruam, multas adolescentiae tuae maiores animi passiones ex assidua carnis suggestione reservavit ad martyrii coronam. Quod licet te audire taedeat et dici prohibeas, veritas tamen id loquitur manifesta. Cui enim superest pugna, superest et corona quia "non coronabitur nisi qui legitime certaverit." Mihi vero nulla superest corona quia nulla subest certaminis causa. Deest materia pugnae, cui ablatus est stimulus concupiscentiae. ("For this I give thanks to the Lord, who both spared you punishment then and reserved you for a crown to come, and who also by a moment of suffering in my body cooled once and for all the fires of that lust in which I had been wholly absorbed through my excessive incontinence, lest I be consumed. The many greater sufferings of the heart through the continual prompting of the flesh of your own youth, he has reserved for a martyr's crown. Though you may weary of hearing this and forbid it to be said, the truth of it is clear. For the one who must always strive there is also a crown; and the athlete cannot win his crown unless he has kept to the rules. But no crown is waiting for me, because no cause for striving remains. The matter for strife is lacking in him from whom the thorn of desire is pulled out.")

41. See Letter 5 (Muckle 4) *Mediaeval Studies* 15 (1953): 92: Plange tuum

reparatorem, non corruptorem, redemptorem, non scortatorem, pro te mor-
tuum Dominum, non viventem servum, immo nunc primum de morte vere lib-
eratum." Just before on the same page, Abelard states: Quid in te, inquam,
quaerit [sc. Christus] nisi teipsam? Verus est amicus qui teipsam non tua
desiderat ("Mourn for your Savior and Redeemer, not for the seducer who
defiled you, for the Master who died for you, not for the servant who lives and,
indeed, for the first time is truly freed from death." And: "What does he seek
in you except yourself? He is the true friend who desires yourself and nothing
that is yours.")

42. See Letter 5 (Muckle 4) *Mediaeval Studies* 15 (1953): 93: Unum quippe
sumus in Christo, una per legem matrimonii caro. Quidquid est tuum, mihi
non arbitror alienum. Tuus autem est Christus quia facta est sponsa eius. Et
nunc, ut supra memini, me habes servum quem olim agnoscebas dominum.
("For we are one in Christ, one flesh according to the law of matrimony. Whatever is yours cannot, I think, fail to be mine, and Christ is yours because you
have become his bride. Now, as I said before, you have as a servant me whom
in the past you recognized as your master.")

43. See Letter 5 (Muckle 4) *Mediaeval Studies* 15 (1953): 90: Abelard here
says that Heloise's producing spiritual daughters far surpasses her earthly
motherhood. In the case of real motherhood: Nec esses plus quam femina nunc
etiam viros transcendis et quae maledictionem Evae in benedictionem vertisti
Mariae. ("Nor would you have been more than a woman, whereas now you rise
even above men, and have turned the curse of Eve into the blessing of Mary.")
See also Letter 7 (Muckle 6) *Mediaeval Studies* 17 (1955): 268-69: Prius quoque
Dominus Evam totius originem mali restauravit in Maria, quam Adam in
Christo reparavit. Et, sicut a muliere culpa, sic a muliere coepit gratia et virginitatis refloruit praerogativa. ("The Lord restored Eve as the origin of all evil
in Mary even before he repaired Adam in Christ. And just as guilt began with
woman, so with woman began grace and has the privilege of virginity flourished again.")

44. See Letter 5 (Muckle 4) *Mediaeval Studies* 15 (1953): 93-94. Abelard
ends his prayer as follows: Coniunxisti nos, Domine, et divisisti quando placuit
tibi et quo modo placuit. Nunc quod, Domine, misericorditer coepisti, miseri-
cordissime comple. Et quos semel a se divisisti in mundo, perenniter tibi coni-
ungas in coelo, spes nostra, pars nostra, exspectatio nostra, consolatio nostra,
Domine, qui es benedictus in saecula. Amen. ("Thou hast joined us, Lord, and
hast parted us, when and in what manner it pleased thee. Now, Lord, what thou
hast mercifully begun, most mercifully end, and those whom thou hast parted
for a time on earth, unite forever to thyself in heaven: thou who art our hope,
our portion, our expectation and our consolation, O Lord, who art blessed
world without end. Amen.")

45. See the end of Letter 6 (Muckle 5) *Mediaeval Studies* 17 (1955) 253: Tibi

nunc, domine, dum vivis incumbit instituere de nobis quid in perpetuum tenendum sit nobis. Tu quippe post Deum huius loci *fundator*, tu per Deum nostrae congregationis es *plantator*, tu cum Deo *nostrae* sis *religionis institutor*. ("It is for you then, master, while you live, to lay down for us what Rule we are to follow for all time, for after God you are the founder of this place, through God you are the creator of our community, with God you should be the director of our religious life.")

46. See Letter 7 (Muckle 6) *Mediaeval Studies* 17 (1955): 253: sicut utrumque sexum vocare venerat [sc. Christus] atque redimere, ita utrumque sexum in vero monachatu suae congregationis dignatus est adunare ut inde tam viris quam feminis huius professionis daretur auctoritas, et omnibus perfectio vitae proponeretur quam imitarentur. ("Just as he came to call and redeem either sex, so he has deemed it worthy to unite either sex in the true monastic mission of his congregation, so that the authority of this profession would be bestowed upon men as well as women, and that the perfection of life is held up to all to be followed.")

47. See Letter 7 (Muckle 6) *Mediaeval Studies* 17 (1955): 253.

48. It is significant that Abelard concludes the Rule for Heloise's community (Letter 8) with a long exposition on the prime importance of the study of scripture by the nuns. See T. P. McLaughlin, *Mediaeval Studies* 18 (1956): 241–92, esp. 285–92. It may be noteworthy with regard to Abelard's role as *plantator* of Heloise's community that the study of scripture is described in "agricultural" terms. Introducing Gregory the Great's recommendation of scripture study, Abelard says: "For that zealous digger of spiritual wells strongly urges us not only to drink of them but also to dig our own"; in the actual quote from Gregory we find many similar expressions, such as "draw living water from your wells." Further, Abelard contrasts the happy man who meditates on the Law day and night and is as "the tree planted by a watercourse (ps. 1)" with the sterility of the monks who give themselves to idle talk ("for a dry tree is also unfruitful, because it is not watered by the streams of the words of God.")

49. Letter 7 (Muckle 6) *Mediaeval Studies* 17 (1955): 261, 269, 273. Among the women who are named are Eve, Deborah, Judith, Esther, Jephtha's daughter, Elizabeth, Mary, Mary Magdalene, the widow Anna, the Samaritan woman (John 4). Abelard also includes Sibylla's prophecy.

50. For text and analysis of Abelard's *Planctus*, see Wilhelm Meyer, *Gesammelte Abhandlungen zur mittellateinischen Rythmik* (Hildesheim and New York: Georg Olms-Verlag, 1970), 340–74. See also Peter Dronke, *Poetic Individuality in the Middle Ages: New Departures in Poetry (1000–1150)* (Oxford: Clarendon Press, 1970), 114–149 for a subtle treatment of Abelard's *Planctus* and their autobiographical nature including problems of dating.

51. See *Planctus* III: (Jephtha's daughter to her father):
Immolare filium volens Abraham

non hanc apud dominum habet gratiam
ut ab ipso puerum vellet hostiam

Puerum qui respuit
si puellam suscipit

Quod decus sit sexus mei, percipe
uteri qui tui fructus, inspice,
quid mihi quid tibi sit hoc gloriae.

("To sacrifice his son was what Abraham wanted;
but he did not find this favor with the Lord
that He wanted the child from him.

Boy that He spurned
if He but receives the girl
What grace this will be for my sex, see
for the uterus that is your fruit, look
for me, for you, what glory will this be!")

52. See Letter 7 (Muckle 6) *Mediaeval Studies* 17 (1955): 263, where Abelard quotes Gregory: et tanto agone sexus fragilis triumphet ut frequentius ipsum *gemina virginitatis et martyrii corona* pollere noverimus? (". . . in so great a contest the fragile sex shall triumph in order for us to know more frequently that it exercises power over the double crown of virginity and martyrdom?") and p. 275: feminae . . . ut pro conservanda carnis pariter ac mentis integritate Deo se per martyrium offerrent holocaustum, et *gemina* triumphantes *corona* agnum sponsum virginum quocumque ierit sequi studerent. ("that to preserve the integrity of the flesh and the mind alike, women offer themselves as a sacrifice through martyrdom, and that, triumphant with a double crown, they attempt to follow the lamb, spouse of virgins, wherever he goes.")

53. See Letter 7 (Muckle 6) *Mediaeval Studies* 17 (1955): 267, where Abelard quotes Jerome to Eustochium: . . . dominam quippe debeo vocare sponsam Domini mei. (". . . the lady whom I owe to call the spouse of my Lord.")

54. See, e.g., Morris, *Discovery of the Individual*, chap. 4, "The Search for the Self."

55. See Brian Stock, *The Implications of Literacy: Written Language and Models of Interpretation in the Eleventh and Twelfth Centuries* (Princeton: Princeton University Press, 1983) esp. chap. 4, "Language, Texts and Reality." Although Stock's approach is quite different, it may nevertheless be helpful in analyzing what I see as the problem underlying my own study: the connection between literacy, individuality, and reading the Bible as a text.

56. See Caroline Walker Bynum, *Jesus as Mother: Studies in the Spirituality of the High Middle Ages* (Berkeley: University of California Press, 1982), 82–109: "Did the Twelfth Century Discover the Individual?"

Soil and Salvation: Theological Anthropology Ecologically Informed

William C. French
Loyola University Chicago

*E*merson in his great work *Nature* wrote: "What is a farm but a mute gospel?"[1] The house in which I grew up was in the woods of my grandparent's farm called Bellevue in central Maryland. We did not know much about this "mute gospel" business. We just thought of it as a dairy farm. My grandmother used to tell us about the old days when every fall the men would butcher the hogs and she would take charge of sausage production.

When my grandfather died my grandmother came to live with us, and the farm management was turned over to a tenant. In the late 1950s the Federal Government decided to relocate a number of its expanding agencies to sites in the Virginia and Maryland countryside surrounding Washington, D.C. In the space of four years the Atomic Energy Commission broke ground five miles up the road, while my grandmother's farm was taken over for the 250-acre campus of the National Bureau of Standards. We were especially fascinated by the construction of the Radiation Physics Laboratory with its special housing for a nuclear reactor. Much of my childhood was spent with my brothers and cousins and dogs in tow wandering all about the construction project. We didn't know what atomic energy or radiation were exactly but they sounded very important.

We began to learn more about the new realities of an atomic era around the time of the Cuban missile crisis when President Kennedy told the nation that it would be prudent to build bomb shelters. My dad, always the patriot and a federal research engineer himself, decided that as long as we were having an addition put on the house we might as well make it a two story affair with a bomb shelter below entered into from the basement. The walls and ceiling were one foot thick reinforced concrete. We were only twenty miles from the White House and the Pentagon and the anxieties of living near likely Soviet missile target zones were felt strongly by people in my region.

Emerson believed nature to be a "discipline," what he calls "a school for the understanding." "The moral law lies at the centre of nature and radiates to the circumference. . . . All things with which we deal, preach to us."[2] He believed: "Each particle is a microcosm, and faithfully renders the likeness of the world."[3] So, too, the story of one farm in Maryland, I believe, in important ways serves as a microcosm for some of the new features of the broader story of the earth in our day. Both stories are shaped powerfully by a vast expansion of human power to transform and sometimes to destroy. In both, humanity grasps nature more tightly within our control and dominance, and in both we bear greatly increased risks. In raising Holstein cows and in splitting uranium atoms we interact with nature and its diverse energies and powers, and are constrained by natural laws. Holsteins must be fed, kept dry, and milked regularly. Nuclear reactors too must be carefully tended. Both cows and reactions must be contained, but it is really not such a big deal if the cows get out. Traffic usually stops. But if the reaction breaches the containment building, a vast region can be rendered uninhabitable for centuries.

In the years since the end of Bellevue there has emerged yet another connection between dairy farming and nuclear power—a chemical connection. In April 1953 university labs around Troy, New York, found that a rain shower was dumping highly radioactive water all over the city. The scientists' guess that the radioactivity had come from secret Nevada nuclear bomb tests was later confirmed. No one had until then believed it possible that fallout could travel so far on the winds. The Atomic Energy Commission rightly argued that the exceedingly slight amounts of the airborne fallout then detected could not penetrate deeply into the body and thus posed no serious health threat. However, scientific concern began to focus on the presence of strontium 90 in the fallout. Strontium 90 proved different because it moves through the food chain in concert with calcium. While the radiation from strontium 90 cannot penetrate more than a fraction of an inch into one's skin from the outside, research came to prove that strontium 90, like calcium, is taken up from the soil by grasses, eaten by cows, passed on through their milk into the bodies of children and adults where it is incorporated into bone structure. This poisoning from the inside greatly increases the danger of cancer. This new scientific awareness eventually led to Kennedy and Krushchev signing the Limited Nuclear Test Ban Treaty in 1963 prohibiting the atmospheric testing of nuclear weapons.[4] More recently, in 1986 we again saw concerns raised about strontium 90 given off in the fallout from the Soviet nuclear reactor disaster at Chernobyl. Herds in the Ukraine, Eastern Europe, and the Scandinavian countries had to be killed and buried. Emerson may have been right that farms are quiet "gospels," but the meaning of such texts takes on new and unnerving twists in a nuclear age.

The history of this century is characterized by a radically altered nature of human power and an accelerating tempo of technological innovation and societal and planetary change. We are witnessing an increasing invasion of nature by human history and we are coming to understand that our well-being is now and has always been dependent on the well-being of the planetary ecosystems. Instead of a sense of autonomy from nature, much of our growing knowledge of pollution, toxins, carcinogens, and nutrition gives rise to a heightened sense of the porousness of the membrane between self and world. While the self acts on, and in, the world, the very matter of the world enters into the self. Indeed, the very scientific prowess that has made possible our vastly increased impact on nature has in the same century remarkably expanded our understanding of the complexity of the natural world with its dynamic relations between and among species, and of the richness of animal life, especially primates, higher mammals, whales, and dolphins. The revolutionary insight of Charles Darwin into humanity's evolutionary development from prehuman strata of life has in this century gained increased confirmation by advances in biology, geology, and the rise of the ecological sciences and ethology, the study of animals in their native habitat. Even as science in this century has helped foster increased industrial and agricultural powers that pose an increased threat to the planetary ecosystem, it too has offered us a new appreciation for humanity's rich naturalness—our animality, our biological connectedness to a vastly ancient and complex genetic history, our thick interparticipation within the biosphere and, of course, our ongoing dependence on the integrity and health of the planetary ecosystem.

Modern Western experience has been shaped deeply by the emerging power of human action. Accordingly, our dominant thought forms in religion, philosophy, and ethics have concentrated on the felt power of human agency—the ability to act in history, to create culture, and to shape the future. The Enlightenment tended to an optimistic reading of human agency leading to progress; the existentialists reeling from the carnage of the World Wars struck a pessimistic note when they stressed that human agency imposed meaning in an otherwise meaningless world; and many postmoderns today embrace understandings of human agency as proliferating multiple cultures, interpretations, and plural truths. But beginning with the Darwinian revolution and gaining weight in this century, an emerging appreciation for the primary activity of nature, the planetary ecosystem, has begun to take hold. From this vantage point the human is neither self-creating nor autonomous, but born out of a vastly complex natural history of the planet. Certainly humans enjoy agency, but our agency arises out of our biological heritage and powers and is constrained also by our inherited limits and our ecological conditions. Human agency arises out of powers given us through evolutionary history, and thus our understanding of human life must be situated within a broad attention to the entire history of life on the planet. Indeed today an adequate account of the "self" must include attention to how the emotional, rational, linguistic, artistic, and spiritual capacities of human selves have a natural base—that is, they are made possible by biological capacities, predispositions, and propensities.[5]

Most people today on some level acknowledge our evolutionary inheritance and our deep rootage in nature. However, for people in industrialized urban cultures the technological richness mitigates against any sustained and richly felt sense of the immediacy and depth of our connectedness to nature. Those of us who do not grow our own food or chop, mine, or drill for our fuel are allowed by an advanced division of labor to focus little of our day-to-day attention on our close dependence on the natural world.

It is not surprising that most theologians and ethicists are more attuned to intellectual discussions within the humanities than with new fields or findings in the sciences. Nor is it surprising that theologians and ethicists have tended to be and remain more attentive to understanding human life as shaped by history, culture, and language, rather than by evolutionary history, genetics, or participation within ecosystems. Sadly, dominant streams of theology and ethics, by continuing to ignore the drama and import of the twentieth-century sciences, especially the findings of the ecological sciences, continue to articulate an unbalanced, inadequate account of the human person. By construing the "self" as having little real connection to the environing natural nexus, theologians and ethicists make it difficult to frame any articulate account of God's relationship to the nonhuman natural world or of God's action, grace, or judgment as operative within that sphere. Interpretations of human life that sharply demarcate us off from the rest of nature render it difficult to take humanity's animality seriously and thus make it more difficult for us to generate moral concern and care for the other animal life forms with whom we share this planet. Understandings of the "self" that stress reason, spirit, and freedom, but not embodiment, reinforce particular emphases on God as transcendent and acting in history, but not immanent and acting in the materiality of nature.

In what follows I examine how broad streams of twentieth-century Christian reflection about humanity have followed the dominant modern tendency, separating humanity sharply from nature and interpreting the human within the spheres of culture and history. An emphasis on history as the distinctive arena of the divine–human encounter, I will suggest, had major impact on biblical theology in the 1950s, 1960s, and 1970s by giving priority to God's mighty acts to Israel, but downplaying God's covenant to the earth and Israel's enjoyment of divine blessings which come to it through the fruitfulness of a good land. A historicist-dominated theological anthropology not only leads to an unbalanced view of the human, but also to an unbalanced understanding of the ways of divine action in the world, and, as I will try to show, an unbalanced way of approaching basic scriptures of the Hebrew Bible.

I briefly examine the emergence in the last two centuries of an ecologically informed understanding of humanity's rootedness in the natural world and consider its implications for revising theological anthropological reflection and for recovering the centrality of the doctrine of creation. This task of revision in light of the ecological "signs of the times" has begun, but by no means has it gone far enough. I will explore the contributions of H. Richard Niebuhr and James Gustafson in their recovery of the doctrines of creation and divine providence, which situate the human encounter with God as much in the sphere of nature as in the sphere of history. Likewise I will examine how this ecologically informed theological anthropology provides an important interpretive vantage point for recovering important scriptural themes stressing humanity's participation within creation and the breadth of God's covenant to the entire community of creation. Where modern theology and ethics has tended to stress the separation of the human from nature, postmodern, environmentally responsible movements in theology and ethics are critically recovering certain premodern emphases on humanity's participation in the order of creation which correlate well with emerging data of the environmental sciences about human dependence on the well-being of the planetary biosphere. Likewise many are explicitly informing their understanding of the ways of divine action in the world with scientific data about how life—including human life—evolved and is, in fact, sustained on this remarkable planet.[6]

Theological Anthropology as if Only God and Humans Mattered

Even though revolutions in industrial and agricultural output have greatly increased human population and global economic growth in this century, Western intellectual attention has been dominated by the two World Wars and the Cold War even as theological attention continued to focus on humanity's encounter with God in history. Given the weight of these historicist and existentialist concerns in Christian theological circles in the 1930s, 1940s, and 1950s, it is not surprising that dominant movements in theology and Christian ethics in the 1960s and 1970s continued to appreciate this view's sharp separation of humanity from nature. Indeed, even while a number of theologians began in the 1970s to take environmental issues seriously and to explore the need to recover the doctrine of creation and a sense of humanity's, and God's, participation in the sphere of nature, most theologians and church people continued and continue today to affirm a strong separation of God and humanity from the sphere of nature.

The revolutionary expansion of humanity's scientific, technological, and industrial power in this century has given rise to an unprecedented range of new capabilities, many positive, sadly many destructive. Unfortunately our religious and philosophical reflection on these new capabilities and the consequent unprecedented expansion of our range of moral responsibilities has been hindered by long-dominant theological traditions that concentrate attention on the divine–human encounter in history and ethical traditions that, by focusing exclusively on the intrinsic value of rational life, narrow the spotlight of moral attention tightly to actions that impact on other humans.[7] We clutch at maps of the old country as if these will help us find our way in the terrain of this new era we have entered.

Modern scriptural interpretation has not been immune from the power of these dominant theological anthropological assumptions. As Walter Brueggemann rightly argues, much of biblical theology has emphasized the categories of time and history over against space and nature. The "mighty acts of God" school of Gerhard von Rad and G. Ernest Wright stressed God's deeds in history as the "normative events around which Israel's faith has clustered."[8] The powerful influence of Rudolf Bultmann and Karl Barth pushed a whole generation to employ existentialist categories of "decision," "crisis," and "event" as keys for thematizing God's relationship to Israel, and Christ's relationship to the disciples and to generations of church members. Peering through these historicist and existentialist screens, biblical scholars in the 1950s, 1960s, and 1970s understandably came to focus on God's decisive acts of providential care for, and judgment against, Israel, not the perduring and consistent dimensions of God's sustaining of creation and nurturing of Israel in its land. Consequently pride of place was accorded to Exodus, the prophets, and the New Testament narratives of the life and death of Jesus, while Genesis and the nature imagery of the Psalms were downplayed as primeval myth.[9]

These historicist and existentialist perspectives lent authority to theological emphases on human freedom in culture, language construction, and historical agency. Until only recently little explicit theological or moral attention was given to the fact that humans are biological creatures who are participants in, and dependent on, a broader natural community of the entire planetary biosphere. The true self was understood often in opposition to what a long heritage dubbed our "animal" nature. Not surprisingly, this theological anthropological model depicted the sphere of persons as sharply separate and distinct from the sphere of nature. Consequently little theological importance was assigned to the latter sphere and it was ceded over to the purview of the natural sciences. However, this seemingly innocent disciplinary division of labor did have the odd and unhappy result of disconnecting theological anthropological reflection from the doctrine of creation, elaborated canonically in Genesis and professed authoritatively down through many centuries of Christian preaching and teaching.

H. Richard Niebuhr has rightly emphasized the direct link between theological anthropology and Christian ethics by noting that our actions always have the character of responsiveness. The moral adequacy of our actions is based on their fittingness to the situation to which we are responding, and such fittingness is dependent on the adequacy of our interpreting and seeing. For Niebuhr a fundamental question is: "To whom or what am I responsible and in what community of interaction am I myself?"[10] By construing the self as a self only in history and culture, the historicist/existentialist hermeneutic fails to situate the self within the broader community of the biosphere. By thus understanding the relevant "community of interaction" as only the community of rational—culture-building, language-using—beings, this hermeneutic anthropocentrically constricts our sense of moral responsibility. Similarly by stressing God's action in history, but not God's action in nature, this hermeneutic under-cuts the force of the traditional affirmations of the sovereignty of God by tightly circumscribing the venue of divine power and action. This oddly affirms that God is Lord of history, but it disconnects human history from its rootedness in broader natural history of the evolution of life on this planet. God's grace is tied to history, but it is an oddly noumenal history disconnected from the primal physical, biological, climatological, and chemical forces that sustain all living organisms—including human selves. This view understands divine grace as active, but as acting thinly only on mind, emotion or spirit, but not thickly within the matter of creation or within selves who require the sustenance of their bodily organism for mental, emotional, or spiritual life.

The Modern Theological Retreat from Creation

In a much noted essay years ago in *Science* magazine, Lynn White charged that Christianity has been the most anthropocentric and anti-nature religion of all. By so emphasizing the transcendence of God over the material world, Christianity, White argued, destroyed animistic belief and thus "made it possible to exploit nature in a mood of indifference. . . ." Christianity stressed a "dualism of man and nature" and insisted that "it is God's will that man exploit nature for his proper ends."[11] This doctrine encouraged an ethic of exploration and use and gave impetus to the rise of modern science, which in turn has led to our emerging "ecologic crisis." Accordingly, White holds that Christianity bears a heavy burden of responsibility for our ecological problems.

While White's critique of Christian anthropocentrism has proved influential, many scholars rightly view his claims as historically reductionistic. White, I believe, errs by according religious doctrine too much historical power and by holding the flow of influence as moving only in one direction from religious belief to cultural attitude. He makes too little of the diversity of historic Christian interpretations regarding God's and humanity's relationships to the rest of creation even as he fails to give due weight to the impact that Renaissance, Enlightenment, and modern cultural forces and intellectual movements have had on the development of Christian theology. Specifically he ignores how the rise of modern science with its picture of the nonhuman natural world as a mechanistic realm encouraged modern theologians to highlight history as the arena of humanity's encounter with God. Nature, construed as a machinelike world of "things," seemed quite removed from the sphere of persons, both human and divine.[12] Accordingly, liberal Protestant theologians began to concentrate attention on God's action in history, on the centrality of Jesus Christ, and on the absolute distinction between humanity and the rest of nature. Christology and eschatology came to take pride of place as the doctrine of creation lost significance. Liberal theology accommodated itself to the emerging authority of science by allowing science free reign in the accounting of nature, while claiming for itself a distinct arena of authority, namely, the realm of the spirit, the sphere of persons in their affectional, intentional, cultural, and historical life.

Catholic theology rooted more deeply in premodern classical metaphysical perspectives continued into the middle of this century to emphasize God's role in creation and God's providential governance over the natural world. This stress on natural law and creation was given impetus in 1879 when Pope Leo XIII formally endorsed Thomism in his encyclical *Aeterni Patris*. Despite this deep appreciation for the divine ordering of creation and despite acknowledging humanity as a participant within this grander community of created life, Catholic theology and ethics inherited the classical and medieval emphasis that the intellectual soul makes humans radically distinct from, and superior to, the rest of nature. Rationality gives to humans the capacity of freedom, the mastery over our acts, while all other creatures act out of instinctual necessity. Catholic thinking rested quite comfortably during the first half of this century with the view that animals and plants exist simply for the sake of the human who may use them as resources in any way.

Revisionist movements in Catholic theology since the 1940s have shown an eagerness to break from the confines of classicist modes of thought to embrace what Bernard Lonergan, S.J., has dubbed "historical mindedness."[13] Concerned to overcome some of the rigid metaphysics of the Thomist natural law tradition, many Catholic theologians came to emphasize Christology, eschatology, and the historical dynamism of human experience. This opening to human experience and historical change was validated by the Second Vatican Council, where central documents were promulgated stressing the dynamism of human history and the need to scrutinize "the signs of the times" and to interpret them in "the light of the gospel."[14] Increasingly Catholic revisionists called for centering Catholic ethics not in appeals to natural law but in responsibility to persons and in the needs for full human relationships.[15] For many Catholic thinkers, appeal to the natural law lost its plausibility even as the category of "nature" ceased to be of particular theological or ethical interest.[16]

If White is correct that the Christian tradition is in a thoroughgoing way aggressively antinature, then there is little point in returning to the tradition or to scripture for theological and ethical resources for developing more ecologically adequate accounts of God's and humanity's relationships to nonhuman nature. If I am correct, though, that the theological depreciation of the order of creation is more of a modern phenomenon—primarily a theological response to the rise of modern science, then a theological anthropology that is more ecologically sensitive might be articulated in part by retrieving certain themes, doctrines, and metaphors of pre-modern Christian and Hebraic thought.

Biblical Theology and Salvation History

The "mighty acts of God" school of biblical theology made up of G. Ernest Wright, William Foxwell Albright, and Gerhard von Rad was strongly influenced by the general theological concentration on history as the realm of the primary disclosure of divine action. As Wright argues, because the genius of the Hebrews lies in the insight that God acts in history, history accordingly is "the chief medium of revelation." Also Wright stresses that God is primarily concerned for and related to "man, society, and history."[17] Von Rad in his project tends to subsume the order of creation within the saving history of Israel. He tends to polarize history as the dynamic arena of free divine and human transformative activity and nature as a static realm of unfreedom, embedded in repetitive cycles. Thus, he tends to depict humanity's dominion over nature as a nearly absolute domination and to downplay God's relationship to, and covenant with, the rest of creation. Von Rad develops a "soteriological understanding of Creation" which subsumes God's creation into the order of salvation history. This historicist hermeneutic pushes von Rad to emphasize humanity's distinctive creation from the rest of nature and to deemphasize nature's covenantal connection to its Creator. Similarly he stresses human dominion as entailing rights of use of nature, while giving little attention to texts which balance human rights of use with notions of stewardship responsibilities for animal and plant life.[18]

This concentration on history and how it often supports a denigration of nature and the order of creation can be seen in the powerfully influential eschatological theologies of Jürgen Moltmann and Wolfhart Pannenberg. As Moltmann puts it with remarkable sweep: "The recognition that man does not have nature but history means an overcoming of all naturalistic or quasi-naturalistic ways of thinking."[19] Pannenberg similarly states that Israel "drew the whole of creation into history. History is reality in its totality." "The theology of history now appears in principle at least as the legitimate heir of the biblical understanding of reality."[20]

Major articulators of liberation theology likewise opted early on for a model emphasizing God's liberating action in history and the Exodus narrative as a critical disclosure of God's nature and will. As Gustavo Gutierrez noted in his early classic: "Other religions think in terms of cosmos and nature; Christianity, rooted in Biblical sources, thinks in terms of history."[21] Again a historicist hermeneutic guides the placement of priority on Exodus, the prophetic accounts, and the New Testament. Displaced is any sustained focus on Genesis and the relationships God and humanity have with the nonhuman natural world.

All of these theological movements as well as broad movements in Catholic revisionist thought share a concentration on the categories of the person and of history. Constructed via metaphor and doctrine choice, propositional statement, and rhetorical associations, this common theological paradigm gives a powerful emphasis on salvation history as the realm of encounter between divine and human persons. Nature, in contrast, is not a dynamic category, and neither the human nor God is related to it in any significant way. Nature is not recognized as having an evolving history, nor is it recognized that the continuation of human history depends on the continued flourishing of natural history. Scripture is not interpreted in a vacuum, and this historicist hermeneutic has long dominated both scriptural interpretation and theological construction.

It is important to note that a number of eschatologically oriented and liberation theologians who most forcefully stressed history and eschatology earlier have begun in the 1980s and 1990s to respond to growing environmental awareness by recovering a more balanced appreciation of creation and God's action in the natural world. The titles of Jürgen Moltmann's *God in Creation*, Wolfhart Pannenberg's *Toward a Theology of Nature*, and Leonardo Boff's *Ecology & Liberation: A New Paradigm* suggest the importance of this emerging paradigm shift and also suggest the hope that the group of biblical scholars and theologians who are beginning to recover Israel's stress on creation and God's action in nature will be joined by others.[22]

Environmental Threat and Ecological Awe

While the rise of nuclear power well illustrates one of the revolutions in human power and ability to cause harm, it is not at all clear that it is the chief threat the planetary community faces. If asked to name the worst ecological scenario we can imagine, most of us would rightly cite a nuclear war. Such a horror is clearly the most dramatic and speedy of environmental cataclysms imaginable. While the continued existence of different national arsenals remains potent and constitutes a massive potential threat, we may gain some comfort with the recognition that no rational national leaders can view a nuclear war as in any nation's interests. In contrast, while current rates of consumption and production cause patterns of ecological degradation that are gradual and much less dramatic or horrific than a nuclear war, still it is unnerving to recognize that almost every national community believes it is in their interest to expand consumption and production. Where no national or corporate engines of interest are revving to have a nuclear war, almost all nations and corporations understand their most fundamental interests pushing for a high growth agenda of expanding production and consumption. Each national community, while acknowledging concern about environmental degradation, is under extreme pressure to let massively voiced interests in short-term economic growth trump long-range concerns about ecological stability and well-being.[23]

To understand rightly our circumstances, we need the moral and intellectual discipline to step back from our feelings that, for all of its perversity, our era is a normal one. Because we know the history of our lifetime best, it is difficult not to take the dynamism of our dominant societal practices, technologies, and trends for granted. Only by stepping back and framing our era and its trends in a historical context may we come to see and feel the genuine revolutionary character of the twentieth century where global human population has tripled and economic production has multiplied fiftyfold.[24] Edward O. Wilson suggests that we see our predicament from the vantage point of an alien space station on one of Jupiter's moons whose scientists have been watching Earth for millions of years. Quietly these watchers have observed the measured rhythms of forest growth, glacier expansion and retreat, climate fluctuations, volcanic eruptions, and spread of species. However, in the last two centuries, a blink in geological time, the watchers see "the Moment" they have been long waiting for, when a species emerges with intelligence and gains a dominant and massive control over the planet. For Wilson, humanity has become a "geophysical force" and is currently "swiftly changing the atmosphere and climate as well as the composition of the world's fauna and flora."[25] The signs of this human juggernaut are visible to the space watchers in the rapid cutback in global forest cover, the rapid rise of atmospheric carbon dioxide, the depletion of the ozone layer, and in the millions of dots of light across the land surface at night.

Humanity's ability to effect change has expanded in its range of impact both ecologically and temporally. We have missiles whose reach is over seven thousand miles. Fallout from Chernobyl was monitored worldwide even as chlorofluorocarbon (CFC) use in the northern hemisphere is increasing the depletion of the ozone layer worldwide. Similarly, given the long half-life of nuclear materials, any release through weapons use or industrial accidents means that the chain of destruction will not be exhausted with its impact on the present generation, but will continue on to damage and sicken future generations for thousands of years. Likewise jungle and forest clearing, in destroying the habitat of many animal, plant, and insect species drives accelerating numbers of species into extinction.[26] Through wilderness degradation and threatened global warming, human action today possesses unprecedented capacities to do significant and permanent harm to key components of the ecosphere.

Western ethics was shaped during the long period when human technology was relatively weak and nature by contrast appeared vast, strong, and essentially imperturbable. Moral attention and concern are limited resources, and it is understandable that earlier generations did not lose much sleep over the fates of animal and plant species, the Amazon, the atmosphere, or future generations who did not appear threatened. These seemed rather to be solid furniture of the world and were taken for granted as givens, as stable structures whose present and future existence could be counted on.[27] Even when religious communities oriented themselves around the belief in an impending end-time, still no generation until our own has been confronted with the possibility of the ending of significant features of the natural world, or of the human species, by its own actions. Thus, millenarian movements, while denying the givenness and imperturbability of the world and living species, viewed the end as coming from God's action, not human action, and thus they interpreted it theologically, not ethically. Thus these movements failed to develop any sustained challenge to the dominant Western ethical system with its focus exclusively narrowed to the value of human life.

Even as new scientific data force us to confront the unsettling facts that much of the natural world that once could rightly be taken for granted is now becoming threatened, science in this century is also uncovering the remarkable and inspiring complexity of nature's ecosystems and generating a deepened sense of the majesty of the history of the universe and of life on this planet. Science is the vehicle by which we chart our fears of progressive ecological degradation, even as it is the vehicle for a heightened sense of our connectedness to the rest of life on this planet. As science discloses the contours of our current and potential ecological losses, it is a generator of a broadened sense of moral responsibility. As science discloses the complexity of the planetary biosphere, the richness of animal genetic structure and social activity, the beauty of climate cycles and Earth's myriad species, it occasions feelings of awe, respect, and gratitude for the multiple forces that have played a hand in the development of this life community.

As Thomas Berry, a Catholic priest and self-styled "geologian," points out in his book *The Dream of the Earth*, contemporary science has given us a great gift in an emerging, comprehensive, empirical account of the origins of the universe and the origins and evolution of life on this planet. As a narrative, Berry rightly believes, this scientific creation account is fully as compelling in inspirational power, spiritual richness, and symbolic association as the Hebraic Genesis story or as the creation accounts of the other world religions. For Berry the scientific account enjoys an advantage as empirical and holding transcultural authority among the worldwide community of scientists. Berry believes that Christians, Jews, and other religious peoples need to appropriate this scientific narrative as a truthful account of the modes of divine presence and creative action in the world. This "new story" of the creation of the universe, Berry feels, if rightly understood cannot help but have a transformative power over people, for it both insists that there exists a continuing intimacy between humanity and the nexus of matter and life out of which we have developed and are sustained and that God is best understood as a numinous energy in the heart of creative material and nonmaterial processes.[28] Science is disclosing the historic dynamism of nature, both the universe and the planetary biosphere, even as it shines an empirical spotlight on the grandeur of divine creative action.

From Social Contract to the Land Ethic

John Rawls's magisterial book A Theory of Justice illustrates the increasingly apparent inadequacies of anthropocentric models of ethics and interestingly suggests the importance of understanding our place in the natural world. He denies that we owe "animals and the rest of nature" duties of strict justice, yet he feels that we should not be cruel to animals and that species extinction is a "great evil." But still he states:

> I shall not attempt to explain these considered beliefs. They are outside the scope of the theory of justice, and it does not seem possible to extend the [social] contract doctrine so as to include them in a natural way. A correct conception of our relations to animals and to nature would seem to depend upon a theory of the natural order and our place in it. One of the tasks of metaphysics is to work out a view of the world which is suited for this purpose. . . . How far justice as fairness will have to be revised to fit into this larger theory it is impossible to say.[29]

Rawls recognizes that we must naturalize our understanding of the human and develop a coherent ethical construal of our relationship to the rest of nature. Problematically, he acknowledges the importance of the task and the inability of his theory to respond adequately, and simply leaves it for others. Like Rawls's acknowledgment of the need to expand our ethical models to account for our broader relationships with the whole world of nature, we in theology need to reexamine scripture and tradition with an eye for new models for understanding both God's and humanity's relationships to nature.

Where Rawls's contract theory of justice restricts its reach only to humans, other theorists have proposed a broader account of community, one where humanity is situated within a wider community of all creation. Aldo Leopold in his little classic A Sand County Almanac charts an influential account of ecological ethics based on expanding our notion of community to include "the land" by which he meant collectively "soils, waters, plants, and animals." Where traditional ethics, like that of Rawls, viewed humanity as radically separate from the rest of nature, Leopold's simple insight was to reconstrue them as all part of one community, the "biotic community." This simple expansion of the boundary of what counts as the relevant community entails a direct expansion of the range of moral attention and concern. As Leopold notes: "In short, the land ethic changes the role of Homo sapiens from conqueror of the land-community to plain member and citizen of it. It implies respect for his fellow-members, and also respect for the community as such."[30] Likewise in theology a recovery of attention to the expansiveness of the divine covenant would help ground a Christian ethical argument for an expansion of our notion of our moral concerns along the lines of Leopold's "Land Ethic."

To understand our kinship with other life forms does not entail an ethical equation between the value of a human life and that of a snail. It is, however, to recognize that snails too have moral value apart from their instrumental value to us.[31] Our need today to interpret human life in continuity with nature and animal life must not lead us to downplay our remarkable distinctions from the rest of nature and the other animal and primate species. While there are now remarkable estimates that common chimps and pygmy chimps share 98.4 percent of the same DNA structure as humans, still the tiny genetic difference allows a tremendous distinction between the capacities and activities of humans and our nearest cousins.[32] Clearly humans enjoy higher capacities of linguistic and complex agency, yet the ecological paradigm might suggest that we take this not solely as a source of pride but also as a rather humbling realization that our new human powers today render the well-being of the entire community of life into our care and responsibility. Today our own powers daunt us with their potential, and this should invigorate a heightened felt need to increase our moral energies of restraint.

Hebrew Scripture and God's Covenant with the Earth

The historically dominant, human-centered view has tended to support an anthropocentric reading of Genesis 1 highlighting how God creates vegetation, fish and birds, animals, and finally crowns this ascent of creation with its apex, namely, humanity. This influential reading has long tended to construe the divine mandate for human "dominion" over the rest of living creation (Genesis 1) as authorizing human superiority and absolute rights of use of the natural world. Similarly this anthropocentric hermeneutic has supported a history-centered reading of the Exodus events as a journey of liberation where divine action in history leads a people out of slavery into freedom.

Beginning in the last twenty years, however, a number of scripture scholars have begun to look at the ancient Hebraic texts with eyes opened to the significant roles creation, soil, floods, land, and other natural events play in these texts. For example, ecologically informed theologians and scholars are renewing interest in the account of creation found in Genesis 2 where Adam is created "from the dust of the ground" (2:7). The author employs a wordplay connecting the human being (Hebrew ʾādām) with the "ground" or "soil" (Hebrew ʾădāmâ). If Genesis 1 suggests that the human is the crown of all creation, Genesis 2 suggests that our humanity is derived from the very material of the earth. Similarly, where the dominant interpretation has stressed humanity's separateness from, and superiority over, nature and God's special covenant with Israel, with humanity in general, or with the church as the successor of Israel, many are now attending to the Noachic Covenant in Genesis 9, where God covenants the entire community of creation, and are stressing its ecological relevance. Bernhard Anderson and others have pioneered a new emphasis on Genesis 9 as containing "an ecological covenant" which marks the narrative conclusion and high point of the story of origins. Arguing against the traditional reading, which tends to lift Genesis 1 out of its narrative context to support a human-centered and dominationist view, Anderson and others hold that Genesis 1 must be read in its context as part of a larger narrative unit which builds up to a culmination after the Flood in God's covenant with the earth "for all future generations."[33] It is not that the notions that God has a special covenant with Israel, humanity, or the church are wrong. It is just that they alone are not the full story and if they are taken to be, imbalance and reductionism results. Just as Rawls's theory of justice is not wrong, but by itself inadequately narrow in failing to chart the moral implications of humanity's broader environing relations with the wider natural world, so too narrow notions of the covenant need to be situated within, and thus qualified by, attention to the broadest and culminating covenant pledge of the Genesis narrative.

While liberation theologians have served in recent decades to energize the appropriation of the Exodus story as a potent text highlighting God's historical activity in liberating oppressed peoples, a number of interpreters are beginning to recover the dominant role that the land and the earth's fertility play in this narrative. As Wendell Berry, the noted poet, essayist, and farmer, nicely reminds us, the journey is not simply a liberation from bondage but a positive movement of a people to claim a divine "gift of good land." The land cannot be sold forever, for God claims that "the land is mine." Humans may use the land, but finally may not own it "for you are strangers and sojourners with me" (Lev. 25:23). The Promised Land is "a land which the Lord your God cares for; the eyes of the Lord your God are always upon it" (Deut. 11:12). The land is no reward for innocence for the people are not innocent (Deut. 9:6). Rather, as Berry notes, it is given with conditions—the people must grow to prove worthy of the land "or they will not continue long in it."[34] They are to be "faithful, grateful, and humble" and to "bless the Lord" for the "good land" (Deut. 8:10). They must be neighborly, and they especially must practice good land stewardship. Every "seventh year there shall be a sabbath of solemn rest for the land" where "you shall not sow your field or prune your vineyard" (Lev. 25:4). Failure to hold to the conditions—moral, ceremonial, or agricultural—of the covenant will mean the unworthiness of the people for the gift of good land and their banishment from it. "You shall therefore keep all my statutes and all my ordinances, and do them; that the land where I am bringing you to dwell may not vomit you out" (Lev. 20:22). The texts repeatedly describe the fruitfulness of the land as the conduit of divine blessing for Israel's faithfulness to the covenant and God's ordinances, and the land's harshness and infertility as a conduit for divine judgment and anger at Israel's forgetfulness and irresponsibility.[35] While the notion that divine blessing and judgment occur through natural events or processes has long grown out of favor as crudely mythic and reductionistic, an ecological age pondering how God sustains life on earth might do well to rethink this dismissal of the idea that God blesses humanity and judges humanity mediated within the natural matrix of substantive material life on earth.

The Sovereignty of God and the Breadth of God's Care

While many have sought to emphasize divine transcendence in order to stress divine sovereignty, some have noted that by construing God as only acting in history we limit the expanse of divine action. In a classic series of essays in *The Christian Century* during 1942 and 1943, H. Richard Niebuhr reflected on what it means to see God acting in the World War. He argued that Christians must see God's action in this war as "redemptive and vicarious, absolute and unified judgment" on the nations. It is a judgment against the "self-centered character of nations, churches, classes and individual men." From this theological intepretation of the current historical situation, Niebuhr drew certain Christian ethical inferences. "To carry on the war under the judgment of God is to carry it on as those who repent of their self-centeredness and who now try to forget about themselves while they concentrate on the deliverance of their neighbors."[36] He argues in his essay "Is God in the War?" that the logic of monotheism necessarily commits one to holding that "God is one and universal," acting in all events both historical and natural. "God" for Christians, he holds, must be understood as "an objective reality."[37]

While Niebuhr in his early writings was at pains to argue that Christians must discern, and respond to, the action of God in all historical events and actions, his later writings make more explicit his arguments that the notion of divine action necessarily entails an affirmation that God is acting as much in natural events and processes as in history. Radical monotheism, by so stressing the sovereignty of God, he believes, must necessarily stress the absolute and universal range of God's creative and sustaining action. All the great religions, like Christianity, are so radical, he believes, precisely because they call "into question our whole conception of what is fitting—that is, of what really fits in—by questioning our picture of the context into which we now fit our actions."[38] For Niebuhr every response to particular natural and historical events includes a responsiveness to "the Transcendent One" who is present in all of those webs of action. "God is acting in all actions upon you. So respond to all actions upon you as to respond to his action." The oneness and sovereignty of God are ultimately the ground for affirming a universal community of creation. "When I respond to the One creative power, I place my companions, human and subhuman and superhuman, in the one universal society."[39] By radicalizing our notion of the community of which we are a part, Niebuhr radicalizes and expands the notion of Christian love of the neighbor. He responds to the question "Who, finally, is my neighbor?" by arguing: "He is the near one and the far one. . . . He is my friend . . . and my enemy. . . . He is . . . the unborn generations who will bear the consequences of our failures. . . . He is man and he is angel and he is animal and inorganic being, all that participates in being."[40] By radicalizing theological anthropology to situate the self within a universal community of being, Niebuhr establishes a warrant for a radical ecological and temporal expansion of our understanding of our moral responsibilities.

James Gustafson, once Niebuhr's student and colleague, has developed Niebuhr's stress on the radical sovereignty of God in a more explicitly ecological way. Gustafson appropriates the Calvinist tradition to condemn anthropocentric models of ethics, which restrict all notions of inherent value to the human, and anthropomorphic language about God, which domesticates God into a warm "friend" of humanity. Gustafson develops Niebuhr's insistence that God acts in the world fully as much within the dynamic processes of nature as in history. Indeed, he forcefully challenges those who dualize history against nature and humanity over against the rest of creation.[41]

For Gustafson, Christian faith demands taking a theocentrically dominated perspective of reality, that is, construing and responding to oneself, others, and the broader world always in relation to their relations to God. As he puts it: "[W]e are to relate ourselves and all things in a manner (or in ways) appropriate to their relations to God."[42] Within the perspective of faith and piety, then, there can be really no nontheological view of reality. Put differently, all intellectual and scientific disciplines are theological if rightly understood. The data of sociology, physics, and ecology from the standpoint of piety are all theological data. Of course disciplines have their own integrity, but in radical fashion Gustafson insists that from the perspective of faith in a Creator God who loves and sustains her/his creation, then all the sciences and disciplines are ultimately theological disciplines which chart the complex ways of divine relatedness to persons, communities, and nonpersons in the world. As Gustafson puts it: "In piety the patterns and processes of interdependence that we perceive and conceptualize are indicators, signals, or signs of the divine governing and ordering of life."[43] Thus, the discernment of such patterns and structures points directly to requirements of human moral responsibility. Attention to the significance of species diversity thus should serve as a moral impetus to attend to the economic and political policies pushing habitat destruction and species extinction. Similarly, evidence of increased rates of lethal skin cancer connected to ozone depletion should serve as a moral stimulus to generate policies which halt human activities which emit CFCs into the atmosphere which begin the ozone depletion cycle in the first place.

Conclusion

No account of the "self" today may be considered adequate if it does not include serious attention to humanity's participation in nature, our animality, our embodied existence, our participation within a remarkable and increasingly endangered planetary biosphere, and our evolutionary legacy connecting us back into ancient streams of life. None of this is meant to suggest that human existence is not also saturated in historical experience, and continuously shaped and empowered by culture and language. To naturalize our conception of the "self" should not suggest some need to turn our backs on history, but rather to extend and radicalize our sense of human historicity by locating personal and social history within a yet grander pageant of the natural history of life on this planet. Nature is historical, and human history continues sustained by the environing matrix of life, oxygen cycles, and stable climate patterns. The rise of the ecological sciences has given us a rich and awe-inspiring picture of humanity's thick relations with the natural world even as increased scientific monitoring suggests the severity of the threat we pose to the planet and in turn to ourselves through increased rates of ecological degradation. Our widening sense of awe and the growing awareness of threat together push us to expand the frame by which we interpret the self and our base community.

Such a reconstrual of the self should help prompt theologians to think through the model of divine selfhood in new ways and perhaps find that thinking of God's action as "thickly" present throughout the material world is not such a dangerous or weird way of thinking after all. Similarly, such a reconstrual of the self for ethicists will help situate the human within a broader community of animal and plant life forms all of whom are bearers of intrinsic value and all of whom make claims on us for respect and care. This expansion of our sense of the border of our "community" will, as Niebuhr put it, expand our understanding of the

range of our "neighbors" whom we are called to love. Likewise this reconstrual of the self for scripture scholars and readers might help encourage
a rereading of texts highlighting new understandings of the centrality of
land and creation in the pageant of God's blessings and judgments and
humanity's situation within a broader covenanted community, the community of all creation, with its sign of divine favor, of course, still marked
by the rainbow.

Notes

1. Ralph Waldo Emerson, *Nature*, introduction by Jaroslav Pelikan (Boston:
Beacon Press, 1985), 53.

2. Ibid., 46, 53.

3. Ibid., 54–55.

4. Barry Commoner, *The Closing Circle: Nature, Man & Technology* (New
York: Bantam Books, 1974), 46–52.

5. See Mary Midgley's concept of "open textured" instincts in her book
Beast and Man: The Roots of Human Nature (Ithaca, N.Y.: Cornell University
Press, 1978), 51–82. For an insightful exploration of the import of evolutionary
biology for Christian ethics, see Stephen J. Pope, *The Evolution of Altruism and
the Ordering of Love* (Washington, D.C.: Georgetown University Press, 1994).

6. See Gordon D. Kaufman, *Theology for a Nuclear Age* (Manchester: Manchester University Press; Philadelphia: Westminster Press, 1985), 42–46.

7. Hans Jonas, *The Imperative of Responsibility: In Search of an Ethics for the
Technological Age*, trans. Hans Jonas with David Herr (Chicago and London:
University of Chicago Press, 1984), 6–8, 21–23.

8. Walter Brueggemann, *The Land* (Philadelphia: Fortress Press, 1977), 3.

9. Ibid., 4–6.

10. H. Richard Niebuhr, *The Responsible Self: An Essay in Christian Moral
Philosophy* (New York: Harper & Row, 1963), 68.

11. Lynn White, Jr., "The Historical Roots of Our Ecologic Crisis," in *Western Man and Environmental Ethics*, ed. Ian G. Barbour (Reading, Mass.: Addi-
son-Wesley, 1973), 25.

12. See Gordon D. Kaufman, "A Problem for Theology: The Concept of
Nature," *Harvard Theological Review* 65 (1972): 337–66.

13. Bernard J. F. Lonergan, S.J., "The Transition From a Classicist World-
View to Historical-Mindedness," in *A Second Collection*, ed. William F. J. Ryan,
S.J., and Bernard J. Tyrrell, S.J. (Philadelphia: Westminster Press, 1974), 1–9.

14. Concilium Oecumenicum Vaticanum II, "Constitutio Pastoralis de
Ecclesia in Mundo Huius Temporis," *Acta Apostolicae Sedis* 58 (December

1966): 1025-1120. Among other places, this can be found in Walter M. Abbott, S.J., gen. ed., *The Documents of Vatican II*, trans. and ed. Joseph Gallagher (New York: Guild, 1966), 199-308. See section 4.

15. See, e.g., Charles E. Curran, *New Perspectives in Moral Theology* (Notre Dame: University of Notre Dame Press, 1974), 14-15.

16. For more on this shift, see my article "Subject-centered and Creation-centered Paradigms in Recent Catholic Thought," *Journal of Religion* 70:1 (January 1990): 48-72.

17. G. Ernest Wright, *God Who Acts: Biblical Theology as Recital* (London: SCM Press, 1952), 13, 49.

18. Gerhard von Rad, *Old Testament Theology*, 2 vols., trans. D. M. G. Stalker (Edinburgh and London: Oliver and Boyd, 1962, 1965), 1:138-47.

19. Jürgen Moltmann, *Hope and Planning*, trans. Margaret Clarkson (New York: Harper & Row, 1971), 118.

20. Wolfhart Pannenberg, *Basic Questions in Theology*, vol. 1, trans. George H. Kehm (Philadelphia: Westminster Press, 1970), 21, 31.

21. Gustavo Gutierrez, *A Theology of Liberation*, trans. and ed. Caridad Inda and John Eagleson (Maryknoll, N.Y.: Orbis Books, 1973), 174.

22. Jürgen Moltmann, *God in Creation: A New Theology of Creation and the Spirit of God*, trans. Margaret Kohl (San Francisco: Harper & Row, 1985); Wolfhart Pannenberg, *Toward a Theology of Nature*, ed. Ted Peters (Louisville: Westminster/John Knox Press, 1993); and Leonardo Boff, *Ecology & Liberation: A New Paradigm*, trans. John Cumming (Maryknoll, N.Y.: Orbis Books, 1995).

23. Jonas, *Imperative of Responsibility*, 202-3.

24. See Lester R. Brown, "The Acceleration of History," in Lester R. Brown et al., *State of the World 1996* (New York: W. W. Norton, 1996), 3-20.

25. Edward O. Wilson, "Is Humanity Suicidal?" *New York Times Magazine* (May 30, 1993): 24.

26. See E. O. Wilson, "The Current State of Biological Diversity," in *Biodiversity*, ed. E. O. Wilson (Washington, D.C.: National Academy Press, 1988), 3-18; and idem, *The Diversity of Life* (Cambridge: Belknap Press of Harvard University Press, 1992).

27. Jonas, *Imperative of Responsibility*, 4-6.

28. Thomas Berry, *The Dream of the Earth* (San Francisco: Sierra Club Books, 1988). See also Brian Swimme and Thomas Berry, *The Universe Story* (San Francisco: Harper, 1992).

29. John Rawls, *A Theory of Justice* (Cambridge, Mass.: Harvard University Press, 1971), 512.

30. Aldo Leopold, *A Sand County Almanac* (New York: Sierra Club, 1966), 239-40.

31. See Lawrence E. Johnson, *A Morally Deep World* (Cambridge: Cambridge University Press, 1991).

32. See Jared Diamond, "The Third Chimpanzee," in *The Great Ape Project: Equality Beyond Humanity*, ed. Paola Cavalieri and Peter Singer (New York: St. Martin's Press, 1993), 95.

33. Bernhard W. Anderson, "Creation and the Noachic Covenant," in *Cry of the Environment*, ed. Philip N. Joranson and Ken Butigan (Santa Fe: Bear and Co., 1984), 45-61.

34. Wendell Berry, *The Gift of Good Land* (San Francisco: North Point Press, 1981), 271-72.

35. See also my essay "Chaos and Creation," *The Bible Today* 33:1 (January 1995): 9-15.

36. H. Richard Niebuhr, "War as the Judgment of God," *The Christian Century* 59 (May 1942): 632.

37. H. Richard Niebuhr, "Is God in the War?" *The Christian Century* 59 (August 1942): 954.

38. H. Richard Niebuhr, *The Responsible Self: An Essay in Christian Moral Philosophy* (New York: Harper & Row, 1963), 107.

39. Ibid., 123-24, 126.

40. H. Richard Niebuhr, *The Purpose of the Church and Its Ministry* (New York: Harper & Row, 1977), 37-38.

41. James M. Gustafson, *Ethics From a Theocentric Perspective*, vol.1 (Chicago: University of Chicago Press, 1981), 62.

42. Gustafson, *Ethics From a Theocentric Perspective*, vol. 2 (Chicago and London: University of Chicago Press, 1984), 2.

43. Ibid., 293.

Narratival Selfhood

John C. Haughey, S.J.
Loyola University Chicago

O ur project has four components: theology and Bible; self as whole and self as divided. By way of introductory comment on how I see these components and their relationship to one another, I would say that the self I experience and observe in others is more divided than whole, though whole is my and our common aspiration. The Bible is a resource for the self becoming whole, though there is a growing division on the use of this resource for that purpose. Theology is an after-the-fact kind of discipline that observes the self that believes or the community of believing selves and does this critically lest faith be a source of naïveté.

My contribution to this volume will be that of an ethicist and a systematician. I will begin autobiographically and then add an anthropological reflection on the self as narratively constituted. These done, the question of the character of our narratives and their impact on our characters will surface. The question of how our primary narrative, the scriptures, can produce wholeness and division, saints and fanatics, literalists and literati-ists, ridicule and reverence, will be examined.

My Self

The self I have chosen to begin this examination with is the one I am most competent to inquire into, my own. It is partly known by others and yet largely unknown, even to me. It is whole, to some extent, and divided, also to some extent. This self, when I examine it reflexively, I find inextricably connected to the Bible and theology. I find this self stacked up in layers like planes over O'Hare or tells under Nineveh.

The first layer is my scripts. I am unmistakably scripted; the passive tense connotes conditioning, the involuntary, a lot of givens I have to work with and work around. Some of these scripts have been positive, some negative. The faith of my Irish Catholic immigrant parents has been a positive while its parochialism has been a negative script. Some scripts I can transcend; others will remain part of who I am, like it or not.

In reaching the age of reason—a stage that has no clear beginning and, I hope, will have no ending—I began inhabiting the cultural narratives that circulated in the milieu in which I was raised. Cultural narratives aren't told the way other narratives are. They are absorbed by living uncritically in a culture. Unless I have something countercultural functioning at the same time, I am a product of my culture. For me there was the cultural narrative of progress, for example, which cashed out as: you will be a success later if you are industrious and studious now. You will be a loser later if you are lazy and careless now. The cultural narrative of the mission of America, which most of us have internalized to some degree,[1] was preceded by the triumphalist narrative of Roman Catholicism and its mission. It was easy to identify with the latter because I was raised in a Pennsylvania Dutch town where people who were in error about their Christianity were the overwhelming majority and I, strongly identifying with Roman Catholicism, was schooled in an ongoing obligation to edify them out of their errors and into the one true church. But then Pearl Harbor came when I was eleven and I entered the mission of the American cultural narrative from that moment since I was very much invested with the righteousness of the American/Allied cause, whatever the cost.

But, in growing to some degree of maturity, I found myself more discriminating and beginning to choose the narratives I would inhabit. I chose to inhabit the narrative of the Jesuits, for example, though not altogether freely, since they were so revered by my family, especially my mother. Even our free choices are not wholly free of the scripts and cultural narratives that are the givens we find our freedom conditioned by. The Jesuit thing is still a narrative I choose and do so with increasing freedom and identification. This choice excluded another way of composing my personal narrative, namely, via marriage/family/career.

A personal narrative is composed from scripts, cultural narrative, and the stories I identify with. With varying degrees of freedom, the composition is chosen. For example, I chose the theology route within which to function as a priest. This was partly a free choice driven by my interests. God and the things of God fascinated me. But it was not wholly free because superiors wanted me to go this route and at the same time I wanted the prestige of having a doctorate. But even more determining was the fact that I identified with the theologians who taught me or whom I knew from what they wrote.

Personal narratives are composed from narratively embodied ideals or models as well as from stories one identifies with. All these shape identity and choices. The experience of identification with stories and the figures in stories were key to my self-understanding and to my self-aspirations. Stories, heard, observed, imagined, are inextricable from developing a self. So are relationships, sufferings, jobs. But is not each of these a story, too?

Lurking behind all of this emergence of my selfhood was a larger story, which I will call a metanarrative or a megastory. It was what drew those with whom I identified into itself. Now that I think of it, everyone I admired had become an inhabitant of it. What was this "it" we had in common? It was and still is a doctrinal, moral, liturgical tradition that evinces identification with and adherence to it. This metanarrative had its beginnings with Israel and underwent a drastic revision with Jesus and his followers. It no sooner wins new inhabitants than it begins to shape them, depending on the depth of their identification with it. In time they can become its carriers and some even begin to author a distinctive version of it.

This metanarrative has been and still is a trove for many doctrines, liturgies, theologies, spiritualities and ideologies. It has been both a producer of the scriptures and produced by scripture. It crafts its denizens by scriptures as these are internalized by each of those who identify with it.

My selfhood is inexplicable if I do not take all of the above terms into account: scripts, cultural narratives, stories, personal narrative, and metanarrative. What looks like history when looked at from the outside in, is from the inside out an endless series of dramas each having these five dynamic, interacting layers as their essential parts. (If I knew anything about biology or neurology or DNA, they would be in there too. But I don't, so the reader ignorant of these is spared. The knowledgeable reader can fill in the gaps.)

Having described briefly what these terms mean in my own repertoire, I intend here to move to a second level of reflection which is less autobiographical and more analytical about this *homo narrans* selfhood I am in touch with. Explicating this understanding of my selfhood will take my study beyond self to some of the recent literature on self that fleshes out the above.

Narratives and Anthropology

If one looks at the language that the self speaks it begins to reveal itself as more than a medium through which the person communicates to others. It is the medium in which I understand my own experience. My experience and, incipiently at least, its meaning are caught in its narration, even if that narration remains interior to the self.

But there is a further question about my narrations. What is the prelinguistic self? Is there a prelinguistic, a prenarrated self? If there is what does it have to say for itself? What is its story? If there is no story it can narrate about itself, in what does this mute reality consist? How can it be known if it is narrative independent? There are some terms for this prenarrative given we call the self: soul, spirit, mind, heart, for example. Each of these terms can be found in biblical and philosophical discourses that attempt to flesh out the image of a prelinguistic self. But which of these discourses is prenarratival? This raises anew the question: Is there a self that is prenarratival?

Ironically, scriptural, religious, philosophical narratives are why most of us have taken for granted that there is a prelinguistic self as the given from which utterances come and by which meanings are assigned to experiences. These scriptural and religious and philosophical accounts were reinforced by metaphysical or ontological categories like person, rational animal, body and soul, the embodied self, flesh and spirit, inner self and outer self, and so on. No less reinforcing were psychological categories like ego, id, superego, the conscious, the collective unconscious, and so on. But what if "acts of self-narration" are not only descriptive of what comes from me but are "fundamental to the emergence and reality of the subject" that is me?[2] What if the self is itself the product of language or "a result of discursive praxis rather than either a substantial entity having priority over praxis or a self with epistemological priority, an originator of meaning"?[3]

In what would a personal identity consist if this line of thinking were affirmed? This question prompts another: When is there a consciousness of self except in the act of narration?! The narration may be very internal or only incipient but does not all experience of anything including the self have a narrative quality to it? "In principle, we can distinguish between the inner drama of experience and the stories through which it achieves coherence. But in any actual case the two so interpenetrate that they form a virtual identity," Stephen Crites observes.[4]

It would seem, then, that if selfhood develops *pari passu* with the stories we identify with and if plural stories are the building blocks of an identity that selfhood is narratively constituted. This thesis stands in opposition to a metaphysical view of self as the substance or the essence to which accidents like narratives can be added or subtracted without vitiating the prior given substance.

More needs to be said about what narratives are if selves are narratively constituted by them. A narrative is something we heard, so it was told. It was told and probably repeatedly told, so its telling has something of history to it either because its contents were presented as history or, more frequently, it was heard by me at some past point in time. As a narrative it has a sequence to it, a beginning and the incidents that follow sequentially. For it to hang together it must have some kind of plot composing it. For it to impact one's identity the hearer has to identify with it in some ways. This identification is an affective thing, a transactional transference takes place in the hearing of it. It swims into my inner self in which place it does not find itself alone. It has prior inhabitants, some of them even prenatal. Most stories I hear never make it to the inner self; they "go in one ear and out the other." But this inner self is nothing if not narratival, constitutively, pluralistically narratival.

It is with these plural stories that one can make sense of one's experience. Personal experiences don't happen to a *tabula rasa*. One reads one's experiences and their meaning through the latticework of already inhabited stories, howsoever indistinctly they are remembered and incoherently connected. The narratives give one language. Language supplies one with many lenses by means of which to read one's experiences.

If my self is narratively constituted, then the stories I inhabit take on a stature and an importance far beyond my simple identification with them. My identity itself is at stake. If my self is narratively constituted then who I am will be better grasped by growth in narrative awareness than by any narrative independent way if indeed there can be any self-knowledge that is narrative-independent.

The issue in not only one of identity but also of character. The character of the stories I inhabit will effect the moral character I have and will have. For both these reasons a look at the narratives I am immersed in is critical. To some extent we have done this by constructing the deconstructionist anthropology above. Here I would like to examine only the role of the metanarrative in character building and character disintegration.

Character and the Metanarrative

Two bothersome questions emerge from the above account. One is why does this self identify with some stories and not with others? What has shaped its affectivity, in other words? I would say, a special narrative or type of narrative. One that early on the hearer attached a special credence to because it appealed to his or her hopes, needs, desires. Even before it functions as a mature canon of judgment by which to assign greater or lesser significance to the plural stories, there is a merely experiential canon that performs the same function. Otherwise a self has such discontinuity that there is no *one* home; there is no home; there is no here, here or there, there.

The second question wonders about the rhetoric used in the section above that spoke about a self that composes itself out of the plural stories it has inhabited. Doesn't this prior self put the lie to the proposed anthropology? I don't believe so. Even the construed self is created from what it receives. "Humans are inescapably traditioned," as Delwin Brown puts it. I would put it: we humans are endemically canonical.[5] We use one narrative to take the measure of and put the rest of the identified with stories in some order. It can and does change, of course, but for someone to be one in any functioning way, there has to be an order making, meaning giving, story.

The American philosophical tradition of radical empiricism is preferable to the linguisticism of a Derrida or a Foucault for grounding these assertions. This radical empiricism sees the composition of selfhood and therefore our affective inclinations to identify with this story rather than that as explained, in part, by nonconscious "feeling tones." While sense data feed our conscious feelings and perceptions, we find ourselves apprehending something "vague, unmanageable . . . heavy with contact of things gone by," in the words of Whitehead. More particularly, "what is inherited is feeling-tone" from a "settled world in the past."[6] "Our primary awareness is of an interrelated matrix of givenness within which we are embedded, to which we are inextricably related." What we find is that we have inherited "forces, values that incline us, influence us, move us . . . they are causative, they are powers. They are the basic realm of causal connectedness in which we dwell."[7]

So even in this process of composing a self and a personal narrative, we are doing so from more than conscious stories. This more is visceral, preconceptual, nonconscious material that our bodies carry more surely than our consciousness. This material might be called traditions. We have this in common with the infra-human creatures who carry their traditions from one generation to the next without the benefit of human consciousness. Gadamer's observation is apropos here: "the role of the past is more being than consciousness."[8]

I have invested metanarratives with all this freight. They are traditions that are carried into the present even before they are seen by their carriers for what they are. But we will pick them up at the point of being sighted. Not only are we carriers of traditions before we even know we are; once we know ourselves we realize we have a dire need for same. Rather than dwell on the psychological need for such which should be intuitively obvious, I will go directly to the philosophical or theological character of mature metanarratives. Although a metanarrative can be a tradition of moral philosophy, the much more frequently inhabited metanarratives are of a religious character. The three metanarratives we are most familiar with are Islam, Judaism, and Christianity. Each of them has a number of versions. Each would claim to be normative vis-à-vis the other narratives one inhabits. What is true of all of them and each of their versions is that the megastory they tell has within it a huge number of smaller stories embedded like so many matriochka dolls. Each doll can be extricated and give meaning in a given circumstance which otherwise remains meaningless or threatening, and so on.

A metanarrative differs from a narrative on several scores. One is its dimensionality. It is a whole milieu of identity-shaping metaphors, beliefs, stories, models, symbols, practices, doctrines, prescriptions. Its heights and depths, its length and breadth, while giving order and meaning "on the ground," also open out to infinity because of its transcendent trajectory. Depending on the depth of one's embrace of it, one will avail oneself of little or much of it. It can function as canonical for the other narratives one inhabits, or simply as competitive with the one that operationally is canonical. Implicit in a religious metanarrative and able to be culled from its appropriation is a comprehensive understanding of one's self.

How to explain how a past account can have such personal and communal relevance in the present and the future for its inhabitants? While every inhabited narrative has to have come from somewhere, some one, some ones, the metanarratives I have in mind claim more. They claim to come not just from history but from a community that carefully composed them over centuries. They have been socially mediated all this time. They further claim that while they mediate their interpretations of history, they reveal more than history because they transcend history. They claim to reveal the living God, the heart, mind, and will of the living God. If these claims are true, believers can stand in their metanarrative and touch the divine in and through it.

Are they true? I can speak for only one, the Christian metanarrative. I could attempt to justify its claims to truth with a rationality that stands on its own, outside the metanarrative. There are many apologists who have done this with some success. I do not choose to go this route because the form of rationality I function with has a hard time putting credence in other forms of rationality that are or claim to be narratively independent.

An alternate way of proving the truth of Christianity's metanarrative is to have recourse to the testimony of those living and dead who can bear witness to its truth by their own experience of it and by the evidence to others of wholeness in their lives which they would ascribe to their embrace of it. This would take us far afield, though I think this cumbersome evidence could be and has been compiled in the various forms of Christian hagiography to which one could have easy access.

The third approach to the truth of the metanarrative is not other-directed before it is self-authenticating. Convinced by personal experience of the truth of the metanarrative I inhabit and that the mystery of my own selfhood is intimately tied up in that font, another will not rob me of it. And by personal testimony the other can be brought to at least inquire of me what it is that makes for growth, meaning truth for me. Of course, it's one thing for my metanarrative to authenticate itself to me, but to be convincing to others they would have to see me as whole and see this wholeness as deriving from that font. So, rather than concern myself with proving the truth to others, I will return to a more introspective "first level of reflection," as Rahner calls it.

The Word and the Self

If selfhood is narratively constituted, then each self has had a beginning in heard words or in deeds, which are observed words. A very early Christian hymn retrojected an understanding of Jesus of Nazareth back into a preexistence as a way of understanding his unique selfhood. "In the beginning was the Word. And the Word was with God and the Word was God" (John 1:1). The connotation here is that the Word that was made flesh in the person of Jesus of Nazareth had its beginning as preexistent Word. There seems to be an intuition here that the selfhood of the second person of the Trinity and, by extension, Jesus' selfhood began as word, wordedly. By extension could not all other selfhood begin this way?

Those who are still in doubt about this anthropology are invited to explicate a pre-word selfhood, one that is narrative-vacant. If that proves impossible, then the way is cleared for seeing the value of this kind of postmodern, deconstructionist approach for religious faith.

It might be more insightful to see it as premodern. Faithful Israel, which didn't have a word for self, seems to have had the experience of living from the narratival font of Torah and the Pentateuch, primarily, and the prophets and the Talmud, which were course corrections and clarifications of Torah and Pentateuch. Christianity developed a way of living from the narratival font of God's revelation different from that of Israel.

Jesus will always be the model for Christians of how both to inhabit the megastory and critique extant versions of it at the same time. His megastory was Israel's, at the heart of which was the covenant. His version of living in this covenant was an implicit and explicit critique of what had become a law-centered formalism with too many of Israel's authorities. The letter of the story had replaced its spirit. According to Mark's Jesus, God's revelation to Israel had been reduced to prescriptions that adherents observed rather than a story it inhabited (e.g., Mark 2:16–3:6).

Later than Mark, Matthew's Jesus comes "not to destroy but to fulfill" the Law and the Prophets (5:17). What one enters into in Matthew is Israel's metanarrative, every bit of which, "even the smallest part of the letter of the law" (5:18), will come true. But the Law and the Prophets are sublated by the reign of God, which is proclaimed and begun in the person of Jesus. The megastory and the reign of God are two different metaphors which begin to describe the same reality. Each admits of different degrees of insertion or identification. For Christians each of these is now personalized, in the sense of centered on the person of Jesus.

By the time of Matthew's Gospel we are already into second- or third-generation Christianity, so it is more concerned with the authoritative transmission of the megastory than Mark was. Church and church authority and building the megastory on rock are some of Matthew's concerns. For example, Matthew's Jesus declares Peter "Rock, and on this rock I will build my church. . . . I will entrust to you the keys of the kingdom of heaven. . . . Whatever you declare bound on earth shall be bound in heaven" (16:17-19).

Luke-Acts probably came to be around the ninth decade of Christianity. The communities from which it took its rise faced, among other issues, the dismaying question of whether God's promised faithfulness could be trusted, given the destruction of Jerusalem and the delay in Jesus' return. Luke is at pains to show that God's faithfulness is not to be called into question, only human presumption about the forms it takes. This faithfulness now includes many who were not in Israel's purview: the Gentiles, the outcasts, the sinners, and so on. The Christianity of Luke-Acts is reconstituted Israel. God has not changed "his mind"; believers have just learned more about the mind of God from Jesus. He saw daughters and sons of Abraham where his hearers had seen only tax collectors or pagans. This Jesus includes in the ranks of the elect those who were discounted and disqualified by the metanarrative's legitimators of his day.

John's Gospel is an example of how Christocentric Israel's metanarrative had become for Jesus' followers. By this time, he is the story in a sense. "I am the resurrection and the life" (11:25), for example, would have never been said in one of the Synoptic Gospels. The reign of God is not something Jesus points to in the Fourth Gospel because his person mediates it, even subsumes it into himself. "I am the way, the truth and the life; no one comes to the Father but through me" (14:6).

The one who comes closest to naming my experience of being invested in this metanarrative is Paul the apostle. "For me to live is Christ, to die is gain" (Phil. 1:21). This captures my sense of both who I am and what I value most. What I value most is my union with Christ. In this union I experience peace. But more than this, in this peace I have a sense of who I am. Beyond or outside of this union I experience anomie. This is not to say that I think I am Jesus of Nazareth redivivus. Rather, the anointing Jesus experienced of being special to God, chosen by God, loved by God, God's own, was something his followers also experienced. The language used early about Jesus names him Christ—he was christed by God. But this names me better than my own name. For me he mediates the heart, mind, and will of God. He embodies perfectly the metanarrative of Judaism and makes it available to those of us who follow him.

I do not feel that this way of experiencing union with God in Christ sets me above anyone else or makes me better than anyone else. On the contrary, this outcome has come about from necessity. This need for a deeper insertion has come because of particular sufferings that have had me throw myself onto God with an abandon proportionate to my total powerlessness and need for God. I am not alone in this, I'm sure. In fact, it would seem that sufferings are among the most important stories for shaping one's identity. Sometimes they are meaning making but usually one can only find meaning in them from beyond them. Hence, the need for a deeper insertion into a metanarrative that can account for otherwise meaningless suffering. The Christian metanarrative has an uncanny way of making the mystery of suffering something that is bearable and given some degree of meaning through Jesus' own sufferings.

The project for which this volume has been done is a study on the whole and divided self. Before there are the academic notions of self as whole and/or divided, there is the experiential question of my own whole or divided self. I would have to say that insofar as there is any wholeness in me, it seems to come from the consonance I regularly experience from using the scriptural texts of Judaism's and Christianity's metanarrative. They or, better, God in some mysterious way speaks to, nurtures, and sustains this selfhood of mine through the Bible. So before I conjure up a problem to be studied, I am first aware of the Bible being more of a solution to the project's subject matter than simply another layer of problem. The Bible seems to make any other way of discovering the mystery of me, of Christ in me, of me as more christed than a separate self, unnecessary or unfruitful. I accord scriptural texts a sacredness and I listen to them as if they were not simply cultural products, though they are also unmistakably that. I initially accorded them a special place because I had been "traditioned" to believe that they were coauthored by the Spirit. "All scripture is inspired of God" (2 Tim. 3:16). But I also regularly experience their specialness so that what started as a belief is now more of a daily, operational principle of my life.

Rather than isolating me from others, this way of being made more whole conjoins me with others as members of a body are conjoined to one another (1 Cor. 12:12). This Pauline metaphor is one of the many that come from the scriptures. As it indicates, wholeness is more than an individual task, aspiration, or destiny. It has to do with being knit together with other denizens of this same metanarrative. The body-of-Christ metaphor confirms my experience of who others are to me and me to them: we are in Christ. The christedness I sense in myself is not peculiar to me. I sense it in others and have found a number of people aware of the same marvel.

And, even more germane to the subject of wholeness is the suggestion that these christed selves are members of a Self that is larger, deeper, and more long-term than I and you and here and now. If it is faith that has made us whole in our individual selves, it is this same faith that has made many selves one whole self, the embodied Christ. This is not simply a belief; it is a reality to me. This reality changes the meaning of wholeness of the self.

Is this an I-and-Jesus or a we-and-Jesus delusion I am in? The megastory itself leads one away from such a privatization and sectarianism even though it invites the total investment of my person in it. A change in the biblical paradigm clarifies this difference. "I have made a covenant with my chosen one, I have sworn to David my servant: Forever will I confirm your posterity and establish your throne for all generations" (Ps. 89:3-4). My experience, though intensely personal, is not individualistic. I am involved in a story that has had a covenanting God choose and embrace a whole people that has been eons in the making. David was the embodiment of the embraced partner. But David was not all that God embraced by making covenant. Since the Son of David had pity on me I am one of those included in that embrace. My selfhood is better understood through this reading and experience of this covenant megastory than through any other process of introspection or conceptual grid or psychological map I have known or studied.

The selfhood that results from a deep identification with Christ differs from that given as the result of any other deep interpersonal narrative I have entered into. The difference has been aptly termed exstantial, in the sense that the self stands forth from where it had been.[9] Luther's way of saying this was *fides ponit nos extra nos*, "faith posits us beyond ourselves." But this experience is closer to one of being intimately accompanied than of ecstasy which is a transitory exodus from self because of the riveting presence of an object. Since in the following of Christ the

experience is neither ecstatic nor transitory, the role of the Spirit as that
is described in the Gospel of John illuminates how this can be. This
other "Paraclete will be with you always" (14:16). This Paraclete enables
one to abide in Christ, to hear Christ's particularized words, to abide in
love of him and of one another. It is as if my own "I am" has begun to
migrate into his "I Am."

Without the Bible this exstantial experience either would not have
taken place or would not be able to be named as I have been taught and
personally learned to name it. Although exegesis in all its forms is an
essential moment in understanding the scriptures and as such endlessly
informative, it would seem to be misused if it were to postpone or obfus-
cate the personal and communal appropriation of the word-as-address.
The best exegesis can deliver is word-as-idea. While this latter is not an
unimportant contribution to understanding the megastory, still it is a
servant of it. Exegesis in all its forms is essential to keeping the megastory from lapsing into versions that are privatized, selective, or simply
ignorant. But exegesis doesn't tell the story; it only helps to make its
telling more precise.

The character of the narratives we inhabit begins to shape the kinds
of persons we are. I have described my previous self as having been in a
sense lost and, over the course of time, I have a sense of having inhabited a new self, one more aligned with who I now think I am. Though
still mystery, it is more authentic than the old self that was more and
more divided by the many conflicting narratives it sought to live in. But
isn't this what the metanarrative has said was the *desideratum?*—that you
find your self by losing your self. Also that your faith will make you
whole. And the whole, it turns out, is a reality considerably more peo-
pled than the previous, solitary, whole-seeking self ever imagined.

Theology, Ethics, and the Self

This is all very well and good for me but there is the lurking question
behind all of this of misreading texts or deceiving oneself. This question
used to be posed in terms of objectivity. Now it is asked in terms of interpretation. Am I interpreting the metanarrative of Christianity correctly?
This is where the fourth component of our project intrudes itself,
namely, theology. Theology is a reflection on faith. It is a reflection on
the doing of faith that seeks to understand it better and more critically.

Theology actively entertains suspicions about faith as it has been acted upon and experienced.

Running alongside the faith metanarrative in the whole course of its elaboration from the beginnings of Israel till the present time there has been theology, theologies—in fact, whole schools of critical reflection on faith and its claims. These seek to keep the metanarrative from falling into pietism or illusory constructs. Theology has a function different from promotion of the faith. It has a function different from authenticating or delegitimating versions of the faith. It does not purport to be official but only constructively critical.

Theological ethics is one of the specializations of Christian theology. Here it would inquire into the character produced by the scriptures and the megastory of Christianity. What kind of character is formed by its texts? Assuming that the megastory has integrity, the issue would be its reception. How explain how it can be used for such contradictory behavior, for example, homophobia/homophilia, anti-Semitism/reverence for Judaism, sexism/gender inclusiveness, sectarianism/interreligious pluralism, and so on.

To answer these questions, recall that while the megastory is radically scriptural it is not exclusively so, at least in the Roman Catholic version of it. It is complemented with what is loosely referred to as Tradition. I combine the two in the terms *metanarrative* or *megastory*. The questions that follow after the basic one of what kind of character this megastory produces are three. (1) Is there something about the scriptural component of the megastory that makes indwelling it too protean to be trustworthy? In other words, can it mean what you want it to mean? (2) Is there a difference in the ethical consequences for those indwellers for whom scripture alone is normative in contrast to those for whom it is only part of what is normative—that is, between evangelical Christianity and scripture-cum-tradition Christianity? (3) Is the Christian metanarrative capable of self correction? Has it done so, in fact?

It would take us far afield to fully answer these questions, so only the general directions of an answer will be given here. First of all, the metaphorical, symbolic character of much of scripture invites a pluralism of interpretations for those who reverence it. Steno texts have a single referent; tensive texts are meant to have plural referents. Scripture's tensivity enables it to speak to readers in their ever-changing, always particular circumstances. This does not make the scriptures untrustworthy; it makes them endlessly fruitful. But the symbolic, metaphorical, tensive nature of the scriptures make their use susceptible of a pluralism that can lead to self-deception, self-interest and neighbor-dangerous behavior. In a word, the scriptures could be a source of unethical behavior.

So, built into their use, there has to be an authorized, authoritative reading of the scriptures that, at the same time, leaves them as free to be tensive as they were meant to be. Yet this use of authority must itself be both "under the Word" and at the same time capable of correcting misreadings of the Word. Some of this correction can be done by those versed in the disciplines germane to understanding the texts in their contexts. But the disciplines themselves have been relatively recent, whereas the telling of the story faithfully has been exigent from the beginning. For Roman Catholic Christianity there has been an authority and a responsibility from the beginning that extends to overseeing the faithful transmission of the megastory through history. The metanarrative must have the wherewithal to be tradition-correcting while remaining faithful to the Word.

Roman Catholicism's understanding of authority claims to function under the word yet from within a living tradition. It claims to function in matters pertaining to faith and morals. Its moral theologians function as a critical voice within that community, critical not only of misunderstandings of the morality entailed in the following of Christ but also of those magisterial understandings that misread or misunderstand the tradition. This combination of actors has functioned well though not without tension over the course of history.

Roman Catholicism would seem to be an example of an authority that has been able to bring a correction to its own misunderstandings—for example, with regard to slavery, usury, or anti-Semitism—at least in its official pronouncements and teaching instruments. It is being pressed at the present time to further course corrections, as it has been through the centuries. The role of the witness of those who "live the story" and represent a marginal voice that eventually becomes the official position is one of the more dramatic subplots of the ever-developing metanarrative. These voices keep the metanarrative from becoming an inert ideology.

The second question above about the difference between Christians whose metanarrative is isomorphic with scripture and those who have tradition as part of their normativity, prompts a brief reminder about the both-and nature of Catholic Christianity. It is a metanarrative that combines reason with revelation, natural law with positive and divine law, culture with faith, freedom with authority. The consequence of this both-and nature of Catholic Christianity's reading of the megastory is that it has more interpretive tools than the texts of scripture alone provide. Roman Catholicism's narratively mediated tradition, though complex, supplies Catholic Christians with a way of developing their metanarrative so they can deal with the questions they face about whether their own reading and telling of the megastory is itself true, good, even ethical.

It is the nature of the living tradition which includes but is not exhausted by scripture that it is always in the process of being received and construed at the same time. The "it" is never final but ever developing. Its receivers are those who have inhabited it. They are its primary developers, but, at the same time, it cannot mean whatever they want it to mean. Hence the role of authority in authenticating one understanding over against another when that has to be done. All I want to do at this point is describe this version of Catholic Christianity's understanding of itself and its authority rather than justify the conclusions that have been arrived at.

What I have done in this article is move the meaning of personal wholeness on to a larger frame of reference. It is about this larger frame that Vatican II observed that there is so essential a linkage between three realities—"sacred tradition," "sacred scripture," and "the teaching authority of the church"—that "one cannot stand without the others" (*Dei Verbum* #10). I cannot comprehend my own selfhood without the word and the word heard within a tradition, a tradition that can authoritatively teach. This may leave the reader with the distinct impression I have never transcended my initial script. They may well be right. But this time it's become where my I has freely gone.

Notes

1. Roger Betsworth, *Social Ethics: An Examination of American Moral Traditions* (Louisville: Westminster/John Knox, 1990). This book is useful for describing the four major cultural narratives that have shaped and are still shaping the character of our citizenry.

2. Anthony Paul Kerby, *Narrative and the Self* (Bloomington: University of Indiana Press, 1991). I have found this book especially useful for this section.

3. Ibid., 4.

4. Stephen Crites, "The Narrative Quality of Experience," *Journal of the American Academy of Religion* (Sept. 1991): 294.

5. Delwin Brown, *Boundaries of Our Habitations* (Albany: State University of New York Press, 1994), 49.

6. Alfred North Whitehead, *Process and Reality* (New York: Free Press, 1978), 119.

7. Brown, *Boundaries*, 51.

8. Quoted in Brown, *Boundaries*, 54.

9. Robert P. Scharlemann, *The Reason of Following: Christology and the Ecstatic I* (Chicago: University of Chicago Press, 1991), 23.

Part Three

Paul Ricoeur on Self and Bible

The Self in the Mirror of the Scriptures

Paul Ricoeur

*M*y final two Gifford lectures form an inseparable whole.[1] In them, I discuss, on the one hand, how the self is instructed by the religious tradition that stems from the Judaic and Christian biblical scriptures and, on the other hand, the inner resources with which the self responds to this instruction, which determines it in the manner of a call that imposes no restraints. The relation between call and response is thus the bond that holds these two lectures together. What is more, this relation also produces a gap between these concluding lectures and those that preceded them. This gap or break needs to be clarified, even if all the determinations of the self traced out in the earlier lectures, and worked out in *Oneself as Another*, are taken into consideration again here, where through this recapitulation they are both intensified and transformed.

I want to lay particular stress on this initial gap between these concluding lectures and what had gone before in order to dispel a possible error in interpretation that might appear to be fostered by the term "response." One might understand this term in the following way: to be a Jew or Christian is to possess the response (or answer) to the questions posed by philosophy but left without a response. Philosophy then would raise the question and theology would provide the answer. But this is not at all what I have in mind. In the first place, I do not set the response over against a question but rather a call. And this changes everything. It is one thing to respond to a question in the sense of resolving a problem that has been posed; it is something else again to respond to a call in the

201

sense of conforming [*correspondre*] to the conception of existence it proposes. Next, this call does not come from philosophy but from the Word, harbored in scripture and transmitted by the tradition and interpretive traditions issuing from these writings. Finally, the response I have in mind is not that of theology, considered as a more or less systematic discourse, but that of the self, which moves from being a self that is called to being a responsive self.[2]

As for the relation between philosophy and faith, if we still want provisionally to use these problematic categories, this is not determined by the relation between question and answer, despite its apparent resemblance to the relation between call and response. First, we can apply the schema of question and answer only within a prior domain of understanding, which is exactly what is at issue if it is a question of the relation between philosophy and faith. Second, if we admit the existence of such a domain, it quickly becomes apparent that philosophy often gives the answer and it is faith that poses the questions. But philosophy responds or answers in a way wholly other than does the believing self, that is, in the sense of resolving problems that it itself raises on the speculative plane that is proper to it. As for faith, it can pose questions as much about those mysteries that it refuses to transform into problems in need of resolution as about those solutions that philosophical speculation proposes out of its foundational and totalizing *hubris*. In short, for philosophy to respond by answering is to resolve a problem. Whereas to respond to the word of scripture is to conform to the proposed meaning that issues from what is given through the Bible. It follows that the relation between these two ways of responding or answering turns out to be immensely complex. It cannot be reduced to the handy schema of question and answer.

In order to give some account, however briefly, of this relation, which is not my real topic here, I shall limit myself to two assertions whose complementarity itself poses problems. On the one hand, the call to which faith responds in so many different ways, as I shall discuss in the following lecture, is born within a setting of human experience and language that have their own structures, whose internal coherence at a specific symbolic level I want to take up here. On the other hand, these originary structures of experience and language have come down to us only thanks to an uninterrupted process of transmission and interpretation that has always implied conceptual mediations that are foreign to the original expressions of the faith of Israel and of the early Christian church—those, for example, contributed successively by Hellenistic philosophy, by Neoplatonism, by scholasticism, and by Cartesian and post-Cartesian, Kantian, Hegelian and post-Hegelian philosophy. As a result, neither Judaism nor Christianity can be thought about today in isolation, but only in relation to the rest of our theoretical and practical culture. This not some kind of contamination that we ought to regret, even less does it represent a perversion. Rather it represents an unavoidable historical destiny that we have to take into account. I am not looking for any easy reconciliation of these two assertions. On the contrary, the tensions that result from this relation between the specific language of faith and the conceptual mediations that have been borrowed from its cultural milieu have animated many of the internal debates within Western thought, whether it accepts or rejects the biblical legacy.

If in this lecture I stress the specificity of the experience of the biblical human person and the coherence of the language at a symbolic level proper to this experience, I do not mean to lose sight of those cultural and conceptual mediations that were practically contemporary with the birth of this experience and its language. In fact, our recognition of the singular status of this experience and language is itself a characteristic of the hermeneutical era of Western reason.[3]

This restitution expresses a way of questioning backward—of *Rückfrage*, to use Husserl's terminology for his inquiry into the *Lebenswelt*, the lifeworld—that in no way means to restore the original immediacy of an originary experience and its language. What this questioning backward brings to light are in fact earlier interpretations whose interpretive import was incorporated into the oldest form of the texts that have come down to us and that are recognizable only within the framework of the self-critique of modern reason. In other words, the reconstitution of expressions taken to be the most original expressions of biblical faith is itself a modern phenomenon, which itself belongs to the history of interpretation. The use of historical-critical method, of structural analysis, of literary criticism, and especially of the theory of symbolism all make evident the modern status of this reconstruction. I shall say nothing more here about the conflictual conjunction between the biblical background of experience and language and those cultural and philosophical mediations from which philosophy was born. If I believe I can abstract from these mediations—given the important reservations just indicated—it is because I am not concerned here with theology properly speaking, which consists of a discourse at a conceptual level that has its own rules and its

own manner of incorporating philosophical concepts and ways of thinking. Instead, I mean to take up expressions of biblical faith that antedate
formal theologies from the very point of view of their capacity to form
the kind of responsive self whose phenomenological description I
attempt to undertake in my final lecture.

This choice explains why I am placing the principal accent on the
specificity of biblical experience and the language that gives it expression
rather than on those cultural and philosophical mediations into which
this specificity tends to disappear owing to a kind of compromise
discourse. This stance also further explains my mistrust as regards the
question-and-answer scheme when it is applied to the relationship
between faith and philosophy, and even more my refusal of any apologetic attitude, whether it be intended to sing the praises of or to defend
some profession of Jewish or Christian faith. I am well aware that my
belonging to this particular field of experience and language is first of all
a biological, geographical, and cultural contingency. However, I also
believe that it can be transformed into a freely assumed destiny by anyone who takes the path of a wager and a risk. The risk is that of responding positively, in one way or another, to the nonconstraining call issuing
from the symbolic field determined by the biblical canon, whether Jewish
or Christian, in preference to any other classical canon.[4] The wager corresponding to this risk involves a letting go of oneself, which calls for
those different figures of selfhood that I shall return to in the next lecture, that we wager will be compensated a hundredfold by a super-
abundant increase in our understanding of ourselves and of others. But I
neither intend to impose nor to excuse myself for introducing this wager.
Certainly I must make sense of it (*logon didonai*), but to do this is something other than to justify oneself—it means accepting and confronting
one's own choice with the other choices made by one's companions in
life and thought, in that "loving struggle" for truth, as Karl Jaspers so
aptly put it.

I turn now to the theme of this next-to-last lecture. Its title is "The Self
in the Mirror of the Scriptures." To convey the sense of this title, I shall
draw on the vocabulary that governed the analyses in my work *Time and
Narrative*. There I used the term "configuration" to refer to the internal
organization of the type of discourse being examined—in that case, narrative—and I called "refiguration" the effect of discovery and transformation this discourse brings about in its hearer or reader through the
process of receiving the text. What I want to consider here is a relation

similar to that between configuration and refiguration. The problem I want to pose is that of how the entirely original configuration of the biblical scriptures can refigure the self, taken in terms of all the determinations I have spelled out in *Oneself as Another*. My title places this relation under the guidance of one telling metaphor from Christian hermeneutics: the metaphor of the Book and the Mirror. *Liber et Speculum*. How does the self understand itself in contemplating itself in the mirror held out to it by this book? For a mirror is never there just by accident. It is held by an invisible hand. On its side, the book remains a dead letter so long as its readers have not become, thanks to it, in Proust's phrase in *Time Regained*, readers of themselves.

What I want to discuss is the internal dynamism that makes the book, made up of the Hebrew Bible and the Christian New Testament, become a mirror for a self who responds to the solicitation of this book.

I shall proceed as follows. In the first step, which is still a preliminary one, I shall say in what sense Christian faith requires a linguistic mediation in general and a "scriptural" one in particular. In a second step, I shall draw upon a purely literary analysis of the Bible, influenced by the great Canadian literary critic Northrop Frye, in order to emphasize both the originality and internal coherence on the plane of verbal imagination of these writings, which Frye, following William Blake, calls the great code.[5] From this follows an initial approach, albeit still an external, extrinsic one, to the relation between book and mirror, or, using my own vocabulary, between configuration and refiguration. In a third step, one more marked by historical-critical exegesis but nevertheless directed toward biblical theology, I want to show how the *theologoumena*, bound to the various literary genres of the Bible, imply a human response that is an integral part of the meaning of these theological motifs. Finally, in a fourth, clearly hermeneutical step, I shall discuss how the dialectic between the manifestation of the Name and the withdrawal of the Name affects the constitution of the self, called at the same time to draw itself together and to disappear, in a decisive way.

The Linguistic and Scriptural Mediation of Biblical Faith

The reader will have noted how in my introductory comments I have repeatedly spoken about religious experience *and* its language, presupposing thereby an intimate union between them. It is time to justify my assertion regarding this inseparable relation. On the one hand, I willingly grant that there exists something like a "religious experience," whose "varieties" William James analyzed in his own well-known Gifford Lectures, published as *The Varieties of Religious Experience*. For my part, the formulations closest and most familiar to me are: a feeling of absolute dependence, in relation to a creation that precedes me; an ultimate concern at the horizon of all my preoccupations; an unconditional trust, which hopes despite . . . everything. These are a few synonyms for what, in the contemporary period, has been termed "faith." And all the formulations we may give attest that faith, as such, is an act that cannot be reduced to any particular word or any piece of writing. In this respect, it marks the limit of any hermeneutics, because it is the origin of any interpretation. But the difficulty that is already evident that it is necessary to "name" this origin of interpretation indicates the necessity of providing a counterpart to the affirmation that faith is more primitive than any language or speech act. If the presupposition of hearing, for example, Christian preaching is that, in faith, everything is not language, it is as well that religious experience is always articulated in language, whether we understand this in a cognitive, practical, or emotional sense. The apparently naked formulations concerning faith given above are already phenomena of language, or, as much theology subsequent to Karl Barth likes to put it, word events. What is at stake in all these formulations is the possibility of "naming God." And however problematic this naming may be, as I shall say, it does constitute the originary linguistic structure of what we nevertheless call a lived faith.

But this is not all. What constitutes the specificity of biblical faith among all the possible linguistic configurations of religious experience is the scriptural mediation that served as an interpretive framework for the religious experience of the members of the Jewish and Christian communities. In these communities, naming God passes through the channel of the biblical writings. It is through them that religious experience attains not only expression, linguistic articulation, but those specific configurations delimited with more or less precision by the biblical canon, whether Jewish or Christian. As religious experience, biblical faith is instructed—in the sense of formed, enlightened, educated—within the framework of those texts that preaching brings back to living speech. This linguistic and textual presupposition of biblical faith precedes anything that may subsequently be said about the relation between the book and the mirror. The self, informed by scripture, will be able to be, as I shall say, a responding self, because, in a certain way, these texts precede life itself. If I can name God, however imperfectly, it is because the texts that have been proclaimed to me have already done so. Or, to use another vocabulary, to which I have already referred above, we can say that biblical faith has its classics, which distinguish it among the cultural choices we make from all other classics. This difference is important for our investigation into the self insofar as the classics of Judaism and Christianity differ on one fundamental point from other classics from the ancient Greeks up to the present: Whereas these other classic texts speak to the readers one at a time, and with no other authority than what these readers choose to confer upon them, the classics that inform Jewish and Christian faith do so across the authority that they exercise over communities that place themselves under the rule—the canon—of these texts. In this way, these texts found the identity of the communities that receive and interpret them. It is against the background of this identity that a responsive self can stand out, following the modalities I shall consider in my final lecture.

The Imaginative Unity of the Bible

Let us now take up in more detail the configuration of scripture, a configuration that governs its power of refiguration. I shall begin by following the path traced out by Northrop Frye in his *Great Code*, relying solely on the resources of literary criticism applied to the Bible considered as literature. Without neglecting the achievements of the historical-critical method, and setting aside the questions of authorship, sources, history of composition, and faithfulness to historical reality, let us simply ask how this text produces its meanings on the basis of its internal textual structures. I have become interested in this kind of reading, one that is foreign to the main currents of exegesis, because it protects the text from the claim that any subject whatever can govern its sense, by stressing, on the one hand, the foreignness of its language in relation to the one we speak today, and, on the other hand, the internal coherence of its configuration in terms of its own meaning criteria. These two features have a decentering influence in relation to any effort to realize the self-constitution of the ego.

Frye begins by stressing the fact that biblical language is entirely for-

208 PAUL RICOEUR

eign to our own in the sense that in order to join it we have to retrace the slope of language that went from being metaphorical in the age of Homer and the Greek tragic poets to becoming argumentative with Neoplatonic theologies and in particular with attempted proofs for the existence of God (from the scholastics to Hegel), finally to become demonstrative with modern mathematics and the empirical sciences. Today, in the midst of this third type of language, only poetry attests to the power of metaphorical language of the first type. This metaphorical language, in fact, says not "this is like that," but "this *is* that." It is by way of such poetry alone that we can move closer to the kerygmatic language of the Bible when it proclaims in a metaphorical mode "the Lord is my rock, my fortress," "I am the way, the truth, and the life," "this is my body . . . ," and so on. By calling this language kerygmatic, we indicate that it is at least metaphorical, pre- or supra-metaphorical, so to speak. What is more, this language possesses complete internal coherence, but this coherence is precisely that of a language akin to that of metaphorical language. It results first of all from the extreme consistency of biblical imagery, which Frye sees organized in terms of two axes, the one paradisiacal or apocalyptic (where these two adjectives are typologically equivalent), the other demonic. We can traverse these two axes, along which are distributed the heavenly powers, heroes, human beings, animals, plants, and minerals, in either direction.

However, the imaginative—not the imaginary—unity of the Bible is assured in a much more decisive way through the thoroughgoing typological functioning of biblical significations. Indeed, Northrop Frye sees in the Bible a vast branching network of correspondences between types and antitypes, to use the language of Saint Paul, correspondences that produce an interconnection of meaning, for example, between the exodus of the ancient Hebrews and the resurrection of Christ, between the Law of Sinai and that of the Sermon on the Mount, between creation according to Genesis and the prologue of John's Gospel, even between the figures of Joshua and Jesus. This typological interpretation circulates not only between the Old and New Testaments for Christians, but within the Hebrew Bible itself, which puts into relation the series of covenants between God and Noah, Abraham, Moses, David, and so on. James Barr says something similar, without attributing such a large role to typological coherence, when he says that in the Bible events, characters, and institutions do not succeed one another in a linear way, where

what comes next simply replaces what went before, but rather in a cumulative and mutually reinforcing way. There is certainly a close tie between
this cumulative process, which works principally on the narrative plane,
and the typological process that is especially characteristic of the
metaphorical language and basic imagery of the Bible.

Frye sees this connection by starting precisely from the typological
process, particularly when it can be unfolded along the sequential and
diachronic line that goes from Genesis to the book of Revelation. In this
way, he sees the Bible as unfolding as a series of U-shaped figures, with
highs and lows, summits and abysses, all described in terms of the, by
turns, apocalyptic or demonic overarching metaphor of the great code,
and linked together by the typological rule that assures its cumulative
character. In this way, along the chain of summits are placed the figures
of Eden, then of the promised land, of the gift of the law, of Zion, the
second temple, the kingdom proclaimed by Jesus, the messiah awaited
by the Jews, and the second coming awaited by Christians. Along the
chain of abysses are the lost paradise and Cain, the captivity in Egypt,
the Philistines, Babylon, the profanation of the second temple, Rome
and Nero, and so on. The typological correspondence is thereby
extended over a temporal sequence, without the close connection broken
between Eden, the promised land, Jerusalem, Mount Zion, the kingdom
of God, and the apocalypse.

If I have given Frye's notion of the Great Code so much importance
in my own presentation, it is to highlight the coherence of a symbolic
field governed by purely internal laws of organization and development—
what Frye characterizes as the centripetal structure that the Bible shares
with every great poetic text. This self-constitution and self-sufficiency of
the Great Code constitutes an important argument for our making sense
of the self corresponding and conforming to it. If we place in parenthe-
ses any eventual representation of real historical events, and with it the
centrifugal and referential movement of the text, which is characteristic
of argumentative language and even more of that demonstrative language that in our culture has largely covered over and repressed metaphorical language, the only relation to reality that counts in a poetic text
is not nature, as in a book of cosmology, or the unfolding of events, as
in a history text,[6] but rather the power to instill in listeners or readers
the desire to understand themselves in light of this Great Code. Precisely
because the text aims at nothing outside itself, it only has us as its out-

side, we who, in receiving the text, assimilate ourselves to it and make
the book a mirror. At this moment, the language which *in itself* is poetic
becomes kerygmatic *for us*.[7]

The Bible, a Polyphonic Text

In the third phase of my investigation I want not to oppose but to add
another vision of the biblical text with the intention of correcting the
first one somewhat. This new approach has important consequences for
the passage from the internal configuration of the text to its refigurative
effect on the self. This new vision of the text is still close to that of literary analysis in the sense that it places its emphasis on the genres to be
found within biblical poetics: narrative discourse, prescriptive discourse,
wisdom discourse, prophetic discourse, hymnic discourse, epistles, parables, and so on. But this approach differs from the preceding one on two
important points. First, the main emphasis is placed on the variety of
genres of discourse, rather than on the imaginative unity of the Bible, as
with a typological reading. Without going so far as slicing apart the text,
one begins, for example, by respecting the triadic structure of the
Hebrew canon—Torah, Prophets, Writings—and then, with James Barr
and Claus Westermann, stresses the absence of any single theological
center to the Hebrew Bible, contrary to the claims of such respectable
attempts at systematization as the theology of the covenant or even that
of the *Heilsgeschichte*. If a unity can be recognized in the Bible, it is that
of a polyphonic rather than a typological order.

The second feature by which this approach differs from the preceding
one shows why they are not hostile to each other. Whereas typological
unity is maintained on the pre- or hyper-metaphorical level of the text,
here articulations in terms of genres are raised to the rank of *theologoumena* through a fortuitous conjunction of a historical-critical type of
exegesis and biblical theology. Northrop Frye would perhaps say that this
way of articulating the biblical domain belies the metaphorical style of
biblical discourse. This is true. But, as I said in opening, it is by way of
the many modes of modernity and with the language appropriate to this
modernity that we attempt to recover something of the significance of
biblical literature. However off-center this significance may be in relation
to the modes of discourse appropriate to our age, this significance
remains a significance for us, however modern we may be. And, in fact,

our search for appropriate *theologoumena* is itself displaced and decentered in relation to past theological constructions imposed on the Bible by our way of asking questions, whether on the anthropological, cosmological, or theological plane. *Theologoumena* are what we shall articulate, but ones governed by language games that are no longer our own, even if they carry familiar names like narrative, prescriptive, and the like. Therefore these *theologoumena* do not resemble the speculations of theological discourse with an argumentative, or even demonstrative, claim, such as that God exists, is omnipotent, absolutely good, the first and last cause, and so forth.

The principal benefit of this new approach for our investigation into the self fashioned by scripture is that it places the eventual unity of the biblical canon beyond what I have above called its imaginative unity. At best, this unity will be a polyphonic unity. This kind of polysemy, which is complementary to the typological unity of the bible, will be reflected in an equally polysemic production of the figures of the responsive self. However, it is initially in the work of naming God that this polyphony of *theologoumena* attached to the various literary genres finds expression, before finding an echo on the plane of the responsive self. The unity of this naming is what first carried over into the secret and silence of the fact that none of the literary genres taken one at a time fully captures this Name.

For example, for a purely narrative perspective, God is the metahero of a metahistory, which encompasses the myths of creation, the legends of the patriarchs, an epic of liberation, wandering, and conquest, a quasi historiography of kings and reigns. God is spoken of here in the third person, as well as in the sense of a superagent or a supercharacter. This narrative naming gives rise to what Gerhard von Rad called a "theology of traditions," which he opposed globally to a "theology of prophecies." God is designated obliquely through the founding events in which the interpreting community recognizes itself inaugurated, instituted, and rooted. In this respect, for Christians the naming of God in the resurrection narratives of the New Testament agrees with that found in the narratives of deliverance in the Old Testament. God is the one who recalled Christ from the dead. Here too God is designated by the transcendence of the founding events in relation to the ordinary course of history.

In the prophetic writings, on the contrary, God is signified as the voice of the Other, behind the voice of the prophet. God is presented in the first person as the one who calls the prophet, who himself speaks in the first person. I return to this theme in my next closing lecture from the point of view of the mission that is implied here. Here I shall confine myself to emphasizing another aspect of the situation, namely, that God is named in a double first person, as the word of another in the prophet's word. It was this model that was, so to speak, hypostatized in those Christian theologies that identified inspiration and revelation, on the model of the double voice of prophecy. But in this way an essential dialectic between the narrative third person and the prophetic first person is overlooked. In this dialectic there is a constant interchange between the pronominal positions. On the one side, for example, narrators do not hesitate to place in God's mouth words taken as equivalent to God's thoughts. These "citations" are equivalent to the prophetic utterances. Conversely, the prophets refer to events, but in another way than the one used by narrators, the collectors of traditions. The prophets have a direct grasp on the imminence of catastrophic events that threaten the very existence of the community. Even more important, the announcement of these events undercuts from within the false security engendered by the recitation of the past. The tension between narration and prophecy engenders a paradoxical understanding of history, as founded on memory yet threatened by prophecy.

I would like to have more time to take up other tensions and other dialectics, such as between the Torah, on the one hand, and the pair narration/prophecy, on the other, both of which are concerned about past or coming events. Let me just note that the gift of the law is in its way a recounted event, while the law in turn gives every narrative an ethical color to the extent that they are narratives of obedience and disobedience. In relation to prophecy, the law is presupposed by the word of judgment; but it is a new law, inscribed on our hearts, that the prophets of the return from exile proclaim, thereby bringing about a tension between an ethics based on prophecy and one based on the traditional prescriptions.

I shall not speak here of what the wisdom writings or even more the Psalms bring to this unfolding of the literary genres. I shall have an opportunity to do so in my next lecture under the rubric of the response of biblical humanity to the call that stems from the narratives of deliverance and settlement, the prophecies of misfortune and liberation, and the multifaceted legislation placed under the emblematic name of Moses. Here I want instead to place the accent on the polyphonic character that results from this interweaving of multiple literary genres. This completes, without contradicting, the kind of imaginative unity that typology assures to the incredible diversity of the writings that make the Bible a library rather than a simple—a relatively simple—poem, like the *Iliad* or the *Odyssey*, or something more simple like Greek tragedy. What makes this complex unity a polyphony is the unique naming of God that takes place from text to text and that circulates among all the forms of discourse whose most visible differences as regards literary structure I have pointed to.

God, we have to say, is named differently in the narration that recounts, the prophecy that speaks in his name, in the prescription that designates him as the source of the imperative, in the wisdom that seeks him as the meaning of meaning, and in the hymn that calls out to him in the second person. This is why the word *God* cannot be understood as a philosophical concept, even that of Being, whether we take this in the medieval sense or following Heidegger. The word *God* says more than the word *Being* because it presupposes the whole context of narratives, prophecies, laws, wisdom writings, psalms, etc. What then does it signify that is of importance to the problematic of selfhood? Two things, it seems to me. On the one hand, the referent God is intended by convergence of all these partial discourses, inasmuch as it expresses the circulation of meaning among all those forms of discourse wherein God is named. On the other hand, the referent God is also the sign of the incompleteness of all the discourses of faith marked as they are by the finitude of human understanding. It is thus both the common aim of all these discourses and the vanishing point exterior to each and every one of them.

From the first perspective, a polyphony of figures of the self can respond to the polyphony of genres. For the second perspective, it is an always deferred unity that corresponds to the unnamable Name.

Let us follow the first of these paths to conclude the present step in our investigation centered on the polyphonic structure of the Bible based on an analysis in terms of literary genres.

The passage from the polyphony of literary genres to the eventual polysemy of figures of selfhood is made easier if we shift the accent from the literary genres as such to the *theologoumena* that can be set forth by a biblical theology, which unlike systematic or dogmatic theology, stays closely attentive to the internal structures of the biblical text. What characterizes these *theologoumena* is that they all imply in their innermost signification a type of *response* on human beings' part. Here we have a note-worthy difference from the earlier literary analysis, where the closure of the text on itself imposed a kind of extrinsic aspect to the mimetic relation that goes from the internal structures of the text to the dispositions of the audience. The *theologoumena*, on the contrary, present a dialogical structure in that they confront the words and acts of God with the response they demand from human beings. This dialogical structure is, ultimately, the only guiding thread for exegesis that rejects the idea of one theological center (and perhaps finds no attraction in the imaginative unity produced by a typological reading).

An example of this kind of approach can be found in Claus Westermann's little book *What Does the Old Testament Say About God?* which attempts to group the various symbolic expressions relating to God around four major themes or schemata, each of which calls for a human counterpart, no longer outside the text, but implied in the very signification of what is said in this way about God.[8] Westermann describes four such themes. First, there is the God who saves, that is, who delivers from external danger. The theology of the *Heilsgeschichte*, which was so dominant in biblical theology earlier in this century, was constructed on the basis of this theme to the detriment of the other schemata. Second is the God who blesses, that is, who dispenses the gift of creation, of fertility, of the promised land, of an existence full of meaning. Third is the God who punishes, that is, who declares himself to be against those who have transgressed the commandments and the specific laws of the community of Israel. Finally, there is the merciful God who suffers because of his own anger, repents, and pardons. Each of these themes offers a dialogical scheme, as can be verified if we take as our guide the literary categories we have already distinguished. One or the other of these themes is predominant, but in each case balanced by a specific response on the human side, whether it be a question of an individual or the elect people, or of humanity as a whole.

For example, to the great narratives centered on the exodus, which valorize the figure of the God who saves, correspond a confession of praise, as we can see in the central text of Deut. 26:5-11, which von Rad places at the center of the Hebraic *Heilsgeschichte*, and which ends with a sacrificial vow as a sign of this praise. What is more, at the very heart of the narrative of deliverance that this passage from Deuteronomy celebrates, it is said of God that he had seen the distress of his people and had heard their cries, and that it was to this lamentation that he replied with a series of liberating acts.

In the narratives of the conquest and settlement of the land, which follow chronologically, and in the prescriptions addressed to a people tied to the promised and given land, it is the figure of the God who blesses that predominates. To it corresponds a soul that itself blesses, in the twofold sense of the Hebrew *bērak*, which means to give thanks for the creative generosity thanks to which the self knows itself forgiven. Within the overall narrative structure constituted by the Deuteronomic historiography, it is the figure of God the judge that dominates. What corresponds to him on the human side is a global attitude of repentance and penitence. As a result, the narration finds itself wholly impregnated by a condemnatory judgment, whose dialogical structure, however implicit it may be, is constantly taken for granted. The reading of this history works like a warning and an appeal.

As for those texts stemming from the prescriptive genre, they are either commandments—that is, simply prohibitions such as: "you shall have no other god before me," "you shall not kill"—or complex laws of the form "if someone does this or that which is wrong, such and such a punishment is to be applied." In both cases, the meaning attached to the word that teaches, the *torah*, is inseparable from the response of obedience or disobedience that goes along with it.

In turn, the condemnation pronounced by the prophets is God's response to the lack of human response that constitutes the apostasy, which is intermingled from the very beginning with the history of salvation, as we can see in the episode of the golden calf, which is so strongly denounced by the prophets of judgment and woe, from Amos and Hosea to Isaiah, Ezekiel, and Jeremiah. But this prophetic word itself calls for a response, whether it announces a judgment or makes a promise: a response of repentance to the judgment of condemnation, a response of confidence and hope turned toward the new future opening beyond all disaster through the promise of pardon and re-creation, a response that blesses a God who will again bless us after having saved and punished.

In this way, the human response to be found in the Hebrew Bible is surprisingly varied. The Psalms, in this regard, are the document where we find brought together, brought to language—to the language of prayer—and articulated according to canonical forms, innumerable nuances of this multiform response. The space of meaning thereby articulated unfolds between the poles of the lament and praise—the praise of one who has been delivered, pardoned, blessed with life, enjoying life in the community and the moments of joy that interrupt the bounds of a generally impoverished existence; the lament of one in peril who calls on a God who saves, the lament of the sinner faced with a God who judges, the lament of someone afflicted with misfortune who calls on God for deliverance and compassion. We should perhaps add memory to this pair of lament and praise, the well-known "remember" of Deuteronomy, which itself replies to a "forgetting" wherein the prophets discern both the cause and the effect of the great apostasy, that internal danger more harmful than any external danger, whether it be the captivity in Egypt or even exile in Babylon, to which responds the God who saves. Forgetting God expresses the dialogical structure of sin as such, which remains, even in its depths, an experience with God.

Limit Expressions

As the last step in our exploration of the relations between the book and mirror, it remains to justify the second perspective opened by the polyphony of literary genres as naming God. The referent "God," I have said, is not only the index of the mutual belonging together of the origi- nary forms of the discourse of faith, it is also the mark of their incom- pleteness.

What prevents our transforming the polyphonic naming of God into knowledge is that God is designated at the same time as the one who communicates and the one who withdraws. In this regard, the episode of the burning bush in Exod. 3:13-15 has a special importance. The tra- dition has rightly called this episode the revelation of the divine name. But this Name is precisely an unnamable name. Whereas outside of Israel, knowing the name of a god was to have power over him, the name confided to Moses is instead one that human beings cannot in fact pro- nounce, that is, submit to the mercy of their language. Moses asked, "'But if they [the children of Israel] ask what is his [the god of the ances- tors] name, what shall I say to them?' God then said to Moses, 'I AM WHO I AM.' And he added, 'This is how you shall addresses the children of Israel, "I AM" has sent me to you.'" The appellation Yahweh—He is—is not a name that defines but rather one that points to the gesture of deliver- ance. Indeed the text continues as follows. "God also said to Moses,

'Thus you shall say to the children of Israel: Yahweh, the God of your ancestors, the God of Abraham, the God of Isaac, and the God of Jacob, has sent me to you. This is the name I shall bear forever, with which all future generations shall call upon me.'" Far therefore from the declaration "I AM WHO I AM" authorizing a positive ontology capable of crowning the narrative naming along with all the other namings, it protects the secret of the for-itself of God. And this secret, in return, refers us to the narrative naming, signified by the names of Abraham, Isaac, and Jacob, and, by degrees, to the others as well.

The text of Exodus finds an echo in the New Testament. Northrop Frye would say that the declaration "I AM WHO I AM" is a type that finds its antitype in an expression that the evangelists attach to Jesus' preaching, namely, the expression *the kingdom of God*. Here we have the limit expression of a reality that escapes all description. The kingdom is signified only by the kind of linguistic transgression that we see at work in the parables, in some proverbs, and in some of the paradoxes of eschatological discourse. This indirect character of naming God is particularly noticeable in the parables of Jesus. As tales, they are just small stories with a metaphorical import: The kingdom of God is like . . . . But it is not the parable that introduces into the plot an implausible, surprising, disproportionate, even scandalous aspect—a grain of wheat that produces a hundredfold, a mustard seed that grows into an immense tree, a worker hired at the last minute who is paid the same as the one who had worked all day, an invited guest who is thrown out because he was not wearing a wedding garment, etc. Through this kind of extravagance, the literal sense is borne toward an ungraspable metaphorical meaning. The extraordinary breaks through the ordinary and points beyond the narrative.

The same transgression of meaning can be observed in the eschatological proclamations where Jesus makes use of forms of discourse common to his day regarding last things in order to subvert such calculations: "The coming of the Kingdom of God cannot be observed and no one can say, here it is, there, for the kingdom is among you." A similar transgression affects the ordinary sense of proverbs, which is to guide life in typical circumstances. Paradoxes and hyperbole dissuade the listener from forming a coherent project and from giving his existence some continuous totality. A paradox: whoever tries to save his life will lose it, and he who loses it will keep it. Hyperbole: if someone strikes you on the right cheek, turn your other to him as well. If someone wishes to bring you to trial and take your tunic, give him your cloak as well. If someone asks for one measure of grain, give him two. Just as the parable, submitted to the law of extravagance, makes the extraordinary stand forth within the ordinary, the proverb, submitted to a law of paradox and hyperbole, reorients by disorienting.

If now we bring together what has been called the unnamable Name indicated by the episode of the burning bush, and the kind of transgression of the usual forms in the parables through the concentrated use of extravagance, a new discursive category unfolds, that of limit expressions. This is not a supplementary form of discourse, even if the parable as such does constitute an autonomous mode of the expression of faith. It is rather a matter of an indication, a modification, that no doubt can affect all forms of discourse by a kind of passage to the limit. If the case of the parable is exemplary, it is because it brings together narrative structure, metaphoric process, and limit expression. In this way, it constitutes an abbreviated form of naming God. Through its narrative structure, it recalls the initial rootedness of the language of faith in narrative. Through its metaphoric process, it makes manifest the poetic character (in the sense already discussed) of the language of faith overall. Finally, in joining metaphor and limit expression, it provides the very matrix of theological language insofar as it conjoins analogy and negation in the way of eminence: God is like . . . , God is not. . . .

This latter comment leads me to express a certain reserve regarding the use of the expression "Wholly Other" to designate God. It served as the emblem of what has been called "dialectical" theology. But, in one sense, it is not sufficiently dialectic, inasmuch as it does not take into account the pulsation among the manifestations of the Name by way of and through the polyphony of kinds of discourse (narratives, laws, prophecies, etc.) and the withdrawal of the Name beyond language, as is borne witness to by the episode of the burning bush and the extravagance of the parables. Yes, for Christians, this pulsation takes on different senses in the Old and the New Testaments, but without a real break between the two testaments. The Old Testament says one thing concerning God, that he is One. Nevertheless, this affirmation has two sides: that of the unnamable—I am the first and I am the last (Isa. 44:6); but also that of the polyphonic unity among all the names of God: God is the same, whether he saves, blesses, judges, takes pity, etc. The continuity between the two testaments is assured in this regard by the typological bond that holds that together. On the side of the manifestation of the name, the resurrection narrative echoes that of the exodus; on the side of the withdrawal of the name, the limit expression concerning the kingdom of God in the parables of Jesus responds and corresponds to what we can retrospectively call the limit expressions of the episode of the Burning Bush. The "newness" of the New Testament is, of course, undeniable. It is summed up in the function of the *center* that the poem of Christ confers on the poem of God. For the impulse toward the center is what, for a Christian reading of the Bible, is at work within the "imaginative unity" of the Bible. The New Testament identifies this center with the person of Christ.[9] Yet this identification in no way abolishes the dialectic of the manifestation and withdrawal of the name. Instead, it intensifies it, to the extent that the kingdom that Jesus preaches is the kingdom *of God*, the resurrection is an act *of God*, and the Jesus of history—as known by way of the Christ of faith—has been interpreted by the confessing community as "the man determined in his existence by the God that he proclaims," as Wolfhart Pannenberg has put it. It is this reference from Christ to God that intensifies without abolishing the dialectic of manifestation and withdrawal.

What results from this dialectic as regards the constitution of the responsive self? Readers of the Bible, I shall say again with Northrop Frye, are finally invited to identify themselves with the book that itself stems from the metaphorical identification between the Word of God and the person of Christ. Through this second-degree identification, readers are equally invited to "repeat"—in the Kierkegaardian sense of "repetition"—the pulsation between the withdrawal of the name and the quest for the center. What corresponds and conforms to the unity of God in the withdrawal of his name on the side of the self is the disappearance of the ego, the letting go of self: who seeks to save his life shall lose it and who loses it will keep it. As for the quest for a personal center, it can only reflect the always deferred "imaginative unity" conveyed by the withdrawal of the Name.

Translated by David Pellauer

Notes

1. See "The Summoned Subject in the School of the Narratives of the Prophetic Vocation," in Paul Ricoeur, *Figuring the Sacred: Religion, Narrative, and Imagination*, ed. Mark Wallace, trans. David Pellauer (Minneapolis: Fortress Press, 1995), 262–75.

2. I adopt the expression "responsive self" from H. Richard Niebuhr's *The Responsive Self* (New York: Harper & Row, 1963).

3. See Jean Greisch, *L'Age Herméneutique de la Raison* (Paris: Cerf, 1985).

4. See David Tracy, *The Analogical Imagination* (New York: Crossroad, 1981), esp. part 1, chaps. 3 and 4: "The Classic" and "Interpreting the Religious Classic."

5. Northrop Frye, *The Great Code: The Bible and Literature* (New York: Harcourt Brace Jovanovich, 1981).

6. In this respect, I believe that Frye is correct in pointing out that the Gospels themselves are more concerned about the correspondence of the events that they recount with this or that prophecy from the Old Testament than in showing the way to some verification of these events by methods external to the text. The Gospel writers seem to have taken particular care to cut off the referential points of their texts, to the point of sealing from within the testimony that they bear to the person of Jesus as the Christ (see Frye, *Great Code*, 42).

7. "Kerygma is a mode of rhetoric, though it is rhetoric of a special kind. It is like all rhetoric a mixture of the metaphorical and 'existential' or concerned but, unlike practically all other forms of rhetoric, it is not an argument disguised by figuration. It is the vehicle of what is traditionally called revelation, a word I use because it is traditional and I can think of no better one" (ibid., 29).

8. Claus Westermann, *What Does the Old Testament Say About God?* (Atlanta: John Knox, 1979).

9. See Frye, *Great Code*, 76-77, 137-38.

Conversation

Paul Ricoeur
David Pellauer, DePaul University
John McCarthy, Loyola University Chicago

Day 1

MCCARTHY: The Bible and Theology project is located at the intersection of three issues: Bible, theology, and the "self." In our discussions we have focused on the topic of "the whole and divided self." What brought us to this topic were the different evaluations that people gave to the self as "whole" and "fragmented." Some saw integrity, a wholeness of the self, as an ideal, as a positive value; others saw the issues of fragmentation, plurality, the divided self, in a very different light. There was a sense that this problem of philosophical, theological, and cultural anthropology was important; at the same time there was a sense that the plurality of texts, ethical options, and theologies inside the biblical material might touch positively on the consideration of the contemporary issues of the whole and divided self. That is what brought us to the questions that our group has discussed. In our discussions what has most divided us are methodological issues. People trained in historical-critical methodologies were suspicious of theological methods and observations; likewise theologians were critical of the self-imposed historical-critical limits and the consequent treatment of biblical texts. That is a brief synopsis of the background of our interests.

I think that the place to begin may be with the question of imagination as it relates to interpreting biblical texts, particularly the relation of imagination to ethics.

221

RICOEUR: But is the question of the self a question about the biblical texts or is it a modern problematic? Do we construe a question and then look for a coherent answer, so to say, displayed in the biblical texts? On the one hand, we have to take into account that we have to do with a culture in which there is no problem of the self as such. Maybe for the prophets; we have strong personalities, and they deserve to be understood in relationship with vocation, strong requirements, threats of a dangerous history, for example, in the case of the exile and the prophets of return. Or we may consider stories, narratives, where character is construed in storytelling. This is a different approach. Here I think of Robert Alter's *Poetics of Biblical Narrative*, where the leading thread was the imperative of history met by the category of the recalcitrant. I like that very much. Here we have short stories, long stories, patriarchs; and the leading thread is the literary genre. I have tried to think along these lines very often. It is difficult to have to do with these strong personalities, these characters in stories, these more or less historical characters like David and Solomon, these more or less fictional characters like Abraham. So I do not see any survey about this problem of the self in the biblical corpus. What you have is the question, "Who am I?" And then in the New Testament you have personalities like Peter. It is very interesting to see the betrayal as well as his conflict with Jesus because he wanted a messiah without suffering. But it is always scattered, dealing each time and in a new way with a certain kind of character, a certain kind of situation, historical or otherwise. I don't see how we could construe something coherent except by borrowing here or there, some important or interesting figure, related to the questions that we raise. So in fact it is more *we* who are raising the question.

McCARTHY: We realized that from the start. None of us approached the biblical material as if it would give a coherent perspective on the modern problem of the self. The studies that I had sent you from our group have not focused on what the text of the Bible can teach us in a unified sense about the self. We have focused on how various authors and readers in the history of interpretation have appropriated a sense of self through the questions that they bring to the text. So, for instance, the work on Abelard and Otloh or Paul. This is precisely a question of the reception of the text. But let's focus on the issue of the contemporary reader of the Bible and the kind of problems that our own fascination with the self, particularly in the West, brings to biblical interpretation.

RICOEUR: In this way we have to be clear about what kind of expectations we bring to these texts as well as the relationship between imagination and ethics. For my part, I would both connect imagination and ethics as well as oppose them. And this is because imagination is a kind of "thought experiment." The sphere of imagination is open, and it is the role of fiction to generate the figures that belong to the field of thought experiments. Yesterday I was discussing that with some friends, saying that in the Bible we have some paradigmatic figures, but not significative figures. We have Abraham presenting his wife as his sister, and Jacob cheating his father, and so on. But these are not ethical models. We have a kind of laboratory of this extraordinary field of possibilities of a way of dealing with situations. In fact *Soi-même comme un autre* is built on the hypothesis that the problem of narrative identity taken in terms of the imagination is an open problem. You may try different configurations, different ways of plotting character, but when you come to ethics we have to take a stand. The opposition between selfhood in terms of promise and ways of keeping a promise is the exact opposite of opening the field and keeping the field open in free imagination. So in a sense there is a contest between imagination and ethics. Nothing is forbidden for imagination, no censorship, but we have to take a stand.

I see that you have had a discussion with Charles Taylor. His notion of "strong evaluation" is very interesting. We have to take a stand, to orient ourselves in what he calls a moral field.

PELLAUER: Let me intervene on this. It is very interesting that Taylor's approach is exactly the reverse of *Soi même comme un autre*. You end up with the ethical self and he starts with the ethical precisely in order to raise the questions. I wonder what you make of that? Is it just two different approaches?

RICOEUR: His problem was the source of the self; it was the ethical problem from the very beginning. His adversary is the claim that a neutral anthropology is possible. In fact, humans immediately have preferences, moral claims, and commitments, and then the problem is to find a hierarchy. If I understand his notion of "sources" as a deep level under the superficial level of strong evaluation, we have, so to say, some predominant ethical interpretation and, for him, there are finally three sources: the Judeo-Christian, the Enlightenment, and the romantic. And he draws political consequences from that, saying that a modern democracy functions to the extent that there is some overlapping between these. So it is very close to John Rawls's notion of overlapping consensus. Taylor wrote to me saying that he had not known what I had done, and that he would take the issue of the sameness of identity and selfhood into account. His problem was with the second stratification of a system of motivations, with the notion of "source" as the basic and ultimate resource.

McCARTHY: In the way that you have described the relationship between imagination and ethics, with imagination opening up possibilities and ethics becoming the place of promise, of limiting and choosing possibilities, does that suggest that the relationship of ethics to imagination is only the relationship of limit to possibility?

RICOEUR: No, it's a kind of polarity, but what is interesting is what is in between. As Peter Kemp has shown also, our moral choices are supported by models, by stories, so, therefore, the narrative furnishes the ethics with concrete models of evaluation. For, to that extent, most stories have ethical stakes. As someone has said, it is like a square: life, death, love, hate; if you take the definition of *mythos* in Aristotle, it has to do with people better than we are, or worse than we are, or equal. The evaluation, the moral evaluation, belongs to the very notion of a character because the experiment is precisely in the ethical field. It's a way of combining, a combinatory system between death, life, love, and hatred.

PELLAUER: Can you expand on that in light of the distinction you make between the ethical and the moral. Is what is at stake really at the ethical level or is it both the ethical and the moral that come into play?

RICOEUR: No, I never said that some problems belong to ethics and some belong to the moral realm. It's a difference of acts of emphasis in ethics, to my mind. For ethics the objective is, How should I like to live? And then we have to do with the moral problems when we are confronted with the prohibition, the negative comment, and so on. But it is very difficult to distinguish the wish from the imperative, and so we are always more or less on the borderline between our deepest wishes and what leads to the good life, the virtues, the paradigms or habits that are supposed to lead to some form of the good life. But the imperative immediately shows up; there is something imperative looming in the wish. Even with Aristotle we are in the middle. But my claim for the sake of ethics is in fact a protest against an overemphasis on mediation, duty, and so on. There is something more fundamental than duty, that "you

ought." We are beings of desire, and I praise Aristotle for having pro-
tected this line of desire. The opposition between desire and duty presented by Kant has broken morality from the social, except when he
speaks of the good will.

PELLAUER: An issue here that brings us back to the biblical question is
that the problem of evil always informs your more recent work on ethics
and morals. In English, analytic ethics that is not a discussion; evil is
always beyond ethics. Would you say that the religious traditions, the
biblical materials, are a better source for reflection on that than the
philosophical traditions?

RICOEUR: Yes, but the problem is to what extent the legislative corpus of
the biblical material forms its center. This is the point that was in fact
raised by the synagogues after the separation between the church and the
synagogue. The rabbinic traditions emphasized written Torah as legislative more than narrative, but you have the *halakah* as a work, and *haggadah*; narrative has never been completely overshadowed. Even in
modern times there is a distinction between Hasidic, which is more on
the side of *haggadah*, the narrative and the hymnic, and rabbinic, the side
of Torah, the legislative, the interpretation of legislative texts—why
should we do this and that. Also Midrash is an interpretive step between
Torah and the Talmud.

McCARTHY: Let me return to the question of ethics and imagination:
specifically the ethics involved in the kinds of questions that we bring to
the texts. A discussion of "the ethics of interpretation" has arisen in biblical circles in the recent past. It is a discussion that raises questions about
the place from which interpretation characteristically arises . . .

RICOEUR: Yes, but if we take biblical studies not as a university or academic task, but as teaching or preaching, then the problems are different.
Preaching is the place where the preacher is, on the one hand, bound by
the text—what text is a problem—but if we have a liturgical order, then a
great diversity of texts show up in time. It is very interesting. Then we
have this change of hues and colors. With the liturgical order of reading
the preacher is compelled not to say what he wants; he has to fight with
the text which leads us where he or she would not like to be lead. It is
then a kind of fight between the world of the text and the world of the
reader, a conflict of two texts. We may have a certain structure of expectation, but it is confronted with a loose structure of propositions that are

coming from the text. All of this is more or less contained by a liturgical order of presentation of the texts.

Last Sunday I attended an excellent sermon. The pastor talked about the problem of birth. He started from the story of one of the two wives of the father of Simeon. The barren wife cries and her prayer is heard. She says, "I give my life to the Lord because he has been given to me." The preacher was very good because he said the problem of barrenness is now often solved by medicine, but we have a problem of barrenness and sterility yet. We have to look at the different kinds of sterility in life, even in those who are unemployed, so there is the sterility of work, all kinds of sterility, barrenness. There is also the problem of lack, and of lack in the religious life. There is a desire to be delivered from a lack, but the gift must be given in time. So it is an interesting way of dealing with the narrative text, using it as an ethical teaching. What would be the analogical situation in our moral life to a problem that is no longer ours because of the problem of a lack of children?

PELLAUER: It is interesting to note that in the essays that you have done with André LaCoque on this question of historical-critical understanding, you have taken a stand that the reader has a right to take a different text from the canon even when historical scholarship has established a hierarchy of texts or quotations. The reader can read texts together because they are generative, productive, even though they may not have been historically linked.

RICOEUR: But also the effect of the canonical order is that it norms the historical order of the production of the texts. Therefore it is a kind of synchronic order, and we have the right to proceed backwards and forwards. I should say that the only constraint would be then the liturgical conditions with the canonical reservations of the synchronic order of texts. The texts are, so to say, extracted from their *Sitz im Leben*, in word, then in text, then in life, and then we have a series of displacements in the text. I belong to a tradition that has interpreted canonical texts. The texts make sense in a canon because they have nourished varied traditions of reading and interpreting and preaching and applications to life.

PELLAUER: Are you pushing here the importance of the liturgical setting having priority over the reflective, historical, theological . . . ?

RICOEUR: Why? Let's say we know what kind of situation a character belonged to. Then I may have an analogical relationship in my own situation to what this character had to his or her own situation. So this kind of analogy forms the terms of the situation and it includes the historical-critical method. We need to know what situation this character belonged to and how he dealt with the situation. It is an analogy of situations and response to situations. This has more to do with practical wisdom. People have often read in my ethics only the two chapters, "ethics" and "morals." But with me there is a third one which is more important—practical wisdom. This is *prudentia*. It has more to do with prudential judgments than with ethical claims or moral rules. For people deal in concrete situations. It is something similar to the situation that we have in historical judgment or in judiciary judgment, namely, to answer the singular situation properly. When we say "imagination and ethics," I need to say, "What do you mean by ethics?" Is it the sense that I give to ethics as something more fundamental or what I take more seriously as the most decisive moment, the moment of concrete decision in the typical situations. This is the *phroenetic*. The "typical situation" is interesting because, as paradigmatic, it is both singular and historically meaningful. It generates an attempt at repetition, in the sense of the German *Nachfolge*. The Germans distinguish between *Nachahmung*, "imitation," and *Nachfolge*, "following." It is a question of *Nachfolge*, not *Nachahmung*. Not repetitious imagination, but inventive imagination.

MCCARTHY: This seems close to the role of decision found in several earlier existential theologies. Are there differences? Where do the differences lie between *phroenesis* and the kind of decision making in unique situation that is part of dialectical theologies?

RICOEUR: I don't see a strong difference. There are historically similar situations that are still very specific and unique, but paradigmatic. This is not the same as law which claims to be immutable. We have to look at something that generates history, that generates historical events, inventiveness, in accordance with this spirit of decision. This is where analogy lies. There will be a certain connection between imagination and ethics; imagination opens the field for some daring behaviors; then they raise the question, Should I act in accordance with this way of dealing with the situation? Then the question is raised, How would I behave in this same situation? So it is not only a moral to follow but a question to reopen by habits, let's say. I am opening a closed, habitual way. This was the problem of Kierkegaard, the problem of the exception, the *Ausnahme*. I was thinking here also of the specific way of providing the models we have in the parables. Twenty years ago I worked on that—the extravagance—how extravagance reorients what has been disoriented, so this is a tricky way of thinking. And also the commands that cannot be obeyed—literally, like to give my shirt, to love my enemies—no politics could be based on that, but the disruptive function is also a part of the structure.

We must discuss concrete cases, either medical or judicial. We cannot speak in general. Then, what is more, we find what would be exemplary in some singular decisions which, in spite of their singularity, provide exemplarity. Exemplarity is not normativity. Exemplarity has something historical. It connects the singularity and universality in a kind of dialectic. Because history is not only the change but also what endures, so there is the capacity to endure, duration, something distinct from change. So I have to do not only with the alternative, either change or changelessness, but also with what can endure, support. But, I think that I must go . . .

Day 2

McCARTHY: Can we talk about the category of liturgy that you raised yesterday? In one of your articles you suggest that liturgy is the place of the purest appropriation of the text.

RICOEUR: I do not use liturgy at all in the sense of ritual but in the sense of the ritualization of the order of reading. I wanted to say that it is within the framework of the situation of preaching that there may be an appropriation of separate small units of texts. But in the liturgical year you have a complete cycle of readings. You have, for example, in some monasteries, 150 Psalms read in one week. This cyclical time of reading is for me very interesting. And the fact that there is a certain agreement between different confessions for people to have the same order of reading on the same day in different churches so that they are all preaching about it—and it is a text which they have not chosen because they like it, but because it is its turn to be read—I like that. Many texts are used in the ritual of the church, the ritual or reading. By liturgy we could mean different things. It is the common good of a community and, so to say, a votive of identifying a community as a community because the whole of the members of the community do the same thing at the same time.

PELLAUER: Can a community read? You go back and forth between "I read a text" and "a community reads a text."

RICOEUR: I don't see why we should raise a special problem because all communities raise the same problem. On the one hand, it is always greater than the individuals; on the other hand there is more to addition than the sum. I think that Husserl solved the problem in the Fifth Cartesian Meditation when he said that through intersubjectivity there is a kind of rectification of the link which generates what he calls personalities of a higher rank. We have to say that with the problem of a shared memory, a collective memory, only individuals have memories but nevertheless we may say that they share a memory, and that commemoration, public commemoration, provides a kind of rectified ritual through this shared memory. We may say that ultimately there are only individuals who evoke this or that event of the past.

I was never impressed by this so-called antinomy of individual and holism. Holism is too often thought of by a mere organicist comparison. An organ which is constituted by cells has no distinct sense that is different than the cells themselves. So the organism comparison is very dangerous. I think Hegel discards it very forcefully. He has the same problem when he rejects the conventional social pact according to the contractualist tradition. It is more than a contract but less than an organism. So in between you have this bond of community as an interweaving of subjectivity and individuality.

MCCARTHY: Back to the issue of liturgy again. In one article you identify tradition, authority and liturgy as what distinguishes a mundane from a sacred narrative. Do these topics have any effect on your understanding of revelation? When you wrote your article on the "Hermeneutics of Revelation" you approached the issue through a consideration of the genres of revelation and a critique of knowledge that leads to hubris. Do these topics of tradition, authority, and liturgy also have a role in understanding biblical texts as revelational?

RICOEUR: Too much in the same question! To start with the concept of tradition: I have always had a discrepancy in the use of the term with Gadamer, for instance. He was speaking of the authority of tradition. First, I insist on the fact that what makes the legitimacy of the concept of tradition is that I am not the starting point, that I receive as a debt, as a deposit, something that has been set, interpreted, believed before me. So there is the element of indebtedness. As for authority, I continue this triadic sequence of exteriority, superiority, interiority, which constitutes the structure of authority that precedes me, that I am not the master of. But the term "revelation" has been reduced to "inspiration" as though someone were speaking to the ear. So it is very crude. Sometimes I try speaking of some basic narrative, like those of the exodus, saying that these are revealed in the sense that they are revealing of a capacity to generate the paradigmatic, of connecting singularity with communicability which is characteristic of the paradigmatic. It then becomes a model of reading history, of reading my own life. The exodus story has been used in this capacity to generate an indefinite number of exemplifications. Before being revealed, it is revealing. We call "revealed" the power of being revelatory, in the sense of generating a capacity of following. But if we take so many stories in the Old Testament—they are exemplary but not edifying . . . this is very interesting..

McCARTHY: What about a difficult story like Genesis 22, the narrative of Abraham and Isaac?

RICOEUR: Precisely it requires an indefinite reflection and many ways of dealing with it. It is interesting to see that there are so many interpretations in the Talmud because they did not like it, and it is against the Torah. But Kierkegaard tried to say that this is the limit—testing the obedience. Maybe the Pauline interpretation follows this. But here it is very important to read good critical literature. What did this story have to do with the prohibition of killing children and so on? The knife is stopped, but it is an absurd obedience. We don't know why it is this way. I have great admiration for the learned people who kept these stories which were embarrassing for them, so it is a kind of modesty for the text transmitted through generation to generation. We don't know what to do with them, but we tell them, and then it's a problem of indefinite reflection. There is a paradox of context for this kind of story: we cannot say that it is a law which says we should do such and such, since it is a suspension of law, or a breaking of a law, or a limit of a law. But you have also the idea that the possession, to the extent that it is renounced, is given twice, twice given. Because excessive relationship to the son is overcome, then that son is given anew. You may try to make sense of the text by placing it among other texts. But there is also respect for those who respected the text by telling it in spite of their own reluctance.

PELLAUER: You said on a text like this that it is important to read the critical literature.

RICOEUR: Even to narrow the inadequate mess of sociological interpretations which flatten the text, to say that it is the end of sacrifice, the last one. Maybe, maybe, but there are many layers of reading here. Here we may follow the principle of the four layers of interpretation. Even if we make a graft from this sociological interpretation to the last sacrifice which has stopped sacrifice to mean the prohibition which retains what is prohibited. Some psychoanalysts would say that, that the criminal move must be retained, preserved, in the prohibition itself.

PELLAUER: What about liturgy as a ritualization of reading? Would you extend that to critical reading? It seems to me as a scholar we read in very regular ways—in a way to criticize the text—to read from a distanced perspective.

RICOEUR: The big difference is that within a school of critical reading it is a personal act. The element of sharing is not decisive in a critical stance: it is more self-distancing. There is a very interesting question here concerning preaching. Preaching cannot be a way of merely retelling the story. It is also an adjustment to a new situation. We spoke yesterday of the analogical. In order first to understand what was specific in the ancient, original situation, and which is no longer mine, what was specific to the situation—this is a critical reading. In that sense the critical distance is implied in the very act of overcoming it. So Gadamer is very good with what he calls *Abstand*, distance. And that comes from Schleiermacher, for whom cultural distance was the reason for hermeneutics. So the critical is implied in the recognition of distance. This may also be connected to what we said yesterday concerning the difference between "imitation" and "following." "Following" implies a critical distance, an overcoming of the critical distance, and then projection of an innovate response. I have spoken several times before about this relation of tradition and innovation.

McCARTHY: Does the idea of "bad imagination" or "bad conscience" play a role in this relation of tradition and innovation? I am thinking of H. R. Niebuhr's notion of "bad imagination" in his book *The Idea of Revelation*. Here the relation of tradition and innovation implies not only overcoming cultural and historical distance but possibly some other set of criteria.

RICOEUR: If I am right, the notion of "bad imagination" has a very peculiar history. Among Jewish theologians, during the time of the proposition of the Torah, there is an alternative to the history of the fall, so bad imagination occurs in Genesis 5, where men were deluded by bad imagination. And there was a Talmudic tradition developing the notion of bad imagination over against the idea of the fall. So it was structural. It was Niebuhr who used it, and I think he had just this in mind, this tradition of overcoming the origin of evil. It has a structural component, to follow in the wrong path, to be attracted—maybe it is a rough psychology of temptation. In Kierkegaard you have this idea of the sliding of consciousness toward evil, a certain fascination between compulsion and arbitrariness, a matter of complacency.

But this is more of an ethical category. In the field of interpretation this may shade over into misreading. What is interesting to evoke here is the controversy in the Pauline church. There was an anomic interpretation of the law—since we are no longer under the law we are allowed to do what we want. So it was a kind of misreading of the overcoming of the law. We say that we are not saved by the law, then there is a necessity to give a new interpretation of the law, and this comes about in a pedagogical sense. Among the reformers this was the famous discussion about the third use of the law. But it is a good example of misreading.

PELLAUER: Could we even say, the mis-imagination, close to the mis-imagination of the life of freedom under the Gospel?

RICOEUR: Anomie as opposed to treason. Before misreading there is something misleading. It is typical of the paradoxical saying that it calls for the creative imagination to apply it properly, in a kind of exploratory way, a tentative way.

McCARTHY: In the North American context the issue of slavery is often used to indicate some of the issues in this relation of tradition and innovation as well as in reading and mis-reading. In the nineteenth century, biblical passages, 1 Timothy for instance, were used to authorize slavery in the debates about abolition. A literal reading of scripture was used to support slavery.

RICOEUR: I think here of some of the arguments of Dutch theologians in the nineteenth century also concerning apartheid, saying that each species was created by God and that they must not be mixed with respect to the laws of nature. So this was a kind of natural theology, misplaced in human biology. But if I am right would not the contemporary exegete say that it was related to a period in which the proximate return of Christ made all moral ethics useless?

MCCARTHY: One issue under consideration in a Catholic context deals with the interpretation of scriptural texts in relation to priesthood and gender, with arguments being made against women becoming priests . . .

RICOEUR: They are very strange arguments. I understand that this was not in the habit of the church but besides that what arguments are there? That Jesus had not chosen women—but then the twelve were not priests.

PELLAUER: Let me raise a question about canonical presuppositions and critical reading here. I was struck that you need to bring in the critical, outside material to the text and what we know about it. In an article that you have written about the Song of Songs you talk about how, within the canonical presupposition, we have the right to use critical reading. At times at least one needs to bring outside material to the canonical text. How much can we do that? In effect, this is a question of the limits of the canon.

RICOEUR: Ah yes, it is an enigmatic question because there is something arbitrary, maybe something violent. There are hard conflicts, but at the same time it was more or less a recognition because there was always a canon. There were never isolated texts; they were in communities; and it was a kind of regulation of this inter-communitary recognition of what could be common that lead to "canons." So, in fact, we are not in front of one decision—that this is canonical—but it is a recognition of a long process, a kind of stabilization of the process. So what is the force behind that? Precisely a kind of intertextuality, I think, a very primitive use of intertextuality, but already—this is what von Rad has shown—as a first intertextual relationship between the narrative traditions of Exodus and the legislative traditions of Sinai. There is now doubt about this Yahwist unity, but nevertheless we take that as typical of the intertextual relationship. And also of the fact that most exegetes acknowledge that nothing was written in its final state that we could read before the Persian period, the fifth to the fourth century. Then there was a gathering of traditions of different periods and also different kinds. It is interesting to see that this was already a kind of intertextuality, both in a diachronic and synchronic order. And this crossing of the diachronic and synchronic is very interesting to the constitution of the canonical institution. But the idea of putting together typical myths of creation with a tradition's stories about patriarchs, and texts of a more historical kind, like the story of David, and to make a whole of that at different levels of historicity is very interesting. This was canonical only later, a way of reading several texts together. But also the fact that they have to choose in a kind of order when there must be a limit to the amount of texts. There is something very concrete here.

PELLAUER: How much right as interpreters do we have to continue this process, in your mind, to confront these biblical texts with outside material, whether they be contemporary materials, or rediscovered materials, or as David Tracy would say, other religious traditions today?

RICOEUR: We must not overemphasize the phenomenon of the canon, but we must also recognize that the canon belongs to a tradition. It has happened that there was a canon and that after that all texts are commentaries. So in our tradition we have canonical writings and commentaries. It is a structural tradition itself. In a sense we may reopen the canon, but for what purpose? We are not in the situation of having to do it; therefore as critical minds we are allowed to bring whatever we think for better understanding of the literature, to better understand why some texts have not been accepted. So, for instance, the reluctance of the early church and also the Hebrews, the Jews, when they closed their canon, either at Babylon or in exile somewhere, that they were reluctant concerning apocalyptic literature. We have a critical obligation not to reverse the canon, but to recognize that texts have been structured in that way. It is part of our instruction to understand the canon in these terms, because it has generated a tradition of reading and we belong to a certain tradition of interpretation that has been shaped by the fact that there is a canon. We are serving in a process to which the canonical belongs, as well as the ending of the canon. So when we accept to be situated in a certain stream of interpretation it belongs to this stream to have the delineation of the canon by the community.

PELLAUER: You would resist removing some things from the canon, some of the nonedifying exemplary stories?

RICOEUR: I do not know what would be the purpose of doing that, because to close the canon was the reply to a certain situation. I would take a more prophetic stance: it is there, the canon is there. It is our job what to do with that and what sense it makes to have the canon. It is wise not to overemphasize the canon, but it is important also not to think that we are in a position of undoing the canon, or doing another canon because canonization is not our problem.

MCCARTHY: But some would say that the canon is indeed our issue, that the canon in fact excludes and has excluded certain possibilities for thinking.

RICOEUR: When we consider that a text deserved to be in the canon then that means for us that this text has some authoritative force for us. But why not other texts also? Why not? We know that they do not fit into the canon, but it has not cut off reading the text. The *Shepherd* of Hermas, for example: it has been included in the liturgy of the Eucharist at times.

It is good to preserve tensions concerning anything that belongs to edification, to deal with the incongruous. But also to create respect for those who closed the canon; they were very generous. I keep returning to the fact that there were four Gospels, and they do not present the same account of the passion. They did not know it perfectly but they did not want to correct it to say that this one is the real Gospel. It belonged to communities whose readers had reverence for those texts. It was not through lack of mutual recognition by communities which had not the same strength of reverence for the same texts. If it is true, as most exegetes agree, that the prophetic writings were gathered after the return from captivity, it is an admirable restraint that they kept these texts which contain damnation—you will be overrun, you will be killed to the last one—they kept these texts. And in regard to narrative traditions, they deserve to be preserved as they are. Maybe because there was a long oral tradition behind them, and this memorization of texts before writing is equivalent to writing. It's a kind of oral writing. So there was an authority over the text before the last redactional stage.

MCCARTHY: Let me turn the conversation away from liturgy, reading, and canon and toward issues of appropriation. I was reading the Twelfth Gifford lecture and noted the role of "conscience." Would you describe "conscience" as important in the imaginative appropriation of the biblical material? What do you see to be the relation between conscience and *phroenesis*?

RICOEUR: I use the term "conscience" in the precise sense of personal conviction in a concrete situation. So this is the way that it is connected to *phroenesis*; first, this element of the singularity of decision making;

then, secondly, a conviction, the call of an injunction of which I am not the master. In *Soi-même comme un autre* it is the last figure of the book because it is the ultimate figure of otherness, of alterity, as completely interiorized. So it is the interiorization of, to use the vocabulary of Levinas, the dimension of height and exteriority.

I am interested here too in the notions of "testimony" and "attestation," because it is Jean Greisch who called my attention to a certain fascination in my use of the terms. I have a precise difference between them since I use the term "attestation" to say the kind of belief and confidence that "I am able to . . . , I am able to speak . . . , I am capable. . . ." I take "testimony" to speak always about the other, the other than oneself, "testimony about . . . ." "Attestation" is always reflexive. I take the term "testimony" exactly as Jean Nabert uses it, precisely as a counterpart of "reflexivity" in the sense that Nabert is coming from a Fichtian background, for whom the problem of consciousness at the level of what he called "originary affirmation" is that of the absolute subject. This distance between empirical consciousness and the self-founding I can never be completely covered. Surely, outside of me there are people, very simple people, who by extraordinary acts of compassion, of courage, give testimony that the extraordinary is possible. This is a testimony to something absolute. It confronts the attestation which remains only a belief in, a confidence that I can be the bearer of this authentic life. What I am looking for in a merely immanent way is done very simply outside of me, and this is in a sense the best use of the term exteriority. It is the exteriority of testimony confirming the interiority of attestation. And then we can say that the prophetic calls are "testimonies" in that sense because they give testimony to the correctness, the height of the source of the call. And so this dialectic between attestation and testimony, I think, is fundamental because it introduces a component of intersubjectivity in conscience, so it is a polarity of conscience, both as inner conviction and also the help of an exemplary life.

We have to see that in my account of the prophetic call there is always this moment of resistance and the need to be reassured. It is a narrative pattern that is repeated and used as a kind of paradigm of "testimony." Precisely through this paradigm there is the first call, the denial, the second call, the resistance, the necessity to see some expectation to be sent—not to be called but to be sent. This is the element of mission. And then there is the reconnection with the expectation of the people—someone needs you. Then the reassurance works. It is a very interesting pattern.

PELLAUER: Is this notion of resistance consistent with what you were saying earlier about the resistance to the notion of absolute choice, the strong existential choice that can do anything? For the prophets it is an acceptance; but it is not absolute freedom in Sartre's sense.

RICOEUR: I should say we have a very poor philosophy of choice, as though we have only two terms in the alternative: either arbitrariness—I choose what I want—or I am determined. But conviction is precisely the juncture of the feeling that now there is only one thing to be done and the approbation which I give to it, which itself is free. It is a free approbation to an inner necessity, a moral necessity.

PELLAUER: Would you link this term "approbation" to what in your earlier work you called "consent"?

RICOEUR: Maybe, but I have connected consent to something quite different. It was what I have not chosen, my own existential constitution, and it has three examples: character, birth/life, and the unconscious, involuntary. "Approbation" has to do with value. I found also this concept of "approbation" in the phrase, "life approves life." Approbation is a recognition of what compels me. And therefore it is a perfect conjunction of arbitrariness and necessity. Intellectual consent has to be duplicated by this elementary consent. I prefer the term, "approbation." I was happy to acquire one more word for "reason."

MCCARTHY: Is "approbation" in that sense then some final moment of hermeneutical appropriation, of textual material?

RICOEUR: Yes, it would be because I recognize something as exterior to me, as one of my basic possibilities. If we use the word "appropriation" technically, meaning what was foreign becomes proper, it is the incorporation into my own experience of something external. And then in that sense appropriation is the way by which the external testimony becomes an inner attestation.

Day 3

MCCARTHY: I would like to suggest an interpretive summary of what we have talked about thus far and raise two more questions.

One way to understand the Bible is as a collection of texts, but to some extent that flattens it. The Bible is also a phenomenon which in itself is a whole series of interactions. So what the notion of "Bible" means may be much larger than simply this collection of texts. It includes interactions between the texts as well as interactions with communities. There is much to be thought of on this score in a project like the Bible and the Self.

For certain issues, then, approaching the Bible as a collection of texts alone is not a good starting point. The starting point that I see you most comfortable with is a starting point through history, that the Bible is part of a tradition. The Bible has played a tremendous role in that tradition. The Bible then is a collection of texts for a community, always read by a community inside of a tradition. It is not simply a series of isolated texts.

Placing the Bible in this framework, inside of the traditions of communities, suggests a hermeneutical moment which would look at the question of what the texts might mean for this specific community, and this would involve at least three aspects: (1) Imagination, with the question, What does the Bible provide for this historical community's understanding of the possibilities for ways of being in the world? (2) Liturgy, or the ritualization of reading, with the question, How does the ritualization of reading, reading texts which are not necessarily the choice of the community, affect the community's way of being in the world? (3) Action and the possibilities for action, with the question, What are the paradigms for action which the history of the Bible provides? and How does one appropriate or exclude these paradigms in specific choices? These three aspects strike me as part of a hermeneutic for the question of the relation of the Bible and the Self.

But aside from this historical and hermeneutical moment would be the moment of approbation, not distinct from the hermeneutical, but certainly not to be confused with simply a better notional or conceptual understanding of the traditions and texts. You spoke of this moment of approbation as a final moment of the text, a dialectical unity of testimony and attestation in choice. The issues surrounding imagination and ethics then are poorly posed if the possibilities of the Bible are understood simply as normative, an implicit understanding of the Bible through the genre of law alone. The relation of Bible and Self comes to completion at this level of approbation, at the point where the Bible and Self meet not only in possibilities but also in approbation of possibilities.

In some of your work you have spoken of the reference of the Bible as the name of God. My sense is that this "name of God" is a reference also to a life lived before the other. Another way of stating this: This life is both a gift and a demand, thus life before God is both gift and demand. This is the context into which any questions of the relation of Bible and Self need to be put. Given this context, here then are my two questions:

(1) When you were talking about modern preaching, you suggested that such preaching could not be simply the rereading of texts. There is the need for a critical moment in modern preaching. You commented on this when you were speaking about an instance of preaching dealing with "sterility." When you spoke about this you used the language of analogy and made a movement to the analogous situations of "sterility." This movement to analogy, of course, has happened often within the history of scriptural interpretation. My question here is, At what point does this analogical move become the creation of a whole new text, not the reading of a text but the reading of a vocabulary suggested by the text to which I then attach myself?

(2) Contemporary academic biblical scholarship has surely recognized that history is an inevitable part of the study of scripture because one of the distances which needs to be accounted for in the study of biblical texts is the historical one. But your own work on the Self suggests that a moment which is equally important in this larger phenomenon of the Self cannot be grasped by the historical-critical approach. It must involve some other ways of study. How is it in contemporary biblical study that you would see the study of the Self to be best carried out? In the context of the academy so many of us realize that one of the reasons why historical-critical methods are useful derives not only from the fact that the texts are historical but because this method provides a style of knowing, something more secure and reliable, comparable to other styles of knowing in the university. But it has often been observed that this style of knowing takes the reader away from the text, tends to alienate the reader from the text, making the movement of second naïveté difficult. The appropriation of the Self seems difficult in the academy, something the academy strays away from. You have located points at which the appropriation of the Bible might occur, for instance, in the community's liturgical reading. But do you think this appropriation has a home in the academy also? Can this aspect of the question of the relation of Bible and Self become a question for the academy in any way?

RICOEUR: Let me begin from the framework of the historical-critical method. Two questions must arise. First, what makes the text important?

Why has it been preserved. Especially when it is discordant with other historical texts? Why did they preserve the text? This is the meaningfulness of the text. And this question has to be linked to the second one: For whom was it meaningful? We cannot imagine when the text was not a part of certain interpretations of the communities, especially in cultures where there was no private reading, the reading that we have become accustomed to do with novels since the seventeenth century. Therefore, within even the historical-critical method there is a problem of being meaningful FOR.

And then we return to the question of analogy. I had a conversation yesterday with some colleagues about the critique of Kant, especially certain problems that are raised in the Third Critique concerning the communicability of the world. This is the whole problem of the critique of the treatment of taste as the connection between singularity and universality. Here we are alerted to a problem which may have some importance for the way in which these stories keep making sense for communities. There is a mode of universalization which does not proceed through normative judgments. Kant speaks of finality without end, or pleasing without consent. Therefore the communicability of the singular may be grasped immediately as paradigmatic. The story about singular events, singular people, singular situations, makes sense for a community without being raised or elevated to the level of generality, normativity, and universality. Once more this is the problem of "the figure" which we have already met, the capacity of the singular to generate through its paradigmatic character, a transposition in situations which would be understood as analogical in those terms of the connection between the singularity and paradigmatic quality, and communicability. This is the problem of how it is possible to have universality without objectivity.

This then was paradigmatic force, the force of the singular. And it may be that it is a kind of reflexive understanding of the community, that such a story has this force of surviving its conditions of protection—not to be a mere effect of social force, but to emerge higher than the situation in which it was produced, the capacity to survive the conditions of production.

McCARTHY: This category of surviving endurance is something important. You mentioned endurance as an essential moment in the issue of *phroenesis* in the first discussion.

RICOEUR: Yes, stories like those of the patriarchs. The capacity to be transposed to new situations may be implied in this capacity to exhaust one's own situation of production, more than appealing to event or language. It brings us to the connection between imagination and ethics. If there is a gap here it is because of imagination, because of the possibilities—the capacity of imagination to grasp and to generate models, not in the sense of norms, but the capacity to enact in new situations—this may be one aspect of historicity keeping the meaning and at the same time, keeping the same sense in a different kind of reading.

Your first question here is good: Is it a new text? Why not? It will be a text if it is received by the community as a kind of paradigmatic, not normative text. It is received as a paradigmatic reading as we have in a paradigmatic text. In a sense, what we call a tradition of reading and interpretation is the capacity to textualize a thread of interpretation.

We can speak of metaphoricity not only in language, but also in narrative, a kind of metaphorization of narrative. Thus we have paradigmatic stories without confusing paradigmatic with normative or universal. And in this gap between the paradigmatic and the normative there is preserved a place for approbations. We took something in the sense that we added something.

What I mean by "naming God"—I insist somewhere that for me this term of "God" is a vanishing point of a plurality and even diversity of approaches. Our different ways of assuming, grasping, and approving this multiplicity generates a vanishing point, by which we mean that the Self is the center of approbation exactly as through all the literary genres there is the vanishing point of God. But our reception has this kind of illusion at the same time. There is a difference between "sameness" and "logical identity." There is a capacity to gather our multiple modes of approbation, our multiple approaches to the text, which themselves point to a vanishing point, a mirroring of the vanishing point beyond the text.

Multiplicity of texts, and multiplicity of graspings. But here I should insist on one thing: it is possible that philosophical approaches to the Self and religious interpretations of the Self do not say the same thing. Maybe this Self assertion must be threatened, in turn, by the sense of losing one's grasp, which is finally care and the moment of unselfishness. I think philosophically. I must go on as far as possible to say that, even at the price of introducing this specificity as I did in the last of the Gifford Lectures. Conscience preserves the possibility of the reverential

Self. There is the dialectic of preserving the self against something, but also losing the Self.

PELLAUER: At the beginning today John talked about the "name of God," but you keep on saying "naming of God." Is it more a process that you recognize. There was a sense that for a long time the tradition tried to name God as being. That is not the only option and it may not be the best option.

RICOEUR: There are many options concerning the meaning of being, and it may be that the Greeks did not exhaust the meaning of being, for in all languages there is the verb "to be." This suggests that there were several possibilities of the verb εἰμί which were not available to any Greeks, even the aristocrats.

The concern is not a particular name of God; the work is not to put forth a name per se. Name in the sense of a personal name, yes, but this was a problem of the Hebrew. Yahweh was an incomparable name. It is very strange because most of these names were proper and common at the same time: a god and God. Sometimes I use an expression by Max Scheler because he was not at ease with the personality of God. God has to be no less than a person, and to that extent it is a personalization. This was his way of putting it, to make being a person inescapable. The source of a person can be no less than a person. But beyond this are the anthropomorphisms of the intelligence. The famous model of the Hittites, where the God and the people form an asymmetrical covenant, preserves both a certain analogy between the partners but at the same time presents an asymmetry which subverts it. In Job this was his problem. "You are looking at me as if to be seen by someone." I am sure we have to struggle with this to resolve it. Is it enough that we say that we have a benevolent glance by a judge, or do we drop this notion of judge and turn to memory which still seems to be more important. Memory in the Hebrew did not mean a relation to the past events as facts, but its care— not to forget to have care, that is the permanence of care.

PELLAUER: How do you see that carrying over into the reading of Scripture and to exegesis. This was something John was talking about, that critical exegesis is almost a separate discipline.

McCARTHY: The issue of memory is interesting here. The relationship to the past through memory as exact recall of events need not be the only relationship that memory can have. In some ways the availability of the past is a problem in dealing with the scripture material. What has often-times happened in contemporary scripture scholarship is that the past has been understood as history, and history as that which is available through a certain method. But this notion of memory as a way of relating to the past as care strikes me as a very productive way of dealing with pastness.

RICOEUR: But Yosef Yerushalmi has written an important book titled *Zakhor: Jewish History and Jewish Memory*, saying that even in the Middle Ages the Jews had no records in certain archives. For example, there was no historical account of the expulsion of the Jews from Spain and Portugal. Perhaps it is because they would tell the story to their young. This is the idea of not forgetting in the sense of telling again, of continuing to tell. History was not an issue of archives. With archives we are confronted with the trace, the trace which has been kept. This is completely alien to the mentality of the Jews and even the early church.

McCARTHY: Earlier I had asked a question about the way of studying the Bible in the academy. Do you have any further thoughts about that?

RICOEUR: Waiting for lessons? No, do not forget that there is a problem because the Bible is being read elsewhere, and only a small segment of the readers are being raised by scientific method. The Bible does not belong to a people with scientific method; it belongs to the people, to the readers, not even to the church.

Index

Socrates, 86, 98
Soliloquia (Augustine), 139
soul-body relationship, 27–28, 59,
   67, 84–85, 91, 94–95, 100,
   102, 104, 109–10, 112, 118–
   19, 125, 185
Stager, L. E., 55, 82–83
Stoicism, 91, 95, 97–98, 103–4,
   112, 114, 125–26
Strodtbeck, F. L., 50, 81, 87–88

Tannous, A. I., 55
Taylor, Charles, 16, 25–27, 29–
   30, 33, 43–45, 51–52, 59,
   71, 81–82, 84, 127, 129,
   148, 223–24
theological studies
   relation to history, 2–4
theology
   and Bible, 1–6, 8–9, 11–15, 19,
   147, 182–183, 221; medieval
   perspective on, 147–48; nonrelation of, 13–15; salvation
   history perspective of, 167–
   69; university context of,
   3–4, 6, 8
   and ethics, 13, 16, 18, 26, 36,
   39, 42–43, 87, 90, 96, 107,
   114, 161–67, 171, 173, 176–
   79, 182, 194–95, 212, 221,
   226–27, 232
   goal of, 11, 13
   self-understanding of, 11–13
   in the university, 3, 6, 8 9,
   11–13, 15, 45, 150, 179–80,
   182
Toennies, Ferdinand, 32, 44

Toulmin, Stephen, 11
Tracy, David, 11–12, 18–19,
   34–35, 45, 220, 234
tradition
   Roman Catholic, 4–5, 197

von Moos, Peter, 139, 151
von Rad, Gerhard, 164, 167–68,
   180, 211, 214, 233

Weintraub, Karl, 25, 30, 44,
   148–49, 151
Westermann, Claus, 210, 214,
   220
Whaling, Frank, 11
White, Lynn, 104, 159, 165–67,
   179
Whitehead, Alfred North, 187,
   198
wholeness, 15, 32–33, 40–41, 63,
   141, 182, 189, 192–93, 197,
   221
Wiles, Maurice, 1, 15, 19
William of Champeaux, 140
Williams, Rowan, 122, 129
Wilson, Edward O., 170, 180
Wolff, H. W., 59, 85, 87
Woods, Charles, 11, 158
Wright, G. Ernest, 54, 82–83,
   164, 167, 180

Xenophon, 98

Yerushalmi, Yosef, 243

Zosimos of Panopolis, 104, 114